Abstracts of the
TESTAMENTARY PROCEEDINGS
of the
PREROGATIVE COURT OF MARYLAND

Volume XXIV: 1744-1746

Libers: 31 (pp. 489-679), 32 (pp. 1-22)

by
V. L. Skinner, Jr.

CLEARFIELD

Printed for Clearfield Company by
Genealogical Publishing Company
Baltimore, Maryland
2010

ISBN 978-0-8063-5471-2

Made in the United States of America

INTRODUCTION

Purpose of the Prerogative Court.

The Prerogative Court was the central point for
probate for Provincial Maryland. It was
mirrored after the Prerogative Court of
Canterbury. There was a judge as well as
clerk(s) of the court. Initially, all probate
was brought directly to the Prerogative Court,
located in the Provincial Capital. As the
Province became more populous, all documents
were still to be filed with the Prerogative
Court; however, administration of probate was
delegated to the various county courts. Even
so, there are documents only in the Prerogative
Court and not in the appropriate county, and
vice versa.

Documents filed in the Prerogative Court.

The following documents were filed in the
Prerogative Court: administration bond, will,
inventory, administration accounts, and final
balances. The testamentary proceedings contain
the administration bond and the docket for the
court. If the administrator is lax in filing
documents, then a summons is also recorded.

Equity Court

The Prerogative Court was also the court for
equity cases--resolution of disputes over the
settlement and distribution of an estate. The
case was brought before the judge and could take
several years to resolve. Often depositions
were taken and recorded in the minutes.

Notes on the Abstraction.

1. The left hand column contains the
    liber/folio number. The folio numbers are
    presented just as they appear in the actual
    document, e.g., 32a, 78½.
2. The right hand column contains the
    abstraction text.
3. Various libers specify a particular session
    for the Prerogative Court, e.g., 1678; or,
    September Court 1742. This information is
    presented as "Court Session:" followed by
    the appropriate session. Should no session
    have been specified, then the phrase "no

date" is used.
4. An ellipsis (...) is used to indicate a continuation of the previous information, but no relevant genealogical information is present.
5. The following symbols are used in the abstraction:
- ? - difficult to read.
- # - pounds of tobacco.
- ! - [sic].

Abbreviations.

The following abbreviations have been used throughout this abstraction:

AA - Anne Arundel Co.
ACC - Accomac Co.
BA - Baltimore Co.
CE - Cecil Co.
CH - Charles Co.
CR - Caroline Co.
CV - Calvert Co.
dbn - de bonis non
DE - Delaware
DO - Dorchester Co.
ENG - England
FR - Frederick Co.
g - gentleman
GB - Great Britain
HA - Harford Co.
IRE - Ireland
JP - justice of the peace
KE - Kent Co. MD
KEDE - Kent Co. DE
LaC - letters ad colligendum
LoA - letters of administration

LoD - list of debts
MA - Massachusetts
MD - Maryland
MO - Montgomery Co.
NE - New England or "non est"
NEI - "non est inventar"
NY - New York
NYC - New York City
p - planter
PA - Pennsylvania
PG - Prince George's Co.
PoA - power of attorney
QA - Queen Anne's Co.
SM - St. Mary's Co.
SMC - St. Mary's City
SO - Somerset Co.
TA - Talbot Co.
VA - Virginia
WA - Washington Co.
WO - Worcester Co.

This volume is a continuation of the series, covering 1744 to 1746. The Court is meeting every 2 months to review the docket, and to take appropriate actions. Except for spurious entries, the information is presented in chronological order, as recorded by the Register.

By 1739, all mainstream processing of probate records has been delegated to the Deputy Commissaries.

31:489 Col. Gabriel Parker (CV) exhibited:
- will of Ambrose Leach. Also, bond of Mary Leach administratrix. Sureties: James Leach, John Lynch. Date: 23 April 1744.
- will of Michael Taney, constituting Michael Taney & Sarah Taney executors. Said executors were granted administration. Sureties: Roger Brooke, John Brooke. Date: 3 May 1744.
- will of Sarah Allnutt. Also, bond of James Allnutt acting executor. Sureties: James Dossey, Michael Catterton. Also, renunciation of William Allnutt (son) executor, recommending his brother James Allnutt. Date: 5 May 1744.
- will of Ann Wood.
- will of John Dorrumple.
- inventory of William Lynch.
- inventory of Aaron Barrs.
- inventory of Thomas Hardisty.
- inventory of John Richards.
- inventory of Henry Smith.
- inventory of Burridge Hutchins.
- inventory of John Tayman.
- inventory of Samuel Young, in CV & BA.
- inventory of Elisabeth Hutchins.
- accounts of Thomas Barrs administrator of Aaron Barrs.
- accounts of Benjamin Johns administrator of Henry Smith.
- accounts of William Dawkins surviving administrator of John Perry.
- accounts of James Kirshaw administrator of Elinor Key.
- accounts of William Hardie administrator of Burridge Hutchins.
- accounts of John Price & his wife Dorcas executrix of Robert Orme.
- accounts of William Holland & William Miller, Jr. administrators of John Couran.
- accounts of Elisabeth Smith administratrix of James Smith.

Exhibited from BA:
- accounts of Elisabeth Rockhold executrix of Charles Rockhold.

Court Session: 1744

- LoD on estate of Luke Stansbury. Also, additional accounts of Tobias Stansbury executor.
- inventory & LoD of Stephen Boddy.
- inventory of Philip Jarvis. Also, accounts of John Robinson & his wife Mary administratrix.

Exhibited from PG:
- accounts of Roger Moody & his wife Abigail administratrix of John Keedle.

Exhibited from AA:
- accounts of Benjamin Wright executor of Henry Wright.
- accounts of Sarah Waterfall (late Sarah Robinson) administratrix of Peter Robinson.
- inventory of William Crouch.
- additional inventory & LoD of Philip Pindall. Also, accounts of Elisabeth Pindall executrix.
- accounts of Joseph Groves administrator of Issitt Groves.

Exhibited from QA:
- additional inventory of Phillip Connor. Also, accounts of John Merridith & his wife Ann administratrix.

31:490   Exhibited from SM:
- accounts of Thomas, William, Benedict, & Henry Spalding executors of William Spalding, Sr.

Exhibited from CH:
- inventory of Jane Browne.

9 May. Exhibited from QA:
- inventory of John Dailey. Also, accounts of Edmund Kelley & his wife Ann executrix.

Exhibited from PG:
- inventory of Henry Butler.
- inventory of Henry Culver.
- inventory of Robert Beall. Also, accounts of Joseph Beall executor.
- accounts of James Haddock Waring executor of Andrew Hoggard.

Court Session: 1744

- accounts of Charles Williams executor of Charles Williams.

Exhibited from QA:
- accounts of Robert Walters & his wife Amelia administratrix of Michael Anderson.

Exhibited from SM:
- accounts of Henry & Barbara Barnes executors of Henry Barnes.
- accounts of James Topping administrator of Thomas Cooke.

Exhibited from BA:
- accounts of Elisabeth Boddy executrix of Stephen Boddy.
- accounts of Thomas Sligh administrator of Edward Cox.
- LoD on estate of Richard Gist.

Exhibited from TA:
- additional inventory & LoD of William Harper.
- accounts of James Priestly administrator of John Hawk.

Exhibited from DO:
- accounts of John Salsbury & his wife Elisabeth administratrix of John Granger.

William Knight (g, CE) exhibited:
- bond of John Baldwin & James Paul Heath executors of Elisabeth Hogins. Sureties: John Veazey, David Ricketts. Date: 20 March 1743.
- inventory of Robert Story.
- accounts of Moses Ruth administrator of Daniel Murray.
- accounts of Thomas Ebtharp administrator of James Collins.
- accounts of Richard Taylor administrator of Robert Woolley.
- accounts of Edward Armstrong administrator of James Wood.
- accounts of William Beetle administrator of James Huston.

31:491   Charles Hynson (g, KE) exhibited:
- bond of Elisabeth Ringgold administratrix of James Ringgold.

Sureties: Edward Worrell, Charles
Ringgold. Date: 5 May 1743.
- inventory & additional inventory of
  Hugh ONeale.
- inventory of John Perkins.
- inventory of George Wetherell.
- additional inventory & LoD of John
  Hall.
- accounts of Sylvester Kelley
  administrator of Katherine Kelley.
- accounts of John Carvill executor of
  Sarah Topping.

Col. Gabriel Parker (CV) to examine
accounts of:
- William Harris executor of George
  Harris (CV).
- Dorcas Gray executrix of John Gray
  (CV).
- Jeremiah Johnson executor of
  Jeremiah Johnson (CV).
- Elisabeth Hambleton executrix of
  Charles Hambleton (CV).
- Mary Hughes executrix of Richard
  Rake (CV).
- Littleton Waters & Richard Young
  administrators dbn of Francis
  Hutchins (CV).
- Littleton Waters acting executor of
  Elisabeth Hutchins (CV).

10 May. Exhibited from PG:
- inventory of Clement Hill.
- 2nd additional accounts of Mary
  Beall & Joshua Beall executors of
  Capt. Charles Rider.
- additional inventory of James
  Mullikin. Also, accounts of Charles
  Mullikin executor.

Exhibited from QA:
- accounts of Thomas Hutchings &
  Thomas Elliott Hutchings executors
  of James Hutchings.
- accounts of Morgin Ponder & his wife
  Ann executrix of Thomas Hines.

Benton Harris (g, WO) exhibited:
- bond of Thomas Coffen administrator
  of Thomas Phippen. Sureties:
  Presgrave Turvill, John Hudson.
  Date: 23 April 1744.

- will of James Townsend. Also, bond of Solomon Townsend administrator. Sureties: Daniel Donohoe, John Donoho. Date: 4 May 1744.
- will of Rowland Hodgson.
- inventory of Thomas Wise.
- inventory of Richard Dillon.
- inventory of William Davis.
- accounts of William Dolby administrator of Thomas Foresith.
- accounts of Rebecca Bratton administratrix of Archibald McNeal.
- accounts of Daniel Steel administratrix of James Steel.
- accounts of Nathan Venatson administrator of William Venatson.
- accounts of Ann Hadock administratrix of Alexander Benston.

Walter Hanson (g, CH) exhibited:
- will of Phillip Lee, Esq.

31:492 11 May. Exhibited from CH:
- additional inventory of Philip Lee, Jr.

Exhibited from DO:
- inventory of Thomas Hunt.

Mr. Benton Harris (WO) to examine accounts of:
- John Notham & his wife Jemima administratrix of Thomas Claywell (WO).
- William Selby & his wife Martha executrix of John Purnell (WO).
- Littleton Townsend administrator of Job Shery (WO).
- Sarah Fletcher administratrix of Rev. Thomas Fletcher (WO).
- Katherine Breeman administratrix of James Breeman (WO).
- William Stephen Hill & his wife Rebecca executrix of John Smith administrator of Thomas Smith (WO).

Exhibited from PG:
- accounts of Mary Sim administratrix of Dr. Patrick Sim.
- accounts of Jane Contee executrix of Alexander Contee.
- additional accounts of Rev. Jacob

Henderson & his wife Mary executrix of Robert Tyler.
- accounts of Rev. Jacob Henderson executor of Martha Duvall.
- 2nd additional accounts of Rebecca Tilley executrix of Capt. John Prichard.

Henry Trippe (g, DO) exhibited:
- bond of Richard Harrington administrator of Joseph Fisher. Sureties: Moses Nicolls, Henry Snowden. Date: 20 January 1743.
- bond of Thomas Loockerman administrator of Robert Ellis. Surety: Henry Trippe. Date: 15 March 1743. Also, renunciation of Grace Spencer (widow of said Ellis). Date: 14 March 1743. Witnesses: William Thomson, William Harper.
- bond of Grace Hooper administratrix of William Hooper. Sureties: Isaac Partridge, Andrew Gowtee. Date: 15 March 1743.
- will of John Hayward. Also, renunciation of 1 executor. Also, bond of Sarah Hayward acting executrix. Sureties: Col. Henry Hooper. Thomas Stewart. Date: 13 April 1744.
- bond of Elinor Lister administratrix of William Lister. Sureties: Nicholas Parish, Henry Wheeler. Date: 16 April 1744.
- bond of William Galloway executor of James Galloway. Sureties: John Meekins, Jr., Thomas Cragg. Date: 1 May 1744.
- will of Sarah Fisher.
- will of Ephraim Trotter.
- inventory of Matthew Traverse.
- inventory of Capt. Charles Rider.
- inventory of Robert Ellis.
- additional inventory of John Stevens.
- inventory of Timothy Graylis.
- inventory & LoD of William Gass.
- inventory & LoD of Josias Mace.
- additional inventory of Mary Carter.
- inventory & LoD of James Moasley.
- additional inventory of Solomon Edmondson.

31:493

- accounts of Elisabeth Deen administratrix of John Deen.
- accounts of Edward Alford executor of Mary Alford.
- accounts of Alice Pullett administratrix of William Pullett.
- accounts of John Stevens administrator of John Stevens.
- accounts of Ezekiel & Priscilla Johnson executors of Robert Johnson.
- accounts of Sarah Thomas administratrix of Simon Thomas.
- accounts of Margery Kennerley administratrix of Thomas Kennerley.
- accounts of Dr. William Murray administrator of Richard Tull.
- accounts of Col. Henry Hooper administrator of Thomas Sumners.
- accounts of Capt. Thomas Nevett administrator of James Moasley.
- accounts of James Carter administrator of Mary Carter.
- accounts of Esther Slayton executrix of James Slayton.
- accounts of Dennis Carey administrator of John Shaw.
- accounts of Titus Hubbart administrator of Humphrey Hubbart.
- accounts of Margaret Edge administratrix of Thomas Edge.

William Tilghman (g, QA) exhibited:
- accounts of Mary Cahell executrix of Edmund Cahell.

12 May. Thomas White (g, BA) exhibited:
- bond of Jane Maxwell administratrix of Samuel Maxwell. Sureties: Joseph Thomas, Nicholas Gay. Date: 28 April 1744.
- bond of James Osborn administrator of Zachariah Smith. Sureties: George Chauncey, John Hughs. Date: 1 May 1744.
- bond of Parker Hall administrator of Lewis Tucker. Surety: Michael Gilbert. Date: 5 May 1744.
- inventory & additional inventory of Robert Gott.
- inventory of Sarah Hanson.
- inventory of John Picton.
- additional inventory of William Cox.

Also, accounts of Thomas Taylor administrator.
- accounts of Thomas White administrator of John Picton.

14 May. Nehemiah King (g, SO) exhibited:
- will of Stephen Tulley, Sr. Also, bond of Benjamin Tulley administrator. Sureties: Edward Bennett, George Bennett. Date: 10-March 1743.

31:494
- bond of Martilda Horner administratrix of George Horner, Sr. Sureties: William Shores, Thomas Martin. Date: 31 March 1743.
- will of William Harris, constituting Frances Harris & William Harris executors. Also, widow's election. Said executors were granted administration. Sureties: Thomas Rencher, Richard Harris. Date: 22 March 1743.
- will of John Howard. Also, bond of Sarah Howard administratrix. Sureties: Joshua Porter, Jacob Morris. Date: 17 April 1744.
- bond of Thomas Browne administrator of David Browne. Sureties: John Woolford, Henry Ballard. Date: 19 April 1744.
- bond of John White administrator of William Richardson. Sureties: Henry Ballard, Robert Givan. Date: 24 April 1744.
- renunciation of Elisabeth Rigsby widow of Levin Rigsby, recommending her son John Rigsby. Date: 12 January 1743.
- assignment by Isaac Crouch of his administration on estate of Joy Hobbs to Absolom Hobbs. Date: 24 September 1743.
- inventory of Joy Hobbs.
- inventory of Lewis Rigsby.
- inventory of Bryan Gilligan. Also, accounts of William Turpin administrator.
- accounts of William Wood administrator of Thomas Wood.
- accounts of Smith Horsey executor of Stephen Horsey.

Court Session: 1744

- accounts of Moses Alexander administrator of Mercillas Fagin.
- accounts of John Elzey executor of Alice Ellis.
- accounts of Samuel Collins administrator of Katherine Billings.

15 May. Mr. Thomas Bullen (TA) to examine accounts of:
- Elisabeth Kirby administratrix of Matthew Kirby (TA).

William Masters (PG) vs. Priscilla Wilson (PG). Sheriff (PG) to summon defendant to render answer.

16 May. M. Macnemara (AA, g) exhibited:
- inventory of Richard Davis.
- inventory of John Rockhold.
- inventory of Hannah Johnson.
- inventory of Thomas Climps.

Exhibited from QA:
- 2nd additional inventory of Benjamin Pemberton. Also, 2nd additional accounts of Grundy Pemberton administrator.

31:495 Mr. Thomas White (BA) to examine accounts of:
- Elisabeth Mathews acting executrix of Roger Mathews (BA).
- Heathcoat Pickett & his wife Elisabeth executrix of William Wright (BA). 2nd additional accounts.

17 May. Mr. Nehemiah King (SO) to examine accounts of:
- Mary Ackworth executrix of Thomas Tate (SO).
- Rebecca Stewart administratrix of Alexander Stewart (SO).
- Mary Hobbs administratrix of Thomas Hobbs (SO).
- Ann Pitts administratrix of John Nelson (SO).
- Christopher Piper executor of Matthew Nutter (SO).
- Sarah Staples administratrix of James Staples (SO).
- Saward Tomlinson administrator of

Court Session: 1744

Solomon Tomlinson (SO).
- Stephen Horsey executor of Hannah Horsey (SO).
- Absolom Hobbs & Mercillas Hobbs administrators of Joy Hobbs (SO).
- Katherine Pitts (alias Katherine Revell) administratrix of Randall Revell (SO).

Mr. Thomas Aisquith (SM) to examine accounts of:
- Charles King executor of Charles King (SM).
- William Leake & his wife Mary administratrix of Hugh Pilkinton (SM).
- Thomas Tarlton & his wife Mary executrix of James Farthing (SM).
- Martha Wheatley executrix of Joseph Wheatley (SM).
- Patrick Lurty & his wife Mary administratrix of William Adams (SM).
- George Daffin & his wife Susannah executrix of William Aisquith (SM).
- Peter Gough administrator of John Leake (SM).
- Alexander Anderson & his wife Henrietta executrix of Thomas Janes (SM).

19 May. Mr. Thomas Aisquith (SM) to examine accounts of:
- John Baker & his wife Elisabeth executrix of Michael Nuney (SM).

Exhibited from AA:
- accounts of Christopher Dixon & his wife Mary administratrix of Benjamin Gardner.
- inventory of Samuel Burgess.

22 May. Exhibited from BA:
- inventory of Edward Fottrell, in BA & AA.
- accounts of Thomas Franklin & his wife Ruth administratrix of Peasley Ingram.

Exhibited from AA:
- inventory of John Watkins.
- inventory of Richard Galloway, in AA

Page 10

& BA.   Also, accounts of Sophia Galloway executrix.

31:496   Exhibited from PG:
- accounts of Leonard Wayman & his wife Deborah administratrix of Abraham Boyd.

24 May.   Exhibited from PG:
- bond of Thomas Lee & Francis Lee executors of Phillip Lee, Esq. Sureties: Edward Sprigg, Osborn Sprigg.   Date: 11 May 1744.

Mr.   Henry Trippe (DO) to examine accounts of:
- Mary Bowen administratrix of John Bowen (DO).
- Charles Layton & Nichollson Layton executors of William Layton (DO).
- James Billings executor of Capt. Charles Rider (DO).
- Thomas Brannock executor of Rebecca Harwood (DO).
- Elisabeth Beachamp administratrix of Robert Beachamp (DO).
- Thomas Long & his wife Rebecca administratrix of Thomas Courson (DO).
- Sarah Owens executrix of William Owens (DO).
- John Hayward, Jr. executor of William Johns (DO).
- Owen Graylis executor of Timothy Graylis (DO).
- William Bradley administrator of Henry Bradley (DO).
- George Griffith & his wife Mary widow & executrix of Capt. Richard Willis (DO).
- Thomas Clarke executor of Thomas Clarke (DO).
- Mary Bramble executrix of John Bramble (DO).
- Benjamin Nicolls administrator of Margaret Nicolls (DO).
- Sarah Stinson administratrix of Alexander Stinson (DO).
- Matthew Hargaton & his wife Mary administratrix of John Bullock (DO). Additional accounts.
- Dennis Carey administrator of James

Court Session: 1744

Melton (TA).

Mr. Benton Harris (WO) to examine accounts of:
- Wheatley Dennis & his wife Elisabeth executrix of Benjamin Holland (WO).

25 May. Mr. Nehemiah King (SO) to examine accounts of:
- Thomas Cooper executor of Gabriel Cooper (SO).
- John Willson & his wife Priscilla administratrix of David Johnson (SO).
- Frances Harris & William Harris executors of William Harris (SO).
- Ann Lackie executrix of Alexander Lackie (SO).

Mr. Peter Dent (PG) to examine accounts of:
- Mary Townley administratrix of John Townley (PG).

Exhibited from PG:
- accounts of Marren Duvall, Jr. administrator of John Soper.

31:497 Mr. Walter Hanson (CH) to examine accounts of:
- Ann Yates administratrix of Robert Yates (CH).
- Mary Briscoe executrix of John Briscoe (CH).
- Ann Maconchie administratrix of John Maconchie (CH).
- Robert Hanson executor of John Coffer (CH).
- Frances Bryan administratrix of Daniel Bryan (CH).

26 May. Petition of Henry Darnall for Henry Trippe. John Vane (TA) died indebted to petitioner. Administration bond on said estate assigned to petitioner.

Exhibited from SO:
- accounts of Jacob Airs administrator of John Outerbridge.

Court Session: 1744

Mr. Walter Hanson (CH) to examine accounts of:
- Rev. Theophilus Swift & his wife Mary executrix of Rev. William Maconchie (CH).

Exhibited from AA:
- inventory of Thomas Lewis. Also, accounts of Elisabeth Lewis executrix.
- accounts of Sarah Wright administratrix of Samuel Wright.

28 May. Exhibited from CV:
- accounts of Lewis Welsh administrator of Burden Crosby.

Exhibited from AA:
- accounts of Sarah, John, Samuel, Edward, Benjamin, & Henry Gaither executors of Benjamin Gaither.

29 May. Exhibited from AA:
- additional accounts of Christopher Dixon & his wife Mary administratrix of Benjamin Gardner.

31 May. Exhibited from AA:
- accounts of William Grimes & his wife Eliza executrix of Robert Bell.

Exhibited from BA:
- accounts of Thomas Coale executor of Aquila Massey.

31:498 2 June. Mr. William Tilghman (QA) to examine accounts of:
- Ann Butler & Thomas Butler executors of Thomas Butler (QA).
- Richard Scrivener & John Lloyd administrators of Elisabeth Bolton (QA).
- John Swift executor of William Swift (QA).
- Margaret Bussell administratrix of John Bussell (QA).
- Ann Scott, John Scott, & Solomon Scott executors of Nathaniel Scott (QA).
- James Dee & his wife Mary administratrix of Jasper Bowden (QA).

Court Session: 1744

- John Collins executor of Richard Collins (QA).
- Elisabeth Nevill administratrix of Walter Nevill (QA).
- Mary Collins administratrix of Thomas Collins (QA).
- Robert Walters & his wife Amelia administratrix of Michael Anderson (QA). Additional accounts.

Exhibited from DO:
- accounts of Henry Stafford administrator of Robert Stafford.

3 June. Thomas Aisquith (g, SM) exhibited:
- bond of Grace Mattinly administratrix of John Mattingly. Sureties: John Mattingly, George Heyden. Date: 1 May 1744.
- inventory & LoD of Peter Jarboe.
- inventory & LoD of James Taylor.
- inventory & LoD of Joshua Guibert.
- accounts of Henry Jarboe executor of Henry Jarboe.
- accounts of John Blackiston executor of Thomas Blackiston.
- accounts of Edward Spink administrator of William Spink.
- accounts of John Dant administrator of Thomas Winard.
- accounts of Joseph Jenkins & his wife Mary executrix of William Coombs.

Exhibited from QA:
- accounts of Letitia Browne executrix of Matthew Browne.

4 June. Col. Thomas White (BA) to examine accounts of:
- Charles Green administrator of Daniel Shaw (BA).
- Elisabeth Lloyd executrix of John Lloyd (BA).
- Bridget Mullhuse executrix of Bartholomew Mullhuse (BA).

Mr. William Knight (CE) to examine accounts of:
- Dr. John Jackson administrator of William Ward (CE).

- Martha Wood administratrix of Joseph Wood (CE).
- Edward Armstrong & his wife Ann administratrix of William Craig (CE).

31:499 Mr. Thomas Bullen (TA) to examine accounts of:
- Margaret Jordon administratrix of Alexander Jordon (TA).
- George Nix & his wife Leah administratrix of John Hutchins (TA).
- Jane Hazeldine administratrix of Francis Hazeldine (TA).
- Thomas Ray executor of John Ray (TA).
- Edward Starkey & his wife Susannah executrix of William Harper (TA).
- Richard Warner executor of Charles Warner (TA).
- Thomas Delihay administrator of Thomas Delihay (TA).
- Anthony Lecompte & his wife Katherine administratrix of William Bennett (TA).
- Mary Dawson & Impey Dawson executors of James Dawson (TA).

Mr. Peter Dent (PG) to examine accounts of:
- Ann Brooke executrix of Leonard Brooke (PG).
- Mary Townley administratrix of John Townley (PG).
- Edward Pye administrator of Walter Pye (PG).

Mr. Charles Hynson (KE) to examine accounts of:
- Esau Watkins & his wife Sarah administratrix of Alexander Johnson (KE).
- Thomas Crow & his wife Sarah administratrix of George Skirvin (KE).
- Ann Hall, Christopher Hall, & George Hall executors of John Hall (KE).
- John Hart & his wife Katherine administrators of John Ange (KE).
- Katherine Smithers administratrix of John Smithers (KE).

- John White & his wife Eliza administratrix of Thomas Rouse (KE).
- Christian Adair administratrix of Alexander Adair (KE).
- Lewis Williams executor of Thomas Williams (KE).
- Rachel Browning executrix of John Browning (KE).
- Richard Kennard administrator of George Barber (KE).
- William Thomas surviving executor of William Thomas (KE).
- Michael Miller executor of Arthur Miller (KE).
- Hanse Hanson & his wife Margaret executrix of Glanvill Rolph (KE).
- Elisabeth Pinar administratrix of Thomas Pinar (KE).
- John Read & his wife Mary executrix of Thomas Mahone (KE).
- Lambert Wilmer executor of Elisabeth Young (KE).
- Christopher Hall surviving executor of Matthias Day (KE).

Mr. Gabriel Parker (CV) to examine 3rd additional accounts of:
- Martha Lingan executrix of Thomas Lingan (CV).

Mr. Walter Hanson (CH) to examine accounts of:
- Robert Froggit & his wife Jane executrix of John Scroggen (CH).
- Rebecca Howard executrix of John Howard (CH).
- George Elgin & his wife Susannah administratrix of Charles Mastin (CH).

31:500   Mr. Thomas Aisquith (SM) to examine accounts of:
- William Taylor & his wife Patience executrix of Philip Evans (SM).

9 June. Exhibited from BA:
- accounts of Charles Green administrator of Daniel Shaw.

Peter Dent (g, PG) exhibited:
- will of Thomas Wilson, constituting Priscilla Wilson executrix. Said

executrix was granted administration. Sureties: James Wilson, Thomas Gordon. Date: 1 May 1744.
- bond of Margaret Mackland administratrix of Matthew Mackland. Sureties: Andrew Cotrell, Michael Jones. Date: 1 May 1744.
- bond of Priscilla Wilson administratrix of Nathan Masters. Sureties: James Wilson, John Cramplin. Date: 1 May 1744.
- inventory of Henry Quando.
- inventory of John Mawdesley.
- inventory of David Candle.
- inventory of Richard Marsham Waring.
- additional accounts of David Crawford administrator of William Green
- accounts of Robert Riddle & his wife Frances administratrix of John Read.

Deposition of Talbot Risteau. He delivered to Mr. Thomas Brerewood a summons, to show cause why LoA should not be granted to some other person on the estate of William Brerewood (SO). Date: 6 June 1744. Before: Charles Ridgely.

11 June. Exhibited from AA:
- inventory of Edward Hall.
- accounts of Henry Darnall administrator of Henry Murray.

John Bowy, William Beanes, & Joshua Boon to appraise estate of Philip Lee, (CH) on the Patuxent River.

Exhibited from PG:
- accounts of Thomas Coleman & his wife Joyce administratrix of Thomas Prather, Sr.

31:501 13 June. Exhibited from AA:
- accounts of William Cotter executor of Jane Sanders.
- inventory of Thomas Reynolds.

Thomas Bullen (g, TA) exhibited:
- will of John Neighbours. Also, renunciation of 1 executor. Also,

widow's election. Also, bond of
Margaret Neighbours acting
executrix. Sureties: John Exley,
John Shannahan. Date: 4 May 1744.
- bond of Elisabeth Skinner
administratrix of William Skinner.
Sureties: James Cockrin, Benjamin
Hopkins, James Colston, Henry
Colston. Date: 4 May 1744.
- bond of Rebecca Clayland
administratrix of Moses Clayland.
Sureties: Isaac Dobson, David Kirby.
Date: 11 May 1744.
- petition & LoA on estate of Mr.
Samuel Simpson to Lewis Jones.
Signed: Thomas Perkins. Date: 14
November 1743.
- will of Sarah Broadway.
- additional inventory of William
Bennett.
- additional inventory of Nathaniel
Fox.
- additional inventory of John Guy
Williams. accounts of Morris
Giddens administrator of Joseph
Williams.

14 June. Exhibited from AA:
- 3rd additional accounts of Edmond
Jenings, Esq. & his wife Ariana
executrix of Thomas Bordley, Esq.

16 June. Exhibited from SO:
- bond of Thomas Caton administrator
of William Brerewood. Sureties
(AA): James Dick, Richard Burdus.
Date: 16 June 1744.

Exhibited from PG:
- additional accounts of John Holmes
surviving executor of William
Holmes.

Exhibited from BA:
- will of Nicholas Fitzsimons.

18 June. Mr. Thomas Bullen (TA) to
examine accounts of:
- Elisabeth Stevens administratrix of
John Stevens (TA).

21 June. Mr. Walter Hanson (CH) to examine accounts of:
- Joseph Milburn Semmes administrator of Ignatius Semmes (CH).
- Walter Scott administrator of James Scott (CH).
- Elisabeth Tarvin executrix of Richard Tarvin (CH). "Error".

Mr. Peter Dent (PG) to examine accounts of:
- Ignatius Howard & his wife Penelope executrix of William Shiercliff (PG).
- Dr. Charles Stewart administrator of Nicholas Brumley (PG). "Error".
- Virlinda Beall executrix of John Beall (PG).

31:502 Mr. Charles Hynson (KE) to examine accounts of:
- David Hull executor of George Wetherall (KE).
- John Carvill executor of Mary Smithers (KE).

Mr. William Knight (CE) to examine accounts of:
- James Foster & John Foster executors of William Foster (CE).
- Richard Ellwood & his wife Martha administratrix of William Boulding (CE).

Mr. Thomas White (BA) to examine accounts of:
- John Parks & his wife Bridget executrix of Bartholomew Millhuse (BA).

Mr. Thomas Bullen (TA) to examine accounts of:
- Jane Harrington, Joseph Harrington, & William Harrington executors of Richard Harrington (TA).

25 June. Peter Dent (g, PG) exhibited:
- will of Charles Digges.
- inventory of Robert Stamper.
- accounts of John Lawrence administrator of Henry Quando.
- accounts of Samuel Selby

administrator of John Bowen.

Exhibited from AA:
- additional accounts of MM Charles Carrolls on estate of James Carroll.
- additional accounts of Clement Mattingly & his wife Burton administrators of Elisabeth Coyle.

26 June. Deposition of John Hadden (BA). He heard Ann Richardson (AA) say that she gave her son Mark Richardson (AA, dec'd) chattel. Date: 26 June 1744.

28 June. Thomas Brereton administrator of Richard Brereton (SO) vs. Wonny McClammy (SO), Solomon Long (SO), & George Benston (SO). Sheriff (SO) to summon defendants to show cause why they conceal estate of dec'd.

29 June. Exhibited from AA:
- accounts of Richard Fowler & his wife Eliza administrators of Stephen Stewart.

Exhibited from BA:
- additional inventory & LoD of John Gardiner.

31:503 9 July. Walter Hanson (g, CH) exhibited:
- bond of Richard Brooke surviving executor of Francis Ignatius Boarman. Sureties: William Neale, James Boarman. Date: 5 April 1744.
- bond of Elisabeth Brawner administratrix of Henry Brawner. Sureties: William Eilbeck, William Nelson. Date: 29 May 1744.
- will of John Posten, Sr. Also, bond of William Posten surviving executor. Sureties: Francis Posten, Thomas Davis. Date: 28 May 1744.
- will of John Wheatley.
- inventory of James Glascock.
- inventory of William Munroe.
- inventory of John Johnson.
- inventory of Thomas Hawkins.
- inventory of John Sutcliff.
- inventory of Samuel Reeves.

Court Session: 1744

- inventory of Richard Brett.
- inventory of William Ansil.
- inventory of John Posten, Sr.
- inventory of Henry Blanchet.
- accounts of Thomas Douglass acting executor of John Garner.
- accounts of John Blanchet administrator of William Milstead.
- accounts of James Freeman & his wife Jennet administratrix of Arthur Westman.
- additional accounts of Barbara Muggleston administratrix of Thomas Muggleston.
- accounts of Ann Swann executrix of Samuel Swann.
- accounts of William Waters & his wife Susannah administratrix of Christopher Cruickshanks.
- accounts of William Boswell & Mary Boswell administrators of William Boswell.
- accounts of Mary Neale executrix of Henry Neale.
- accounts of Ann Howard administratrix of James Howard.
- accounts of James Plant administrator of Thomas Haile.
- accounts of John Groves administrator of Matthew Groves.
- accounts of John Groves administrator of William Till.

Benton Harris (g, WO) exhibited:
- bond of Benton Harris as Deputy Commissary (WO). Sureties: James Martin, Abraham Outten. Date: December 1743.

Nehemiah King (g, SO) exhibited:
- will of John More, constituting Tabitha More executrix. Said executrix was granted administration. Sureties: William Giles, Thomas Byrd. Date: 5 May 1744.
- will of John Kellam, constituting Sarah Kellam executrix. Said executrix was granted administration. Sureties: Bell Maddux, Henry Potter. Date: 21 May 1744.

Court Session: 1744

- will of John Roberson, constituting Joseph Cottman executor. Said executor was granted administration. Sureties: John Sirman, William Cottman. Date: 26 May 1744.
- bond of Sarah Gray one of executors of William Gray. Sureties: William Miles, William Smith. Date: 26 May 1744.
- bond of Matthew Kemp administrator of Thomas Howard. Sureties: Robert Givan, Robert Caldwell. Date: 20 June 1744.

31:504 Also, renunciation of Eliza Howard (widow), recommending Matthew Kemp (greatest creditor). Date: 19 June 1744.

- bond of George Hardy administrator of Christopher Nutter. Sureties: Solomon Hitch, Thomas Acwortt. Date: 3 July 1744.
- inventory of Randolph Smullen.
- inventory of Teague Riggen.
- inventory of Ambrose Riggen.
- inventory of Margaret Lindow.
- inventory of Thomas Ralph.
- inventory of John Howard.
- inventory of William Vaughan.
- inventory of George Horner.
- accounts of Ann Lackey administratrix of John Evans.
- accounts of John Jones executor of James Burne.
- accounts of Ann Lackey executrix of Alexander Lackey.
- accounts of Mary Ackworth executrix of Thomas Tate.
- bond of Isaac Mitchell administrator of Solomon Mitchell. Sureties: Woney McClamey, Stephen Mitchell. Date: 9 July 1744.

Mr. Thomas White (BA) to examine accounts of:
- George Chauncey & John Hanson administrators of Sarah Hanson (BA).
- Dr. Josias Middlemore executor of William Cawthren (BA). Additional accounts.

Sheriff (SO) to summon Samuel Collings (SO) surviving executor of Richard

Court Session: 1744

Chambers (SO) to take LoA.

Mr. Nehemiah King (SO) to examine accounts of:
- Wilson Rider executor of Thomas Ralph (SO).
- Margaret MacKready executrix of Alexander MacKready (SO).
- Christopher Piper executor of Matthew Nutter (SO).
- Ellin McGram executrix of John McGram (SO).

Court Session: 10 July 1744

31:505 Docket:
- William Cumming, Esq. procurator for John Johnson Sothoron (g, SM) vs. Stephen Bordley procurator for Dryden Forbes executrix of Henry Peregrine Jowles (g, SM). Text of libel. Plaintiff married Mary Jowles one of daughters of dec'd, by whom he has several children living. She is since dec'd; plaintiff was granted LoA on her estate on 4 March 1741. Said Henry Peregrine Jowles made his will, with legatees: Dryden Jowles (wife), 4 children: Kenelm Jowles, Mary Jowles who married plaintiff, Rebecca, & Sibella Jowles. Said Sibella died after her father & before the plaintiff's wife. Said Dryden Jowles has married John Forbes (g, SM).
31:506 Mentions: William Cartwright (sheriff, SM).
Text of answer.
31:507 Mentions: Thomas Truman Greenfield (g, SM, dec'd).
31:508 Ruling: plaintiff. Mentions: Negro Penn (woman), MM William Wilkinson, Allen Davis, Jonathan Davis.
- Capt. James Hall creditor to estate of Edward Hall (PG) vs. Mary Hall executrix of said dec'd. Sheriff (PG) to summon defendant to render accounts.
- H. Darnall & W.C. procurators for Clebburn Semmes father & guardian of Clebburn Semmes (infant, under age

21, PG) vs. Stephen Bordley
procurator for Christian Lemaster
widow & administratrix of John
Lemaster (CH).
Text of libel. Said infant is the
only son of Eleanor Semmes who was
the only daughter of John Lemaster
(CH).

31:509   Mentions: George Tarvin (sheriff,
CH).
Text of demurrer by defendant.

31:510   Text of amended libel.
31:511   Text of answer.
31:512   Ruling: plaintiff. Mentions: Negro
Nan.

- John Hellen administrator dbn of
Margaret Banks (CV) vs. Young
Parran & Esther Parran
administrators of John Parran (CV).
Sheriff (CH) to summon said Young
Parran & sheriff (CV) to summon said
Esther Parran to show cause why they
detain effects of dec'd. Struck
off.

- W.C. for Charles Hynson, Jr. & his
wife Phebe (KE) vs. S.B. for John
Carvill executor of Mary Smithers.
Libel, answer.

- John Shermedine & his wife Sarah one
of daughters of John Davie (SM) vs.
Thomas Wilson (carpenter, SM)
administrator of said dec'd
unadministered by Ann Davie.
Sheriff (SM) to summon defendant to
render full inventory & to pay
plaintiff his wife's share.

- William Roberts administrator of
William Ghiselin (Annapolis, AA) vs.
Rebecca Johnston wife of Archibald
Johnston (Annapolis, AA). Sheriff
(AA) to summon defendant to testify
regarding concealment of estate of
dec'd. Struck off.

31:513   - Williams Roberts administrator of
William Ghiselin (Annapolis, AA) vs.
Robert Lusby (KE) & Milcah Lusby
(KE). Sheriff (KE) to summon
defendants to testify regarding
concealment of estate of dec'd.
    - Robert Lusby, age 41, deposed on
21 April 1744.
    - Milcah Lusby (spinster), age 18,

Court Session: 10 July 1744

deposed on 31 July 1744.
Discontinued.
- William Roberts administrator of
William Ghiselin (Annapolis, AA) vs.
Reverdy Ghiselin (PG). Sheriff (PG)
to summon defendant to testify
regarding concealment of estate of
dec'd.
  - Reverdy Ghiselin, age 16 years 8
    months, deposed on 10 April
    1744.
  Discontinued.

31:514 - Sheriff (WO) to summon the following
to take LoA:
  - Alexander Buncle administrator
    of John Long (WO). Left off.
  - Alexander Buncle administrator
    of James Euart (WO). Left off.
  - Margaret Davis administratrix of
    William Davis (WO). Inventory
    exhibited. Discontinued.
  - John Wildman executor of Richard
    Dillon (WO). Inventory
    exhibited. Discontinued.
- S.B. for William Masters (PG) vs.
Priscilla Wilson. Libel.
- Thomas Brereton administrator of
Richard Brereton (SO) vs. Woney
McClammey (SO), Solomon Long (SO), &
George Benston (SO). Sheriff (SO)
to summon defendants to show cause
why they conceal effects of dec'd.
  - Woney McClamey deposed on 10
    July. Discontinued.

Court Session: 1744

31:515 Exhibited (omitted from p. 96):
- inventory of William Mockbee
exhibited on 8 October 1736 & no
accounts. Therefore, distribution
to legal representatives by Mattheu
Mockbee administrator. Date: 14 May
1740.

10 July. Mr. Walter Hanson (CH) to
examine accounts of:
- Abigail Swann administratrix of
Thomas Swann (CH).
- Arthur Lee & his wife Ann
administratrix of Robert Yates (CH).
- Francis Ware & John Doncastle

Page 25

executors of Ann Ebernethy (CH).
Additional accounts.
- John Boswell & Walter Dodson
executors of Allen Henton (CH).
Additional accounts.
- William Brent, William Neale, &
Henry Neale executors of William
Chandler (CH). Additional accounts.

Exhibited from BA:
- accounts of William Hamilton & Luke
Trotten executors of John Gardiner.

Exhibited from PG:
- LoD on estate of William Digges.
Also, accounts of Ignatius &
Nicholas Digges executors.

Mr. Benton Harris (WO) to examine
accounts of:
- Spence Hall executor of Robert Hall
(WO).

Exhibited from TA:
- inventory of William Dehortee.
Also, accounts of John Potts & his
wife Rachel executrix.

Mr. Peter Dent (PG) to examine accounts
of:
- William Robinson & his wife Diana
administratrix of John Williams
(PG).

11 July. Benton Harris (g, WO)
exhibited:
- will of Mary Fassitt, constituting
Rouse Fassitt executor. Said
executor was granted administration.
Sureties: Benjamin Tull, Whittington
Bowen. Date: 23 May 1744.
- bond of Elisabeth Dennis executrix
of John Dennis. Sureties: Daniel
Dennis, Lazarus Dennis. Date: 5
June 1744.
- will of Nathaniel Rackliff,
constituting William Wale executor.
Said executor was granted
administration. Sureties: Paul
Alexander, John Dale, Jr. Date: 6
June 1744.
- bond of Ann Merida Godfrey

administratrix of Charles Godfrey.
Sureties: James Mumphord, William
Jarman. Date: 8 June 1744.
31:516 • bond of Ann Merida Godfrey
administratrix of Joseph Godfrey.
Sureties: James Mumphord, William
Jarman. Date: 8 June 1744.
• will of Joseph Schoolfield. Also,
widow's election.
• will of Thomas Peele.
• inventory of Mary Bedard.
• inventory & LoD of Christopher
Topham.
• inventory of Adam Wood.
• accounts of Sarah Henderson
executrix of John Henderson, Jr.

12 July. Exhibited from QA:
• additional accounts of Robert
Walters & his wife Amelia
administratrix of Michael Anderson.

Exhibited from KE:
• accounts of William Butcher executor
of Edmond Butcher.

13 July. Mr. Benton Harris (WO) to
examine accounts of:
• William Stephen Hill & his wife
Rebecca executrix of John Smith
(WO).

14 July. Exhibited from KE:
• accounts of Sarah England & Richard
Agway executors of Daniel Greenwood.

17 July. Exhibited from QA:
• additional accounts of Letitia Brown
executrix of Matthew Brown.

18 July. Exhibited from DO:
• accounts of John Crittchett
administrator of William Critchett.

20 July. Thomas Bullen (g, TA)
exhibited:
• bond of Frances Wiles administratrix
of Thomas Wiles. Sureties: John
Hewes, John Wiles, John Harrington.
Date: 12 June 1744.
• bond of Thomas Barnett & his wife
Phebe administrators of Richard

Giles. Sureties: Samuel Abbott, Morris Giddens. Date: 15 June 1744.

- additional inventory of Matthew Kirby. Also, accounts of Elisabeth Kirby administratrix.
- additional accounts of Thomas Clark & his wife Sarah administratrix of John Guy Williams.
- additional accounts of William Carey executor of Nathaniel Fox.

Mr. Thomas Bullen (TA) to examine accounts of:
- Thomas Bounton administrator of Joseph Bounton (TA).
- Rachel Ardery administratrix of William Ardery (TA).
- Mark Markland administrator of Charles Markland (TA).

17 July. William Thomas (AA) vs. William Holland (CV) surviving executor of William Holland (AA). Sheriff (CV) to summon defendant to render answer.

31:517 23 July. Thomas Aisquith (g, SM) exhibited:
- bond of Henry Lyon administrator of Thomas Morris. Sureties: Joseph Wood, John Chunn. Date: 6 June 1744.
- bond of James Richardson administrator of Daniel Daggens. Sureties: William Richardson, William Clarke. Date: 13 July 1744.
- will of Wilfred Gardner.
- inventory & LoD of Samuel Tennison.
- inventory & LoD of John Riley.
- inventory & LoD of Bowles Billingsley.
- inventory & LoD of John Mattingley.
- inventory & LoD of William Barnes.
- inventory & LoD of Greenfield Jowles Kenelm.
- inventory of Monica Monarks.
- inventory & LoD of William Smith.
- inventory & LoD of James Crackson.
- inventory & LoD of Capt. John Gardner.
- inventory of Henry Gardner.
- inventory of Dr. David McGill.
- inventory & LoD of Benjamin

Stephens.
- accounts of Ann Doyne executrix of Joshua Doyne.
- accounts of William Orr administrator of John Chieverell.

Exhibited from QA:
- bond of John Osborn administrator of Hannah Osborn. Surety: Joseph Nicholson (KE). Date: 13 July 1744.

Exhibited from AA:
- accounts of Richard Smith & his wife Priscilla administratrix of Henry Austin.

William Tilghman (g, QA) exhibited:
- will of William Ford, constituting Winefred Ford executrix. Also, widow's election. Said executrix was granted administration. Sureties: John Fouracres, William Monsieur. Date: 31 May 1744.
- bond of John Mumford administrator of John Mumford. Sureties: William Carman, William Austin. Date: 6 June 1744.
- additional inventory of Jasper Bowden.
- additional inventory & LoD of William Jackson.
- inventory of George Spark.
- additional inventory of John Cullens.
- inventory of Henry Fortune.
- inventory of Jacob Deford.
- accounts of John Salloway administrator of William Jackson.
- accounts of Abraham Boon administrator of Moses Boon.
- accounts of Ambrose Wright administrator of James Ward.
- accounts of William Greenwood administrator of James Case.
- accounts of Henry Costin executor of Finley Camron.
- accounts of Richard Buckley administrator of Charles Hinesley.
- accounts of Margaret Berry administratrix of Elisabeth Matthews.
- accounts of Mary Collins

administratrix of Thomas Collins.
* accounts of Valentine Green administrator of John Cullens.
* accounts of Margaret Bussell administratrix of John Bussell.

25 July. Mr. Thomas White (BA) to examine accounts of:
* William Hollis executor of William Snelson (BA).

31:518 28 July. Exhibited from AA:
* inventory of Capt. Joseph Shakespear.
* LoD on estate of Henry Murray.
* accounts of Thomas Cheney administrator of Susannah Browne.
* accounts of William Cumming administrator of Joseph Shakespear.

Exhibited from CV:
* additional accounts of John Smith executor of Thomas Smith.

30 July. Exhibited from CV:
* accounts of Job Hunt executor of Sarah Hunt.

Exhibited from SM:
* bond of Thomas Aisquith as Deputy Commissary (SM). Sureties: Richard Hopewell, Robert Ford. Date: 3 November 1742.

Thomas Wilson administrator of Ann Davie (CH) vs. Joseph Hine & his wife Arabella. Sheriff (CH) to summon defendants to testify regarding concealment of estate of dec'd.

31 July. Exhibited from PG:
* accounts of Benjamin Ricketts & his wife Eliza executrix of Hugh McDoggle.

1 August. Mr. Nehemiah King (SO) to examine accounts of:
* John Rigsby administrator of Lewis Rigsby (SO).

2 August. Exhibited from SO:
* inventory of Levin Gale, Esq.

Mr. Gabriel Parker (CV) to examine accounts of:
- Elisabeth Vaughan executrix of John Vaughan (CV).

7 August. Exhibited from TA:
- additional accounts of John Carslake administrator dbn of James Horney.
- additional accounts of John Carslake administrator dbn of John Kersey.

12 March. [Omitted from f. 45.] Martha Laking executrix of Abraham Laking (PG) was granted continuance.

14 April. [Omitted from f. 463.] Mr. Richard Burdus on behalf of Thomas Caton attorney for Alexander Black (merchant, London) vs. estate of William Brerewood (SO). Caveat on estate. Notice sent to Mr. Thomas Brerewood (BA) on 19 April 1744.

31:519 25 May. [Omitted from f. 496.] Notice sent to Mr. Thomas Brerewood (BA) regarding LoA on estate of William Brerewood (SO). Date: 15 May 1744.

13 June. [Omitted from f. 501.] Tobias Stansbury executor of Luke Stansbury executor of Francis Brown (BA) was granted continuance.

28 June. Thomas Brereton administrator of Richard Brereton (SO) was granted continuance.

1 August. [Omitted from f. 518.] Caleb Dorsey & Edward Dorsey vs. estate of Joshua Dorsey (son of Caleb). Caveat regarding granting LoA.

7 August. Mr. Thomas Bullen (TA) to examine accounts of:
- Sarah Reynolds (formerly Sarah Lenard) executrix of John Lenard (TA).

8 August. Exhibited from QA:
- additional accounts of Dr. John Smith & his wife Sarah executrix of William Osborne.

Mr. Henry Trippe (DO) to examine
additional accounts of:
- Ezekiel Johnson surviving
  administrator of Robert Johnson
  (DO).

6 August. Thomas Wilson administrator
of Ann Davie (CH) vs. Arabella Hines
wife of Joseph Hines (CH). Sheriff (CH)
to render attachment to defendant to
testify regarding concealment of estate
of dec'd.

13 August. Thomas Aisquith (g, SM)
exhibited:
- will of Peter Mills. Also, widow's
  election.
- accounts of Samuel Lee administrator
  of John Lee.
- accounts of James Watson
  administrator of Joseph Watson.

14 August. Exhibited from AA:
- additional inventory of Sarah
  Harrison.

31:520   Exhibited from DO:
- accounts of Isaac Meekins executor
  of Thomas Pattison.

15 August. Exhibited from CV:
- additional accounts of John Skinner
  & his wife Elinor executrix of Capt.
  Posthumus Thornton.

Judith Crow widow of John Crow (BA) vs.
James Crow (BA). Sheriff (BA) to summon
defendant to show cause why LoA granted
to him on estate of dec'd should not be
revoked & granted to plaintiff.

16 August. Exhibited from AA:
- inventory of John Chocke. Also,
  accounts of George Chocke
  administrator.
- accounts of Edward Steward
  administrator of David Steward.

21 August. Exhibited from BA:
- accounts of Sarah Legoe
  administratrix of Thomas Legoe.

Court Session: 1744

25 August.   Gabriel Parker (g, CV)
exhibited:
- will of John Gough. Also,
  renunciation of 2 executors. Also,
  bond of Elisabeth Young
  administratrix. Sureties: Benjamin
  Sedwick, Ellis Slater. Date: 19 May
  1744.
- will of Sarah Ogleby, constituting
  John Ogleby & John Sedwick
  executors. Said executors were
  granted administration. Sureties:
  James Brinkley, Thomas Devan. Date:
  10 July 1744.
- will of Jonah Whinfield,
  constituting Dorcas Whinfield
  executrix. Said executrix was
  granted administration. Sureties:
  Newman Harvey, John Whinfield.
  Date: 20 July 1744.
- will of Thomas Morsell. Also, bond
  of William Tayman & his wife
  Elisabeth executrix. Sureties: John
  Lynch, Richard Deal, Jr. Date: 20
  July 1744.
- bond of William Hardie administrator
  of Thomas Stallings. Surety:
  William Miller, Jr. Date: 24 July
  1744.
- bond of Mary Leach administratrix of
  William Leach. Sureties: Thomas
  Hardesty, John Lynch. Date: 27 July
  1744.
- bond of Elinor & John Dorrumple
  executors of John Dorrumple.
  Sureties: William Dawkins, Benjamin
  Ellt. Date: 2 June 1744.
- will of Samuel Little, constituting
  Daniel Talbott executor. Said
  executor was granted administration.
  Sureties: Richard Talbott, Joseph
  Talbott. Date: 30 July 1744.
- bond of Clarana Winall
  administratrix of William Winall.
  Sureties: John Young, James Bowen.
  Date: 7 August 1744.
- inventory of Sarah Hunt.
- inventory of Rev. John Vaughan.
- inventory of Edward Wood.
- inventory of Michael Taney.
- inventory of Sarah Allnutt.
- inventory of Ambrose Leach.

- accounts of Richard Young & Littleton Waters administrators dbn of Francis Hutchins.
- accounts of Elisabeth Hambleton executrix of Charles Hambleton.
- accounts of Dorcus Gray executrix of John Gray.
- accounts of William Harris executor of William Harris.
- accounts of Jeremiah Johnson executor of Jeremiah Johnson.
- accounts of Littleton Waters executor of Elisabeth Hutchins.
- 3rd additional accounts of Martha Lingan executrix of Thomas Lingan.
- accounts of Elisabeth Vaughan executrix of Rev. John Vaughan.

31:521 27 August. Exhibited from BA:
- inventory & LoD of William Galloway. Also, accounts of Priscilla Galloway executrix.

Exhibited from PG:
- additional accounts of Elisabeth James Drane executors of Samuel Pottinger.

Exhibited from AA:
- inventory of Gilbert Yealdhall.

3 September. Gabriel Parker (g, CV) exhibited:
- accounts of Thomas Reynolds administrator of John Tayman.

Peter Dent (g, PG) exhibited:
- bond of Elisabeth White administratrix of Joseph White. Sureties: William Wallace, James Willson. Date: 27 June 1744.
- bond of Elianor Jones administratrix of Edward Jones. Sureties: Charles Jones, Luke Ray. Date: 28 June 1744.
- LoD on estate of John Townley
- additional inventory of John Taylor.
- inventory of Joseph Waters.
- inventory of John Deak.
- inventory of Benjamin Osborn.
- inventory of Samuel Parker.
- inventory of John Cooper.

Court Session: 1744

- accounts of Bartholomew Field & his wife Sarah administratrix of John Taylor.
- accounts of James Rimmer administrator of John McCounell.
- accounts of William Price administrator of William Paul.
- accounts of Ann Hugoe executrix of Israel Hugoe.
- accounts of John Lawrance administrator of Joseph Waters.
- accounts of Stephen Pickrin administrator of Robert Stamper.
- accounts of William Mauduit administrator of James Chambers.
- accounts of George Scott administrator of John Foster.
- accounts of William Robinson administrator of Samuel Parker.
- accounts of Mary Townley administratrix of John Townley.
- 2nd additional accounts of David Crawford administrator of William Green.
- accounts of Richard Brightwell & his wife Eliza executrix of William Watson.

4 September. William Knight (g, CE) exhibited:
- bond of Edward Ryan administrator of Thomas Walker. Sureties: John Holthun, James Redus. Date: 14 August 1744.
- will of Lawrence Gailshiott.
- LoD on estate of William Rumsey.
- additional inventory & LoD of John Cooper.
- inventory of James Simmons.
- inventory of John Piggott.
- inventory of Isaac Clements.
- inventory & LoD of Jeffery Beaseley.
- LoD on estate of Peter Poleson.
- inventory of Robert Patton.
- accounts of Esther Hamm administratrix of Abraham Hamm.
- accounts of William Thompson administrator of George Thompson.

31:522 5 September.
- accounts of Ann Williams, Nathaniel Williams, & David Thomas executors of Elias Williams.

Page 35

- accounts of Rachel Poleson administratrix of Peter Poleson.
- accounts of Sabina Rumsey executrix of William Rumsey.
- accounts of Richard Boulding executor of Richard Boulding.
- accounts of Thomas Saunders administrator of Albert Cox.
- accounts of John Cooper administrator of John Cooper.
- accounts of Christian Bell administratrix of John Bell.
- accounts of William Mill, John Pennington, & Francis Bonner administrators of Mary Mathiason.
- accounts of Richard Ellwood & his wife Martha administratrix of William Boulding.
- accounts of James & John Foster executors of William Foster.

Gerrard Hopkins (AA) & John Sellman (AA) to appraise estate of Richard Goodman (AA).

Exhibited from PG:
- will of Alexander Beall, constituting William Beall, Ninian Beall, & John Jackson executors. Said executors were granted administration. Sureties: John Merridith, John Phillips. Date: 5 September 1744.

22 August. [Omitted from f. 520.] Notice given to Mrs. Mary Hammond (AA) that Mr. Thomas Baldwin has applied for LoA on estate of her husband Mr. Nicholas Hammond.

5 September. Exhibited from CV:
- inventory & additional inventory of Jeremiah Pattison.

Walter Hanson (g, CH) exhibited:
- bond of Mary Neale executrix of Raphael Neale. Sureties: Francis Hamersley, Edward Digges. Date: 1 August 1744.
- bond of Charles Spalding administrator of James Hamblin. Sureties: Samuel Turner, Jr.,

William Leak. Date: 27 August 1744.
- will of John Cadell.
- additional inventory of John Howard. Also, accounts of Rebeccah Howard executrix.
- inventory of George Hatton.
- inventory of Samuel Perrie.
- inventory of George St. Clare.
- inventory of John Brayfield.
- inventory of Richard Tarvin, Sr. Also, accounts of Eliza Tarvin executrix.
- inventory of Benjamin Robey.
- inventory of Francis Ignatius Boarman.
- inventory of Henry Brawner.
- additional inventory of John Scroggen. Also, accounts of Robert Froggel & his wife Jane executrix.
- accounts of Mary Briscoe executrix of John Briscoe.

31:523
- accounts of Frances Bryan executrix of Daniel Bryan.
- accounts of William Brent, William Neale, & Henry Neale executors of William Chandler.
- accounts of Ann Maconchie administratrix of John Maconchie.
- accounts of Jane Woodard executrix of John Woodard.
- accounts of John Boswell & Walter Dodson executors of Allen Henton.
- accounts of Robert Hanson executor of John Coffer.
- accounts of Abigail Swann administratrix of Thomas Swann.
- accounts of George Egan & his wife Susannah administratrix of Charles Mastin.

6 September. Exhibited from KE:
- additional accounts of Walter Dougherty & his wife Ann executrix of Hugh ONeale.
- accounts of Walter Doughterty executor of Henry Evans executor of James Tibbett.

Exhibited from CV:
- additional accounts of Jane & Jacob Pattison executors of Jeremiah Pattison.

Court Session: 1744

7 September. Mr. Peter Dent (PG) to
examine accounts of:
- Priscilla Covington administratrix
  of Leonard Covington (PG).

8 September. Matthew Guibert (SM) vs.
Thomas Coode & James Dunbar
administrators of Jane Guibert (SM).
Sheriff (SM) to summond defendants to
render answer.

Col. Henry Ridgely vs. estate of John
Alstone (AA). Caveat exhibited against
granting LoA.

10 September. Ann Jenkins
administratrix of Thomas Jenkins (CH)
vs. Susannah Jenkins (CH) widow of said
dec'd. Sheriff (CH) to summon defendant
to show cause why she conceals estate of
dec'd.

Court Session: 11 September 1744

Docket:
- William Cumming, Esq. procurator for
  Capt. James Hall creditor to estate
  of Edward Hall (PG) vs. Mary Hall
  executrix of said dec'd. Struck
  off.
31:524 - W.C. for Charles Hynson, Jr. & his
  wife Phebe (KE) vs. S.B. for John
  Carvill executor of Mary Smithers.
  Libel, answer. Daniel Cheston to
  summon Paul Whichcoat & Cornelius
  Dunnahow to testify for plaintiffs.
- William Cumming, Esq. procurator for
  John Shermedine & his wife Sarah one
  of daughters of John Davie (SM,
  dec'd) vs. Thomas Wilson
  (carpenter, SM) administrator of
  said dec'd, unadministered by Ann
  Davie. Sheriff (SM) & sheriff (CH)
  to summon defendant to render
  inventory & to pay plaintiff's wife
  her portion. Struck off.
- Attachment rendered to Andrew Scott
  (PG) administrator of John Watts to
  render accounts.
- S.B. for William Masters (PG) vs.
  William Cumming, Esq. procurator for
  Priscilla Wilson. Libel. John

Court Session: 11 September 1744

Cooke (sheriff, PG) to summon
defendant to render answer.
- Sheriff (SO) to summon Samuel
Collings (SO) surviving executor of
Richard Chambers (SO) to take LoA.
- S.B. for William Thomas (AA) vs.
William Cumming, Esq. procurator for
executors of Col. Holland. Libel.
G. Parker (sheriff, CV) to summon
William Holland to render answer.

31:525 • Thomas Wilson administrator of Ann
Davie (widow, CH) vs. Joseph Hines
& his wife Arabella. G. Tarvin
(sheriff, CH) to summon defendant to
testify regarding concealment of
estate of dec'd.
- Joseph Hine (p, CH) deposed on 6
August 1744. The dec'd is the
mother of his wife.
- Said Wilson deposed that said
Arabella is well able to ride &
that she is not near time of
delivery.
- Judith Crow widow of John Crow vs.
James Crow (AA). John Risteau
(sheriff, BA) to summon defendant to
show cause why LoA on estate of said
dec'd, granted to him, should not be
revoked & granted to plaintiff.
Discontinued.

31:526 • William Cumming, Esq. for Matthew
Guibert (SM) vs. Thomas Coode &
James Dunbar administrators of Jane
Guibert.
Text of libel. Joshua Guibert
(brother of plaintiff) made his
will, constituting his wife Jane
Guibert executrix. Said Jane took
LoA, & died on 12 August last,
intestate. 3 or 4 days later,
Thomas Coode (brother of whole blood
of said Jane) & James Dunbar
(brother by the mother's side of
said Jane) took LoA on her estate.
Philip Key (sheriff, SM) summoned
defendants.
Ruling: LoA on estate of said Jane
revoked. LoA on estate of said
Joshua granted to plaintiff.

31:527 • Ann Jenkins administratrix of Thomas
Jenkins (CH) vs. Susannah Jenkins
(CH). G. Tarvin (sheriff, CH) to

Court Session: 11 September 1744

summon defendant to show cause why
she conceals estate of dec'd.

Court Session: 1744

11 September. Mr. Gabriel Parker (CV)
to examine accounts of:
• William Kidd & John Lynch
  administrators of William Lynch
  (CV).
• James Allnutt executor of Sarah
  Allnutt (CV).
• Henry Lee & Robert Lee executors of
  Robert Lee (CV). Additional
  accounts.
• Mary Dawkins executrix of James
  Dawkins, Jr. (CV).

Exhibited from AA:
• will of William Richardson.

Gabriel Parker (g, CV) exhibited:
• inventory of William Winall.

Benton Harris (g, WO) exhibited:
• bond of William Jarman, Jr.
  administrator of John Jarman, Sr.
  Sureties: William Jarman, Sr.,
  George Truitt. Date: 9 August 1744.
• bond of Alexander Massey
  administrator of William Massey.
  Sureties: Joseph Porter, James
  Porter. Date: 7 September 1744.
• will of Rowland Evans.
• inventory of Charles Godfrey.
• inventory of Thomas Phipps.
• inventory of Mary Fassitt.
• inventory of John Henderson.
• accounts of Ann Maglamery executrix
  of Edward Maglamery.
• accounts of Tabitha Sturgis
  administratrix of Thomas Slingoe.
• accounts of Tabitha Satchell
  executrix of Thomas Mitchell.
• accounts of Jemima Notham
  administratrix of Thomas Claywell.
• accounts of John Sturgis
  administrator of Littleton Sturgis.
• accounts of Elinor Smith
  administratrix of John Taylor.

31:528 13 September. Exhibited from PG:
- bond of James Plummer administrator of Philemon Plummer. Sureties: James Edmondston, Samuel White. Date: 13 September 1744. Also, renunciation of Elisabeth Plummer (widow), recommending James Plummer.
- bond of James Edmondston administrator of Jane Edmondston. Sureties: James Plummer, Samuel White. Date: 13 September 1744.

Nehemiah King (g, SO) exhibited:
- bond of Susannah Tulley administratrix of James Tulley. Sureties: John Hufington, Joseph Tulley. Date: 11 August 1744.
- will of Richard Chambers. Also, bond of Samuel Collings surviving executor. Sureties: Solomon Long, William Smith. Date: 11 August 1744.
- will of Benjamin Tulley. Also, bond of Elisabeth Tulley administratrix. Sureties: John Phillips, Richard Tulley. Date: 18 August 1744.
- will of William Mister. Also, widow's election. Also, bond of Patience Mister one of executors. Sureties: Nehemiah Dorman, John Evans. Date: 22 August 1744.
- bond of Judah Langston administratrix of William Langston. Sureties: James Hardy, Zachariah Read. Date: 22 August 1744.
- bond of Richard Waller administrator of Nathaniel Cottman. Sureties: Thomas Cooper, Charles Hacker. Date: 22 August 1744. Also, renunciation of Ebenezar Cottman, recommending his son Richard Waller.
- will of Sarah Horsey.
- inventory of William Harris.
- inventory & LoD of William Gray.
- additional inventory of Francis Thurrowgood Drummond.
- inventory of Stephen Tulley, Jr.
- inventory of
- inventory of John Moore.
- inventory of John Robertson.
- inventory of Stephen Tulley.
- inventory of David Brown.

Court Session: 1744

- accounts of Thomas Lambden administrator of William Booth.
- accounts of Frances & William Harris executors of William Harris.
- accounts of Mary Hobbs administratrix of Thomas Hobbs.
- accounts of Jennet Nairne executrix of Francis Thurrowgood Drummond.
- accounts of Mercillas & Absolom Hobbs administrators of Joy Hobbs.
- accounts of Stephen Horsey acting executor of Hannah Horsey.
- accounts of John & William Shores sureties for Alice Kenney executrix of John Kenney.
- accounts of John Pitts & his wife Ketherine administratrix of Randall Revell.
- accounts of John Wilson & his wife Priscilla administratrix of David Johnson.

31:529
- accounts of Rebecca Stewart administrator of Alexander Stewart.
- accounts of Thomas Cooper executor of Gabriel Cooper.
- accounts of Sarah Dashiell administratrix of Priscilla Dashiell.
- accounts of Sayward Tomlinson administrator of Solomon Tomlinson.
- accounts of Margaret McCready (alias Margaret Worthylake) executrix of Alexander McCready.

Exhibited from AA:
- bond of Thomas Reynolds administrator of John Alston. Sureties: Samuel Smith, John Howard. Date: 13 September 1744.

Mr. Thomas Aisquith (SM) to examine accounts of:
- James Thompson, Sr. & James Thompson, Jr. administrators of William Barnes (SM).

19 September. James Kingsbury executor of Elisabeth Kingsbury was granted continuance.

William Tilghman (g, QA) exhibited:
- bond of Eleanor Murphy

administratrix of William Murphy.
Sureties: John Say. Blake, Philamon
Charles Blake. Date: 26 July 1744.
- will of Henry Covington,
  constituting John Covington & Henry
  Covington executors. Said executors
  were granted administration.
  Sureties: James Knotts, Charles
  Bradley. Date: 31 July 1744.
- will of John Elliott, constituting
  Susannah Elliott executrix. Also,
  widow's election. Said executrix
  was granted administration.
  Sureties: Joseph Elliott, John
  Carter. Date: 1 August 1744.
- will of Thomas Smith (joiner).
  Also, bond of John Smith
  administrator. Sureties: Andrew
  Price, Jr., Thomas Hutchings. Date:
  31 August 1744. Also, renunciation
  of John Say. Blake. Date: 29 August
  1744. Witness: R. Porter.
- inventory of Hercules Cook.
- accounts of William Dudding
  administrator of William Taylor.
- accounts of James Dean & his wife
  Mary administratrix of Jasper Bowden
- accounts of John Collins, Jr.
  executor of Richard Collins.

Exhibited from SM:
- additional accounts of Stourton
  Edwards administrator of John
  Edwards.

15 September. Thomas Bullen (g, TA)
exhibited:
- will of Nathaniel Grace,
  constituting Alice Grace executrix.
  Said executrix was granted
  administration. Sureties: Nathaniel
  Grace, Robert Spencer. Date: 28
  July 1744.
31:530 - inventory & LoD of John Neighbours.
- inventory of Moses Clayland.
- inventory of Thomas Wiles.
- additional inventory & LoD of John
  Stevens.
- accounts of Jane Hazeldine
  administratrix of Francis Hazeldine.
- accounts of Thomas Ray executor of
  John Ray.

- accounts of Thomas Delihay administrator of Thomas Delihay.
- accounts of Mary Markland administratrix of Charles Markland.
- accounts of Margaret Jordon administratrix of Alexander Jordon.
- accounts of George Nix & his wife Leah administratrix of John Hutchins.
- accounts of Edward Starkey & his wife Susannah executrix of William Harper.
- accounts of Anthony Moore administrator of James Moore.
- accounts of Elisabeth Stevens administratrix of John Stevens.

17 September. Exhibited from AA:
- accounts of John Gassaway administrator of Capt. John Dixon.

19 September. Dr. William Murray who married executrix & Thomas Hollyday executor of Col. Leonard Hollyday were granted continuance.

Tobias Stansbury executor of Luke Stansbury (BA) was granted continuance.

Tobias Stansbury executor of Luke Stansbury (BA) executor of Francis Brown was granted continuance.

Exhibited from AA:
- will of William Wootton.

20 September. Exhibited from AA:
- bond of Elisabeth Wootton executrix of William Wootton. Sureties: James Dick, James Deale. Date: 19 September 1744.

Exhibited from TA:
- inventory & additional inventory of Michael Howard, Esq.

21 September. Thomas White (g, BA) exhibited:
- bond of Mary Woodward administratrix of Thomas Woodward. Sureties: John Ensor, John Hunt. Date: 6 June 1744.

Court Session: 1744

- will of Ann Bond. Also, bond of
  William Andrews administrator.
  Sureties: George Presbury, Thomas
  Lloyd. Date: 14 June 1744.
- bond of James Crow administrator of
  John Crow. Sureties: Richard
  Perkins, William Perkins. Date: 16
  June 1744.
- will of Joshua Starkey, constituting
  Jonathan Starkey executor. Said
  executor was granted administration.
  Sureties: Heathcoat Pickett, John
  Starkey. Date: 21 July 1744.
- will of Aquila Paca. Also, widow's
  election. Also, bond of Rachel Paca
  acting executrix. Sureties: Nathan
  Rigby, Richard Johns, Peregrine
  Frisby. Date: 28 July 1744. Also,
  renunciation of John Hall executor.
  Date: 14 June 1744.

31:531
- inventory & LoD of William Lacy.
- inventory of Bartholomew Millhuse.
- inventory of Zachariah Smith.
- accounts of Samuel Smith executor of
  William Smith.
- 2nd additional accounts of Heathcoat
  Pickett & his wife Eliza executrix
  of William Wright.
- accounts of Eliza Matthews executrix
  of Roger Matthews.
- accounts of John Williamson & Edward
  Cantwell sureties on estate of John
  Bailey.
- accounts of John Parks & his wife
  Bridget administratrix of
  Bartholomew Millhuse.
- accounts of Benjamin Curtis & his
  wife Avarilla administratrix of
  Nicholas Gorswick.

Mr. William Knight (CE) to examine
accounts of:
- James Knox & Jane Knox
  administrators of Edward Usher (CE).
- John Baldwin & his wife Mary
  administratrix of Dominick Carroll
  (CE). Additional accounts.

22 September. Exhibited from AA:
- bond of William Rogers as Deputy
  Commissary (AA). Sureties
  (Annapolis): John Carpenter, Robert

Court Session: 1744

Gordon. Date: 13 September 1744.

Mr. Thomas White (BA) to examine accounts of:
- Margaret Lacy administratrix of William Lacy (BA).
- Samuel Watkins executor of Samuel Watkins (BA).
- John Whiteaker administrator of Charles Whiteaker (BA). Additional accounts.

27 September. Thomas Aisquith (g, SM) exhibited:
- bond of Thomas Coode & James Dunbar administrators of Joshua Guibert. Sureties: Justinian Jordan, James Dunbar. Date: 9 August 1744.
- will of Richard Griffen, constituting Mary Griffen executrix. Also, widow's election. Said executrix was granted administration. Sureties: Isaac Pavett, Daniel Suliven. Date: 16 August 1744.
- will of Anthony Evans, constituting Winefred Trippe executrix. Said executrix was granted administration. Sureties: John Baker, Thomas Pearce. Date: 3 September 1744.
- inventory & LoD of George Whitter.
- inventory & LoD of Thomas Morris.
- inventory of Charles Griffen.
- accounts of Leah Ward administratrix of Benjamin Ward.
- accounts of Martha Wheatley executrix of Joseph Wheatley.
- accounts of Patrick Lurty & his wife Mary administratrix of William Adams.
- accounts of Thomas Tarlton & his wife Mary executrix of James Farthing.
- accounts of Peter Gough administrator of John Leak.
- accounts of Alexander Anderson & his wife Henrietta executrix of Thomas Janes.
- accounts of Paul Grugun & his wife Ann administratrix of Peter Thompson.

- accounts of Rebecca Dillon administratrix of Lawrence Dillon.
- accounts of William Aisquith executor of William Aisquith.
- accounts of William Leak & his wife Mary administratrix of Hugh Pilkinton.
- accounts of John Baker & his wife Eliza executrix of Michael Nuney.
- accounts of Charles King on estate of Charles King.
- accounts of Catherine Pain administratrix of Ezekiel Pain.
- accounts of William Taylor & his wife Patience executrix of Philip Evans.
- accounts of Ann Peacock administratrix of Paul Peacock.

31:532 28 September. Mr. Thomas Bullen (TA) to examine accounts of:
- Samuel Tharp & his wife Ann administratrix of Christopher Birckhead (TA).
- Catherine Kinnimont administratrix of Ambrose Kinnimont (TA).
- Anthony LeCompte & his wife Catherine administratrix of William Bennett (TA).
- Peter Caulk & John Booker administrators of John Barwick (TA).
- Peter Caulk & his wife Eliza administratrix of Joseph Porter (TA).

29 September. Exhibited from PG:
- bond of Richard Snowden administrator of Edward Gilmore. Sureties: Samuel Richardson, Patrick Doran. Date: 29 September 1744.

1 October. MM Josias Green (AA) & Samuel Soumain (AA) to appraise estate of William Ghiselin (AA).

Mr. Charles Hynson (KE) to examine accounts of:
- Hanse Hanson & his wife Margaret executrix of Glanville Rolph (KE).
- Joseph Ricketts & his wife Elisabeth administrators of Nathaniel Ricketts (KE).

2 October. Col. Gabriel Parker (CV) to examine accounts of:
- Margaret Peirce executrix of Charles Somerset Smith (CH).
- Rebecca Young & Roger Boyce executors of Samuel Young (CV).

Mr. Thomas Aisquith (SM) to examine accounts of:
- Mary Slye executrix of Gerrard Slye (SM).
- Elisabeth Clark administratrix of Robert Clark (SM).
- Thomas Price & his wife Elisabeth administratrix of Nicholas Poore, Jr. (SM).
- Luke Mattingly & his wife Priscilla administratrix of George Knott (SM).
- Thomas Wimsett administrator of Dorothy Smith (SM).
- William Field & his wife Mary executrix of John Alney (SM).
- Sarah Casel administratrix of John Casel (SM).
- James Howard & his wife Henrietta administratrix of James Clark (SM).

8 October. Mr. Walter Hanson (CH) to examine accounts of:
- William Poston surviving executor of John Poston (CH).
- William Williams & Sarah Rozar executors of George Johnson (CH).
- Elisabeth Hatton administratrix of George Hatton (CH).
- Mary Robinson administratrix of William Robinson (CH).
- Alexander McLaran & his wife Janet executrix of Peter Mitchell (CH).

31:533 9 October. Exhibited from CV:
- will of John Rousby, Esq., constituting Samuel Lloyd, John Rousby, & Abraham Barnes executors.

10 October. Exhibited from AA:
- inventory of Azell Davidge.

Exhibited from BA:
- inventory & LoD of Edward Fell.

Exhibited from CV:
- bond of Edward Lloyd, John Rousby, & Abraham Barnes executors of John Rousby, Esq. Sureties: Philip Thomas, Esq. (AA), Philip Key (g, SM). Date: 10 October 1744.

Exhibited from SM:
- Abraham Barnes (g, SM) deposed that he is passing his promissory note payable to John Edwards. Date: 10 October 1744.

11 October. Exhibited from KE:
- bond of Mary Chew administratrix of Dr. Samuel Chew. Sureties (AA): Joseph Cowman, John Galloway. Date: 9 October 1744.

Exhibited from PG:
- accounts of Elisabeth Duvall executrix of Mareen Duvall.

8 October. Elisabeth Wintersell administratrix of William Wintersell (AA) was granted continuance.

11 October. Mr. Peter Dent (PG) to examine accounts of:
- Blanford Beavan acting executor of Dr. John Kirkwood (PG).
- Ann Frazer executrix of Rev. John Frazer (PG).
- Elisabeth Condle executrix of David Condle (PG).
- Alexander Norton & his wife Ann administratrix of Henry Jones (PG). Additional accounts.
- William Pritchet & his wife Elinor administratrix of James Herbert (PG). Additional accounts.
- Allen Bowie & his wife Priscilla administratrix of William Finch (PG). Additional accounts.

15 October. Sheriff (PG) to render attachment to Lingan Wilson (PG) administrator of Joseph Wilson (PG) to render inventory.

31:534 Exhibited from KE:
- 2nd additional accounts of John

Spencer & his wife Sarah
administratrix of Hanse Hanson.

16 October. Exhibited from AA:
• will of Samuel Glover. Also,
  widow's election.

17 October. Mr. Charles Hynson (KE) to
examine accounts of:
• Christian Adair administratrix of
  Alexander Adair (KE).
• Jonathan Turner administrator of
  Mary Forbush (KE).

Mr. William Knight (CE) to examine
accounts of:
• Hermana Vanbebber executrix of
  Matthias Vanbebber (CE).
• Mary Holton administratrix of George
  Holton (CE).
• Hugh Terry administrator of Rosamond
  Terry (CE).
• Thomas Severson administrator of
  Isaac Clements (CE).
• Adam Vanbebber & his wife Mary
  executrix of Dr. John Knight (CE).
• Archibald Douglass administrator of
  Mary Douglass (CE).
• John McWhorter administrator of Hugh
  McWhorter (CE).
• John Harper & Cornelius Wooliston
  administrators of William Cook (CE).
• James Redus & his wife Catherine
  administratrix of William Sarson
  (CE).
• John Harper administrator dbn of
  Robert Whithers (CE). Additional
  accounts.

Maj. Henry Trippe (DO) to examine
accounts of:
• Ann Shehawn administratrix of Thomas
  Shehawn (DO).
• Thomas Woollford administrator of
  Solomon Taylor (DO).
• Ann Wing administratrix of Robert
  Wing (DO).

18 October. Gabriel Parker (g, CV)
exhibited:
• inventory of John Parran.
• inventory of John Gough.

Court Session: 1744

- accounts of James Allnutt executor of Sarah Allnutt.
- accounts of Mary Dawkins executrix of James Dawkins, Jr.
- additional accounts of Henry & Robert Lee executors of Robert Lee.

20 October. Exhibited from AA:
- LoD on estate of Richard Davis. Also, accounts of Ruth Davis executrix.

22 October. Peter Dent (g, PG) exhibited:
- bond of Jane Martin administratrix of Stephen Martin. Sureties: William Pain, William Berry. Date: 28 August 1744.
- bond of Rignall Odell administratrix of Richard Butt. Sureties: William Denune, Ninian Mariartee. Date: 29 August 1744.
- will of James Bowie, constituting Thomas Bowie executor. Said executor was granted administration. Sureties: John Bowie, Allen Bowie. Date: 28 September 1744.
- will of James Dickinson.
- will of James Trueman.
- inventory of Thomas Wilson.
- inventory of John Brawner.
- inventory of Nathan Masters.
- accounts of John Evans administrator of John Evans.
- accounts of William Pritchet & his wife Elinor administratrix of James Herbert.
- accounts of William Robinson & his wife Diana executrix of John Williams.
- accounts of Nathaniel Hays administrator of Thomas Hays.
- accounts of Ann Brooke executrix of Leonard Brooke.

31:535

Mr. Peter Dent (PG) to examine accounts of:
- John Orme executor of Amy Groome (PG).

23 October. Mr. William Tilghman (QA) to examine accounts of:

Page 51

- Benjamin Hines administrator of Jacob Deford who married Ann Crupper administratrix of Thomas Crupper (QA).
- Ann Scott, John Scott, & Solomon Scott executors of Nathaniel Scott (QA).
- John Baynard & his wife Eliza administratrix of Joshua Clarke (QA).
- Morgan Ponder & his wife Ann executrix of Thomas Hines (QA).
- Richard Scrivener & John Lloyd administrator of Elisabeth Bolton (QA).
- John Rogers & his wife Ann executrix of Thomas Butler executor of Thomas Butler (QA).
- Elisabeth Nevill administratrix of Walter Nevill (QA).

Exhibited from QA:
- additional accounts of Christopher Wilkinson & his wife Eliza executrix of Joseph Earle.

Exhibited from BA:
- accounts of Christopher Gist administrator of Richard Gist.

26 October. Exhibited from PG:
- additional accounts of William Young executor of Mary Young.

29 October. Charles Hynson (g, KE) exhibited:
- bond of Sarah Griffith administratrix of Charles Griffith. Sureties: Charles Smith, John Kenslaugh. Date: 2 June 1744.
- bond of Jane Clark administratrix of Benjamin Clarke. Sureties: Robert White, James Smith. Date: 21 July 1744.
- bond of Elisabeth Ringgold administratrix dbn of William Buckland. Sureties: Edward Worrell, Charles Ringgold. Date: 16 September 1744.
- will of John Tennant.
- will of Edward Holman.
- will of Richard Wethered.

- inventory & LoD of John Lynch.
- additional inventory of Matthias Day.
- LoD on estate of Matthias Day.
- additional inventory of Thomas Mahone.
- inventory of Robert Key.
- additional inventory of John Young.
- inventory & LoD of James Ringgold.
- inventory of Charles Griffith.
- additional inventory & LoD of Mary Forbush.
- LoD on estate of William Thomas.

31:536
- accounts of Richard Knight administrator of John Knight.
- accounts of Francis Spearman & his wife Hester administratrix of Thomas Wyate.
- accounts of Benjamin Ricaud & his wife Mary & James Roberts executors of William Roberts.
- accounts of Lewis Williams executor of Thomas Williams.
- accounts of William Johnson & his wife Eliza administratrix dbn of William Johnson.
- accounts of David Burk administrator of James Burk.
- accounts of Christopher Hall surviving executor of Matthias Day.
- accounts of Rachel Browning executrix of John Browning.
- certificate of no allowances to crave of John Hall.
- accounts of John Hart & his wife Charity administratrix of John Anger.
- accounts of Lambert Wilmer executor of Elisabeth Young.
- accounts of Katherine, William, & Thomas Massey executors of Thomas Massey.
- accounts of Peter Jones & his wife Mary administratrix of Francis Bellos.
- accounts of David Hall executor of George Wetherell.
- additional accounts of Lewis Williams executor of Thomas Williams.
- accounts of Katherine Smithers administratrix of Thomas Smithers.

- accounts of Richard Kennard administrator of George Barber.
- accounts of John Read & his wife Mary executrix of Thomas Mahone.
- accounts of William Thomas surviving executor of William Thomas.

Exhibited from TA:
- accounts of William Ridgeway acting executor of John Pearson.

Henry Trippe (g, DO) exhibited:
- bond of Rachel Sexton administratrix of Andrew Sexton. Sureties: James Vaulx, Florance Sulivane. Date: 8 June 1744.
- will of Leonard Jones, constituting Elisabeth Jones executrix. Also, widow's election. Said executrix was granted administration. Sureties: Leonard Jones, John Noble. Date: 12 June 1744.
- will of William Williams, constituting Monica Williams executrix. Said executrix was granted administration. Sureties: Richard Adams, William Bradley. Date: 18 June 1744.
- bond of Adling Cannon administratrix of William Cannon. Sureties: Arthur Whiteley, Richard Bradley, Joseph Bond. Date: 16 July 1744.
- bond of Elisabeth Collings administratrix of Patrick Collings. Sureties: Noah Pearson, Summer Adams. Date: 16 August 1744.
- bond of Summer Adams administrator of Morgan Adams. Sureties: Noah Pearson, Ezekiel Johnson. Date: 16 August 1744. Also, renunciation of Elin Adams (widow), recommending her son Summer Adams. Date: 14 August 1744. Witness: Thomas Adams Foxwell.
- will of Henry Edgar, constituting Ruth Edgar executrix. Said executrix was granted administration. Sureties: John Harper, John Gowtee. Date: 3 September 1744.

31:537
- bond of William Adams administrator of William Adams, Jr. Sureties:

Thomas Hackett, Henry Windows.
Date: 5 September 1744.
- inventory of William Hooper.
- inventory of Elinor Hart.
- inventory & LoD of James Spencer.
- additional inventory & LoD of Timothy Graylis.
- inventory & LoD of William Lister.
- inventory of John Hayward.
- inventory & LoD of William Williams.
- inventory of Andrew Sexton.
- inventory of Leonard Jones.
- inventory & LoD of James Galloway.
- additional inventory & LoD of William Johns.
- inventory of William Cannon.
- inventory & LoD of William Williams.
- accounts of John Traverse & Matthew Traverse executors of Matthew Traverse.
- accounts of Thomas Long & his wife Rebecca administratrix of Thomas Courson.
- accounts of Thomas Brannock executor of Rebecca Harwood.
- additional accounts of Matthew Hargaton who married Margaret Bullock administratrix of John Bullock.
- accounts of George Griffith & his wife Mary executrix of Capt. Richard Willis.
- accounts of Sarah Owens executrix of William Owens.
- accounts of George Griffith administrator of James Slone.
- accounts of Elisabeth Beachamp administratrix of Robert Beachamp.
- accounts of John Hayword executor of William Johns.
- accounts of Owen Graylis administrator of Timothy Graylis.

Mr. Henry Trippe (DO) to examine accounts of:
- Mary Williams executrix of William Williams (DO).
- William Galloway executor of James Galloway (DO).
- Rachel Jones administratrix of Walter Hunter (DO).
- Monica Williams executrix of William

Williams (DO).

30 October. Mr. Thomas White (BA) to examine accounts of:
- John Ramsey, Jr. & his wife Hannah administratrix of William Poteet (BA).
- James Harrison & his wife Mary administratrix of Gilbert Crocket (BA).

2 November. Exhibited from CH:
- accounts of Theophilus Swift & his wife Mary executrix of Rev. William Maconchie.

3 November. Exhibited from AA:
- accounts of Elisabeth Browne administratrix of John Elliott Browne.

Mr. Peter Dent (PG) to examine accounts of:
- Martha Waring acting executrix of Martha Greenfield (PG).
- Elisabeth Waring executrix of Richard Marsham Waring (PG).
- Mary Ashcom Brooke executrix of Walter Brooke (PG).
- Thomas Letchworth & his wife Eliza administratrix of Nathaniel Skinner (PG).

31:538 9 November. Exhibited from AA:
- accounts of Thomas John Hammond executor of John Hammond.

William Rogers (g, AA) exhibited:
- additional inventory of John Hammond.

12 November. M. Macnemara (g, AA) exhibited:
- bond of Elisabeth Burgess administratrix of Samuel Burgess. Sureties: William Disney, John Burgess. Date: 12 January 1743.
- bond of Edward & John Hall executors of Edward Hall. Sureties: James Meek, Charles Stevens. Date: 23 February 1743.
- bond of Margaret Hopkins executrix

Court Session: 1744

of Gerrard Hopkins. Sureties:
Gerrard Hopkins, Philip Hopkins,
Samuel Hopkins, Richard Hopkins,
John Hopkins. Date: 16 March 1743.
- bond of Nicholas Maccubbin
administrator of John Taylor.
Surety: Philip Thomas. Date: 2
April 1744.
- bond of Joanna Birkhead
administratrix of Eleazar Birkhead.
Sureties: Charles Drury, Francis
Crandall. Date: 9 APril 1744.
- will of Nehemiah Birckhead,
constituting Nehemiah Birckhead &
John Birckhead executors. Said
executors were granted
administration. Sureties: Richard
Randall (AA), Dr. John Hamilton
(CV). Date: 26 July 1744.
- renunciation of Margaret Goodman
widow of Richard Goodman
(carpenter), recommending James Dick
(greatest creditor). Mentions:
Francis Day. Date: 1 August 1744.
- bond of Patrick Creagh administrator
of John Wabby. Surety: Horatio
Samuel Middleton (Annapolis, AA).
Date: 7 August 1744.
- bond of Caleb Dorsey & John Dorsey
administrators of John Dorsey (son
of Caleb). Surety: John Lomas.
Date: 10 August 1744.
- bond of Philip Hammond administrator
of James Williams. Surety: Thomas
Hammond. Date: 16 August 1744.
Also, renunciation of Mary Williams
(widow), recommending Mr. Philip
Hammond. Date: 19 July 1744.
Witness: James Williams.
- will of Thomas Donaldson
- will of James Wilson.
- inventory of Eleazar Birckhead
- inventory of John Brandon. Also,
accounts of William Cumming, Esq.
administrator.
- accounts of John Simpson
administrator of Elinor Rawlings.

31:539   William Rogers (g, AA) exhibited:
- bond of Mary Hammond administratrix
of Nicholas Hammond. Sureties:
Mordecai Hammond, William Cumming.

Court Session: 1744

Date: 1 October 1744.
- bond of Elisabeth McLeod administratrix of William Jones. Sureties: James Dick, Simon Duff. Date: 5 October 1744.
- bond of Edward Parish & Thomas Norris administrators of Thomas Esdell. Sureties: John Norris, Thomas Williamson. Date: 10 November 1744.
- will of Samuel Burman.
- inventory of Nehemiah Birckhead.
- additional inventory of Mark Richardson.
- inventory of John Taylor.
- accounts of Capt. John Carpenter administrator of John Davis.

10 November. Sheriff (PG) to summon Thomas Lee (PG) surviving executor of Philip Lee, Jr. (CH) to render accounts.

Court Session: 13 November 1744

Docket:
- William Cumming, Esq. procurator for Charles Hynson (g, KE) & his wife Phebe (formerly Phebe Carvill) one of daughters of Mary Smithers (gentlewoman, KE, dec'd) vs. Stephen Bordley procurator for John Carvil executor of said dec'd. Text of libel. Abstract of dec'd's will: legacies: daughter Phebe Carvill Negro Phillis (woman) & Negro Toney (boy) & Negro Patience (girl) & Negro Dido (woman) & her child & Negro Grace (girl). Mentions: Mr. John Hanbury (merchant),

31:540   son John & daughter Phebe Carvill, Phebe's Aunt Paca. Executor: John Carvill (son, g, KE). Plaintiffs married 9 months after the decease of said Smithers.

31:541   Mentions: W. Harris (sheriff, KE). Text of answer.

31:542   Said dec'd died in January/February 1738. Mentions: Charles Hynson & William Hynson as 2 uncles of plaintiff,

31:543   Capt. Samuel Jarrold.

Court Session: 13 November 1744

Daniel Cheston (sheriff, KE) to
summon Paul Whichcoat & Cornelius
Dunahane.

31:544
- Ruling: agreed.
- S.B. for William Masters (PG) vs.
W.C. for Priscilla Wilson. Libel.
- Sheriff (SO) to summon Samuel
Collings (SO) surviving executor of
Richard Chambers (SO) to take LoA.
Deputy Commissary (SO) has granted
LoA on said estate. Discontinued.
- Stephen Bordley procurator for
William Thomas (AA) vs. William
Cumming, Esq. procurator for William
Holland as one of executors of Col.
William Holland (g, AA).
Text of libel. Defendants are:
Elisabeth Holland (DO), Thomas
Holland (CV), & William Holland
(CV). Abstract of will of dec'd.
Legacy to his grandson William
Thomas (under age 21). Plaintiff
was a minor at the time of the death
of dec'd, but has since arrived at
age 21.

31:545
Mentions: G. Parker (sheriff, CV).
Ruling: agreed.
- Thomas Wilson administrator of Ann
Davie (CH) vs. Arabella Hines wife
of Joseph Hines. Sheriff (CH) to
summon defendant to testify
regarding concealment of estate of
dec'd.
- Ann Jenkins administratrix of Thomas
Jenkins (CH) vs. Susannah Jenkins
(widow, CH). Walter Hanson
(sheriff, CH) to summon defendant to
show cause why she conceals estate
of dec'd.
    - Susannah Jenkins, age 52,
    deposed. She is the mother of
    the dec'd & the dec'd married a
    daughter of

31:546
James Middleton. Mentions:
Negro Poll (girl).
    - Matthew Barnes, Sr., age 74,
    deposed.
    - Mary Manning, age 37, deposed.
    - Henrietta Semmes (daughter of
    Susannah Jenkins), age 31,
    deposed.
    - John Manning, age 27, deposed.

Page 59

Court Session: 13 November 1744

- John Jenkins, age 24, deposed.
- Edward Jenkins, age 63, deposed. Mentions: James Middleton & his wife.

31:547
- Marmaduke Semmes, age 43, deposed. Mentions: Negro Solomon (boy).

Ruling: discontinued.

- B.Y. for Richard Watts & John Carr executors of John Watts (PG) vs. S.B. for Andrew Scott administrator of John Watts. Sheriff (PG) to render attachment to defendant to render final accounts.
- Sheriff (PG) to render attachment to Lingan Wilson (PG) administrator of Joseph Lingan (PG) to render inventory. Said Lingan exhibited that he requested James Wilson (brother) & Turner Wootton (guardian to (N) Wilson (minor, nephew)) to sign the inventory & they have refused.
- Sheriff (PG) to summon Thomas Lee (PG) surviving executor of Philip Lee, Jr. (CH) to render accounts.

Court Session: 1744

13 November. Exhibited from BA:
- additional accounts of William Hamilton & Luke Trotten executors of John Gardner.

Exhibited from CV:
- accounts of Ephraim Gardner administrator of Robert Lyles.

31:548 Thomas White (g, BA) exhibited:
- will of Thomas Woodward.
- additional inventory of Samuel Watkins.
- additional accounts of Josias Middlemore executor of William Cawthren.
- accounts of George Chauncey & John Hanson administrators of Sarah Hanson.
- accounts of Margaret Lacey administratrix of William Lacey.
- accounts of Samuel Watkins executor of Samuel Watkins.

Page 60

Court Session: 1744

William Rogers (g, AA) exhibited:
- bond of Margaret Richardson & Daniel Richardson executors of William Richardson. Sureties: Joseph Richardson, Sr., Joseph Richardson, Jr., Joseph Hill. Date: 13 November 1744.

14 November. Exhibited from AA:
- additional accounts of Elisabeth Wintersell administratrix of William Fish.
- additional accounts of Elisabeth Wintersell administratrix of William Wintersell.

15 November. Exhibited from PG:
- bond of Richard Snowden administrator of Edward Rawlings. Sureties: William Kirkland, Thomas Sparrow. Date: 15 November 1744.

Thomas Bullen (g, TA) exhibited:
- bond of Mary Snelling administratrix of Thomas Snelling. Sureties: Henry Burgess, Thomas Burgess. Date: 5 October 1744.
- will of John Reynolds, constituting Sarah Reynolds executrix. Also, widow's election. Said executrix was granted administration. Sureties: John Carslake, William Gary. Date: 26 October 1744.
- will of Varty Sweat. Also, renunciation of 1 executor. Also, bond of Elisabeth Sweat acting executrix. Sureties: John Sweat, David Fitzpatrick. Date: 26 October 1744.
- bond of Francis Armstrong, Jr. administrator of Bennett Peck. Sureties: John Davis (Miles River), Elijah Skillington. Date: 5 November 1744.
- additional inventory & LoD of Joseph Bounton.
- inventory of William Ardery.
- inventory of William Skinner, Sr.
- inventory of John Camper.
- inventory of Nathaniel Grace.
- inventory & LoD of William Skinner, Jr.

Court Session: 1744

- accounts of Jane, Joseph, & William Harrington executors of Richard Harrington.
- accounts of Thomas Bounton administrator of Joseph Bounton.
- accounts of Sarah Reynolds (formerly Sarah Lenard) executrix of John Lenard.

Mr. Thomas Bullen (TA) to examine accounts of:
- Mary Dawson & Impey Dawson executors of James Dawson (TA).
- Philemon Hambleton executor of William Hambleton (TA).
- Peter Harwood, Jr. & his wife Susannah administratrix of John Stewart (TA).

31:549 16 November. Exhibited from BA:
- bond of Burridge Scott administrator of James Powell. Sureties: William Mattingly, William Ensor. Date: 16 November 1744.

17 November. Mr. Charles Hynson (KE) to examine accounts of:
- Elisabeth Pinar administratrix of Thomas Pinar (KE).

21 November. Exhibited from PG:
- accounts of James Kingsbury executor of Elisabeth Kingsbury.

Exhibited from KE:
- additional accounts of William Butcher executor of Edmund Butcher.

Exhibited from DO:
- 2nd additional accounts of Rosannah Loockerman executrix of Jacob Loockerman.

22 November. Exhibited from PG:
- additional accounts of William Smith executor of Mary Demall.

Exhibited from AA:
- additional accounts of Sarah, John, Samuel, Edward, Benjamin, & Henry Gaither executors of Benjamin Gaither.

Court Session: 1744

<u>26 November</u>. Exhibited from PG:
- inventory of Philemon Plummer.

Gabriel Parker (g, CV) exhibited:
- will of Martha Lingan, constituting Thomas & George Lingan executors. Said executors were granted administration. Sureties: John Hamilton, John Smith. Date: 29 October 1744.
- inventory of Sarah Whinfield.
- inventory of Thomas Morsell.
- inventory of Samuel Little.
- inventory of Sarah Ogleby.
- accounts of William Kidd & John Lynch administrators of William Lynch.

Mr. Thomas White (BA) to examine accounts of:
- Patrick Lynch & his wife Sarah executrix of Benjamin Bowen, Sr. (BA).

<u>27 November</u>. Exhibited from PG:
- inventory of Mary Demall.

Exhibited from BA:
- additional accounts of Samuel Bowen acting executor of John Bowen.

31:550 <u>29 November</u>. Peter Dent (g, PG) exhibited:
- bond of Mary Riley administratrix of Terrance Riley. Sureties: John Hillary, Leonard Piles. Date: 15 October 1744.
- bond of William Flintham administratrix [!] of John McCoye. Surety: Capt. Charles Higginbotham. Date: 19 October 1744.
- bond of William Flintham administrator of James Bensford. Surety: Capt. Charles Higginbotham. Date: 20 October 1744.
- will of Eleanor Deveron.
- additional inventory of David Hennes.
- inventory of Rev. John Frazer.
- inventory of Edward Jones.
- additional inventory of Amy Groome.
- inventory of Matthew Markland.

Page 63

- inventory of Richard Butt.
- accounts of Elisabeth Condle executrix of David Condle.
- accounts of Allen Bowie & his wife Priscilla administratrix of Capt. William Finch.
- accounts of Dr. Charles Stewart administrator of Nicholas Brumley.
- accounts of Ann Frazer executrix of Rev. John Frazer.
- accounts of Priscilla Covington administratrix of Leonard Covington.
- accounts of George Scott administrator of David Hennes.
- accounts of Edward Pye administrator of Walter Pye.
- accounts of Alexander Morton & his wife Ann administratrix of Henry Jones.

5 December. Exhibited from AA:
- additional accounts of Joseph Williams administrator of William Brewer.

Exhibited from PG:
- inventory of Alexander Beall.

Walter Hanson (g, CH) exhibited:
- bond of Sarah Hall administratrix of Thomas Hall. Sureties: James Riley, John McCoye. Date: 6 September 1744.
- bond of William Smallwood Taylor administrator of Ann Taylor. Sureties: Edward Maddox, Benjamin Maddox. Date: 18 September 1744.
- bond of William Butler administrator of John Butler. Sureties: John Biggs, Thomas Ash. Date: 23 September 1744.
- will of John Chunn. Also, bond of Richard Chunn acting executor. Sureties: Andrew Chunn, Thomas Birch, Sr., Joseph Allen. Date: 25 October 1744.
- will of William Carter.
- accounts of John Reyley administrator of Edmund Devene.
- accounts of Joseph Milburn Semmes administrator of Ignatius Semmes.
- accounts of Walter Scott

administrator of James Scott.
- accounts of Arthur Lee & his wife Ann administratrix of Robert Yates.

31:551 10 December. William Tilghman (g, QA) exhibited:
- bond of Amy Powell administratrix of John Powell, Jr. Sureties: Stephen Andrews, James Sutton. Date: 4 October 1744.
- bond of Mary Hollingsworth administratrix of Vincent Hollingsworth. Sureties: John Bolton, Albert Johnson. Date: 15 November 1744.
- will of William Burton. Also, widow's election.
- inventory of William Ford.
- inventory & LoD of John Mumford.
- inventory & LoD of William Murphy.
- inventory & LoD of Capt. John Elliott.
- inventory of Samuel Osborne.
- inventory of Henry Covington.
- inventory of John Primrose.
- inventory of John Smith.

Exhibited from PG:
- will of Mordecai Coleman. Also, bond of Mordecai Coleman administrator. Sureties (AA): James Dick, Samuel Preston Moore. Date: 10 December 1744.

Exhibited from AA:
- accounts of William Allen & his wife Catherine executrix of William Crouch.

11 December. Appointment of Mr. Ennalls Hooper as Deputy Commissary (DO), in the room of Maj. Henry Trippe.

20 July. [Omitted from f. 311.] Exhibited from TA:
- Thomas Barnett (TA), age 55, deposed that he was an appraiser of the estate of Richard Holmes (p, TA). Date: 13 July 1744. Signed: James Barnett.

11 December. Petition of John Coursey
(p, QA). Administration of estate of
James Coursey (QA, d. 1714) was granted
to James Coursey & William Turbutt.
Administration bond assigned to
petitioner.

31:552 Mr. William Tilghman (QA) to examine
accounts of:
- Rachel Primrose executrix of John
  Primrose (QA).
- James Powell executor of Thomas
  Powell (QA).
- Andrew Carrer administrator of Henry
  Fortune (QA).

13 December. Mr. Charles Hynson (KE)
to examine accounts of:
- Sarah Kennard administratrix of John
  Kennard (KE).
- Oliver Caulk, Isaac Caulk, & Jacob
  Caulk executors of Mary Pearce (KE).

15 December. Maj. Thomas White (BA) to
examine additional accounts of:
- Robert Bishop & his wife Elisabeth
  executrix of Nicholas Day (BA).

17 December. Col. Gabriel Parker (CV)
exhibited:
- will of James Hungerford,
  constituting Elisabeth Hungerford
  executrix. Said executrix was
  granted administration. Sureties:
  Daniel Rawlings, John Simons. Date:
  3 December 1744.
- will of James Shanks. Also, bond of
  James Sommervelle administrator.
  Sureties: Peter Hellen, Benjamin
  Ellt. Date: 3 December 1744.
- will of John Phillips, constituting
  Jane Phillips executrix. Said
  executrix was granted
  administration. Sureties: Thomas
  Hardesty, William Hardesty. Date:
  11 December 1744.

Exhibited from BA:
- 3rd additional accounts of William
  Savory administrator of James
  Maxwell.

19 December. Exhibited from AA:
* additional accounts of Richard Harrison administrator of Sarah Harrison.

21 December. William Rogers (g, AA) exhibited:
* bond of Ann Burman executrix of Samuel Burman. Sureties: Thomas Reynolds, Francis Crandall. Date: 15 November 1744.
* bond of John Hall administrator of Benjamin Prickyard. Sureties: Joseph Chew, John Connor. Date: 28 November 1744.
* will of Francis Crandall, constituting Joseph Crandall executor. Said executor was granted administration. Sureties: Jacob Franklin, John Norris. Date: 30 November 1744.
* inventory of Thomas Howell.
* inventory of Gerrard Hopkins.
* accounts of Henry Hall executor of Thomas Howell.
* accounts of John Rawlings & his wife Margaret administratrix of Nathaniel Fairbrother.

31:553   Thomas Bullen (g, TA) exhibited:
* bond of Susannah Clark administratrix of William Clark. Sureties: Pearce Fleming, John Abbott. Date: 19 November 1744.
* bond of Jacob Gore administrator of John Sankston, Jr. Sureties: John Harrington, William Harrington. Date: 30 November 1744.
* accounts of Anthony Lecompte & his wife Catherine administratrix of William Bennett.
* accounts of Solomon Sharp & his wife Ann administratrix of Christopher Birckhead.

22 December. M. Macnemara (g, AA) exhibited:
* will of Edward Hall.

25 December. Col. Gabriel Parker (CV) exhibited:
* will of Benjamin Harris,

constituting Sarah Harris executrix.
Said executrix was granted
administration. Sureties: Richard
Harrison, Samuel Harrison. Date: 24
December 1744.

3 January. Exhibited from BA:
• will of John Wright.

William Rogers (g, AA) exhibited:
• will of Dennis Ryan, constituting
  Elinor Ryan executrix. Also,
  widow's election. Said executrix
  was granted administration.
  Sureties: Abraham Simmons, Sr.,
  William Simmons. Date: 3 January
  1744.

5 January. Samuel Smith, Esq. & Francis
Mapp executors of Alice Andrews (AA) vs.
Joseph Hill (g, AA). Richard Burdus (g,
one of coroners of AA) to summon
defendant to show cause why will of
dec'd should not be proved.

7 January. William Rogers (g, AA)
exhibited:
• additional inventory of Mark
  Richardson.
• accounts of William Hollyday & his
  wife Mary administratrix of Mark
  Richardson.

Court Session: 8 January 1744

31:554 Docket:
• Stephen Bordley procurator for
  William Masters (PG) vs. William
  Cumming, Esq. procurator for
  Priscilla Wilson.
  Text of libel. Plaintiff had 2 sons
  Nathan & Robert married to (N)
  Wilson daughter of Priscilla Wilson
  (widow, PG), having 3 children
  (infants). Said Nathan is dec'd.
  Said Priscilla falsely alleged that
  said Robert Masters, residing in VA,
  had renounced administration. Said
  Robert resided in the Province & did
  not renounce until he renounced in
  favor of plaintiff.
31:555 Mentions: John Cook (sheriff, PG).

Court Session: 8 January 1744

Ruling: agreed.

- Thomas Wilson administrator of Ann Davie (CH) vs. Arabella Hines wife of Joseph Hines (CH). Sheriff (CH) to render attachment to defendant to testify regarding concealment of estate of dec'd.
- B.Y. for Richard Watts & John Carr executors of John Watts (PG) vs. S.B. for Andrew Scott administrator of John Watts.
- Sheriff (PG) to render attachment to Lingan Wilson (PG) administrator of Joseph Wilson (PG) to render inventory.

31:556 • Sheriff (PG) to summon Thomas Lee (PG) surviving executor of Philip Lee, Jr. (CH) to render accounts. Accounts exhibited. Discontinued.

- Samuel Smith, Esq. & Francis Mapp executors of Alice Andrews vs. Joseph Hill (g, AA). Richard Burdus (g, coroner of AA) to summon defendant to show cause why the will of dec'd should not be proved. Said will has been proved. Discontinued.

Court Session: 1744

9 January. Benton Harris (g, WO) exhibited:

- bond of Joseph Schoolfield executor of Joseph Schoolfield. Sureties: Adam Bell, John Notham. Date: 26 October 1744.
- bond of George Jarman administrator of Absolom Bessicke. Sureties: Ishmael Davis, Joseph Nicholson. Date: 7 November 1744.
- bond of Naomi Smasha administratrix of William Smasha. Sureties: Richard Blizard, William Hook. Date: 7 November 1744.
- will of Selby Claywell, constituting Peter Claywell executor. Said executor was granted administration. Sureties: John Sheldon, Adam Bell. Date: 18 December 1744.
- will of Affradozi Johnson.
- will of Samuel Hopkins.
- inventory of Clement Beach.
- inventory of Martha Walton.

- inventory & LoD of John Jarman.
- accounts of Spence Hall executor of Robert Hall.
- accounts of William Gillett executor of John Gillett.
- accounts of William Stephen Hill & his wife Rebecca executrix of John Smith.
- accounts of Martha Selby executrix of John Purnell.
- accounts of James Martin administrator of Clement Beach.
- accounts of Margaret Davis administratrix of William Davis.

Exhibited from AA:
- additional accounts of Benjamin Wright executor of Henry Wright.

31:557 Mr. Benton Harris (WO) to examine accounts of:
- Littleton Townsend administrator of Job Shery (WO).
- Catherine Breeman administratrix of James Breeman (WO).
- William Burton administrator of Christopher Topham (WO).
- Rachel Wheeler executrix of William Wheeler (WO).
- Margery Morris administratrix of William Morris (WO).
- Ann Merrida Godfrey administratrix of Charles Godfrey (WO).
- Matthew Wise administrator of Thomas Wise (WO).
- Wheatley Dennis & his wife Elisabeth executrix of Benjamin Holland (WO).
- Ebeneazar Evans & his wife Sophia administratrix of Thomas Simpson (WO). Additional accounts.

10 January. Exhibited from CH:
- accounts of Thomas Lee surviving executor of Philip Lee, Jr.

Exhibited from AA:
- will of Thomas Henderson.

12 January. Exhibited from AA:
- accounts of Thomas Richardson surviving executor of Richard Richardson.

- will of Alice Andrews.

18 January. Exhibited from CV:
- 5th additional accounts of John Smith surviving executor of Thomas Smith.

21 January. Exhibited from PG:
- inventory of Philip Lee, Esq.

Exhibited from AA:
- accounts of Aaron & William Rawlings executors of Aaron Rawlings.

22 January. Robert Freeland & his wife Sarah executrix of Thomas Holland were granted continuance.

28 January. Gabriel Parker (g, CV) exhibited:
- bond of Mary Crompton administratrix of Thomas Crompton. Sureties: John Skinner, Edward Gantt. Date: 14 January 1744.
- bond of John Griffin administrator of Abraham Clark. Sureties: Newman Harvey, John Dew. Date: 16 January 1744.
- bond of Benjamin Johns administrator of Francis Stallings. Sureties: William Harris, Samuel Harris. Date: 18 January 1744.
- bond of Capell King administrator of William Malden. Sureties: John Mackall, Robert Roberts. Date: 19 January 1744.
- additional inventory of Samuel Young. Also, accounts of Rebecca Young & Roger Boyce executors.

31:558 Mr. Walter Hanson (CH) to examine accounts of:
- Ann Jenkins administratrix of Thomas Jenkins (CH).

Exhibited from AA:
- LoD on estate of Caleb Dorsey. Also, accounts of Richard & Edward Dorsey executors.

31 January. Thomas White (g, BA) exhibited:

- bond of John Hall administrator of Thomas Johnson. Sureties: James Taylor, Gabriel Browne. Date: 3 November 1744.
- will of James Tolley, constituting Walter Tolley executor. Said executor was granted administration. Sureties: Thomas Gittings, James Maxwell. Date: 6 November 1744.
- will of Mary Tolley, constituting John Hammond Dorsey executor. Said executor was granted administration. Sureties: Vincent Dorsey, John Day (son of Edward). Date: 17 November 1744.
- bond of Nicholas Gay administrator dbn of Samuel Maxwell. Sureties: George Brown, Robert Dutton. Date: 13 December 1744.
- will of Thomas Hooker.
- additional probate of will of John Murphy.
- inventory of William Annis. Also, accounts of John Hall administrator.
- inventory & LoD of Samuel Maxwell.
- inventory of Thomas Woodward.
- additional accounts of John Whitaker administrator of Charles Whitaker.
- accounts of John Ramsey, Jr. & his wife Johannah administratrix of William Poteet.
- accounts of Patrick Lynch & his wife Sarah executrix of Benjamin Bowen.
- accounts of James Harrison & his wife Mary administratrix of Gilbert Crockett.

4 February. Walter Hanson (g, CH) exhibited:
- will of Andrew Sympson, constituting Juliana Sympson executrix. Said executrix was granted administration. Sureties: Joseph Milburn Semmes, William Hagar. Date: 3 December 1744.
- will of John Clubb, constituting Matthew Clubb executor. Said executor was granted administration. Sureties: William Atchison, Edward Murphey. Date: 3 January 1744.
- will of Barton Smoot, constituting Ann Smoot & Thomas Smoot executors.

Said executors were granted
administration. Sureties: Alexander
Hawkins, Charles Smoot. Date: 16
January 1744.
- additional inventory of Thomas
Jenkins.
- inventory of John Chunn.
- inventory of James Hamblin.
- inventory of Ann Taylor.
- inventory of John Butler.
- accounts of Elisabeth Hatton
administratrix of George Hatton.
- accounts of Mary Robison
administratrix of William Robison.
- accounts of James Mankin
administrator of George Hope.
- accounts of William Posten surviving
executor of John Posten.
- accounts of Alexander McLaran & his
wife Janet executrix of Peter
Mitchell.

Mr. Walter Hanson (CH) to examine
additional accounts of:
- Francis Ware & John Doncastle
executors of Ann Ebernethy (CH).

Exhibited from AA:
- will of Margaret Quinley.

31:559   Peter Dent (g, PG) exhibited:
- bond of Richard Clements
administrator of Thomas Jaco.
Sureties: William Miles, Benjamin
Swann. Date: 14 January 1744.
- bond of William Middleton
administrator of Thomas Middleton.
Sureties: James Keach, James
Griffin. Date: 28 January 1744.
- accounts of Virlinda Beall executrix
of John Beall.

5 February. Peter Dent (g, PG)
exhibited:
- inventory of Joseph White.
- inventory of Terrance Riley.
- accounts of John Orme executor of
Amy Groome.
- accounts of Stephen Lewis
administrator of William Blake.
- accounts of Charles Robinson
executor of George Gentle.

Court Session: 1744

- accounts of Thomas Marshall administrator of James McFall.
- accounts of Elisabeth Waring executrix of Richard Marsham Waring.

Col. Gabriel Parker (CV) to examine accounts of:
- Elisabeth Young administratrix of Joseph Gough (CV).

6 February. Thomas Bullen (g, TA) exhibited:
- will of Jacob Williams, constituting Rachel Williams executrix. Also, widow's election. Said executrix was granted administration. Sureties: John Sweat, James Sanders. Date: 11 January 1744.
- nuncupative will of Catherine Newnam.
- will of Elisabeth Collison.
- additional inventory & LoD of James Dawson.
- inventory & LoD of William Clarke.
- inventory of John Sankston, Jr.
- inventory of John Reynolds.
- accounts of Peter Calk & his wife Elisabeth administratrix of Joseph Porter.
- accounts of Mary & Impey Dawson executors of James Dawson.
- accounts of William Ryan & his wife Hannah administratrix of James Maclendon.

Thomas Sligh & (N) Morgan sureties on estate of Buckler Partridge (BA) vs. Jane Partridge administratrix of dec'd. Sheriff (BA) to summon defendant to render accounts.

12 February. Mr. Thomas Bullen (TA) to examine accounts of:
- Rebecca Stacey administratrix of William Stacey (TA).

John Lang vs. Richard Snowden (AA) administrator dbn of Thomas South (PG). Sheriff (AA) to summon defendant to render accounts.

Court Session: 1744

Mr. Thomas White (BA) to examine accounts of:
- Avarilla Hall executrix of Col. Edward Hall (BA).
- Lewis Lafee & his wife Sarah executrix of William Lowe (BA).

31:560 Nehemiah King (g, SO) exhibited:
- bond of Joseph Bounds administrator of John Richardson. Surety: Wilson Rider. Also, renunciation of Rachel Richardson (widow), recommending her friend Joseph Bounds. Date: 22 September 1744. Witness: Willson Rider.
- bond of James Train administrator of James Train, Jr. Sureties: William Smith, Col. George Dashiell. Date: 12 January 1744.
- will of Robert Dashiell, constituting Esther Dashiell executrix. Said executrix was granted administration. Sureties: Col. George Dashiell, Capt. Isaac Handy. Date: 12 January 1744.
- will of Thomas Walker, constituting Mary Richardson & Sarah Fletcher executrices. Said executrices were granted administration. Sureties: Col. George Dashiell, Dr. Patrick Stewart. Date: 12 January 1744.
- bond of Milcah Gale administratrix of John Gale. Sureties: George Gale, Matthias Gale. Date: 24 January 1744.
- will of James Jones, constituting Sarah Jones executrix. Also, widow's election. Said executrix was granted administration. Sureties: Joseph Callaway, William Waller. Date: 25 January 1744.
- will of James Deane.
- will of James Bleuer. Also, widow's election.
- inventory & LoD of Christopher Nutter.
- inventory of William Langsdall.
- inventory & LoD of William Mister.
- inventory of Benjamin Tulley.
- inventory of Nathaniel Cottman.
- inventory & LoD of James Tulley.
- accounts of Willson Rider executor

Page 75

of Thomas Ralph.
- accounts of Ann Nelson (alias Ann Pitts) administratrix of John Nelson.
- accounts of John Rigby administrator of Lewis Rigby.

13 February. Mr. Nehemiah King (SO) to examine accounts of:
- Joseph Riggen administrator of Ambrose Riggen (SO).
- Mary Riggen & James Riggen executors of Teague Riggen (SO).

14 February. William Tilghman (g, QA) exhibited:
- bond of Frances Wright administratrix of Fairclough Wright. Sureties: John Scott, Thomas Roe, Jr. Date: 17 January 1744.
- will of Jacob Winchester, constituting Mary Winchester executrix. Said executrix was granted administration. Sureties: John Smith (surgeon), Andrew Price, Jr. Date: 30 January 1744.
- will of Alice Lloyd.
- additional inventory & LoD of Thomas Butler.
- accounts of John Larwood & his wife Mary administratrix of Nathaniel Hinesley.
- accounts of John Lloyd & Richard Scrivener administrators of Elisabeth Bolton.
- accounts of Elisabeth Nevil administratrix of Walter Nevil, Jr.
- accounts of Ann, John, & Solomon Scott executors of Nathaniel Scott.
- accounts of John Baynard & his wife Elisabeth administratrix of Joshua Clarke.
- accounts of John Rogers & his wife Ann executrix & Thomas Butler executor of Thomas Butler.
- accounts of Benjamin Hines who married Ann Crupper administratrix of Thomas Crupper.
- accounts of Andrew Carrer administrator of Henry Fortune.
- accounts of Elisabeth Jones administratrix of Henry Jones.

31:561 Exhibited from BA:
- bond of Jannette Janssen Bourdillon administratrix of Benedict Bourdillon. Sureties: John Risteau, Henry Morgan. Date: 22 January 1744.

Capt. William Jones & Capt. Robert Jones to appraise estate of Col. Levin Gale (SO), in room of Capt. John Handy (dec'd).

Thomas Harrington (QA) son of Thomas Harrington (TA, dec'd) vs. James Slaughter (QA) & his wife Elisabeth executrix of said dec'd. Sheriff (QA) to summon defendants to show cause why they withhold legacy from plaintiff.

16 February. M. Macnemara (g, AA) exhibited:
- will of William Ross.
- bond of Burridge Scott & his wife Rebecca executrix of Elinor Herbert. Sureties: Henry Dorsey, Richard Burk. Date: 3 May 1744.

18 February. Mr. William Knight (CE) to examine accounts of:
- Rachel Piggot administratrix of John Piggot (CE).
- Elisabeth Beazley administratrix of Jeffery Beazley (CE).
- Elisabeth Alricke administratrix of Sickfredus Alricke (CE).
- John Gibbony administrator of John Archibald (CE).
- Elisabeth Frisby administratrix of Peregrine Frisby (CE). Additional accounts.

19 February. Mr. Charles Hynson (KE) to examine accounts of:
- Nicholas Linch executor of John Linch (KE).
- James Smith administrator of Richard Reading (KE).
- Elisabeth Ricketts & Joseph Ricketts administrators of Nathaniel Ricketts (KE).
- John Read & his wife Mary executrix of Thomas Mahone (KE). Additional

Court Session: 1744

accounts.

<u>22 February</u>. Benton Harris (g, WO)
exhibited:
- will of Richard Badard, constituting
  Ann Badard executrix. Said
  executrix was granted
  administration. Sureties: Gammage
  Evans, Benjamin Davis. Date: 19
  January 1744.
- bond of Martha Harvey administratrix
  of John Harvey. Sureties: Andrew
  Collins, David Smith. Date: 30
  January 1744.
- bond of Mary Smith administratrix of
  William Smith. Sureties: James
  Stephen Bredell, John Burton. Date:
  4 February 1744.
- accounts of Wheatley Dennis & his
  wife Elisabeth executrix of Benjamin
  Holland.
- additional accounts of Ebineazer
  Evan & his wife Sophia executrix of
  Thomas Simpson.
- accounts of Ann Merida Godfrey
  administratrix of Joseph Godfrey.
- accounts of Ann Merida Godfrey
  administratrix of Charles Godfrey.

31:562 Mr. Benton Harris (WO) to examine
accounts of:
- Isaac Bell & John Rickards executors
  of Elisabeth Smith (WO).
- Alexander Massey administrator dbn
  of William Massey.

Charles Hynson (g, KE) exhibited:
- will of Bowles Green. Also, bond of
  John Green administrator. Sureties:
  Joseph Mason, John Clarke, William
  Simmonds. Date: 22 December 1744.
- will of Jane Ball. Also, bond of
  Margaret Kelley acting executrix.
  Sureties: Joseph Garnett, Robert
  George. Also, renunciation of
  Abraham Milton (executor),
  recommending Margaret Kelley. Date:
  9 February 1744.
- bond of William Taylor administrator
  of Francis Wetherell. Sureties:
  William Clark, Abraham Milton.
  Date: 2 February 1744.

Page 78

- will of William Thomas.
- will of Lawrence ONeil.
- inventory & LoD of Rev. Arthur Holt.
- inventory of Henry Thomas.
- additional inventory of Mary Pearce.
- inventory of Benjamin Clark.
- additional inventory of Robert Key.
- inventory & LoD of James Harris, Esq.
- accounts of Michael Miller executor of Arthur Miller.
- accounts of Hanse Hanson & his wife Margaret executrix of Glanville Rolph.
- accounts of Sarah Kennard administratrix of John Kennard.
- accounts of Elisabeth Pinar administratrix of Thomas Pinar.
- accounts of Jonathan Turner administrator of Mary Forbush.
- accounts of Christian Adair administratrix of Alexander Adair.

1 March. Exhibited from KE:
- LoD on estate of James Harris.

Rosannah Loockerman executrix of Jacob Loockerman (DO) was granted continuance. Date: 24 February 1744.

4 March. Mr. Charles Hynson (KE) to examine accounts of:
- Thomas Crow & his wife Sarah administratrix of George Skirven (KE).
- Mary Key administratrix of Robert Key (KE).

31:563 5 March. William Fell & Walter Dallas to appraise estate of Rev. Mr. Benedict Bourdillon (BA).

Exhibited from AA:
- additional accounts of Thomas Richardson surviving executor of Richard Richardson.

Mr. William Tilghman (QA) to examine accounts of:
- Eleanor Murphy administratrix of William Murphy (QA).

- John Baynard & his wife Elisabeth administratrix of Joshua Clarke (QA). Additional accounts.

Col. Gabriel Parker (CV) exhibited:
- bond of Archable Freeman administrator of Catherine Hollyday. Sureties: Martin Driver, Obed Dixon. Date: 26 January 1744.
- will of Edward Reynolds, constituting Thomas Reynolds executor. Said executor was granted administration. Sureties: James Heighe, Job Hunt. Date: 29 January 1744.
- bond of Elisabeth Skinner administratrix of William Skinner. Sureties: James Skinner, Leonard Skinner. Date: 30 January 1744.
- bond of Thomas Brome administrator of Francis Spencer. Surety: Moses Parran. Date: 9 February 1744.
- bond of Benjamin Ellt administrator of Thomas Brittain. Sureties: William Dawkins, John Dorrumple. Date: 11 February 1744.
- bond of Elisabeth Williams administratrix of John Williams. Sureties: Richard Talbott, Richard Roberts. Date: 11 February 1744.
- bond of Elisabeth Newton administratrix of Henry Newton. Sureties: Obed Dixon, Archable Freeman. Date: 16 February 1744.
- bond of Thomas Goldsbury administrator of Michael Hassett. Sureties: Obed Dixon, John Dorrumple. Date: 16 February 1744.
- will of Richard Pierce. Also, bond of William Pierce administrator. Sureties: Obed Dixon, John Dorrumple. Date: 16 February 1744.
- will of Stephen Dickerson, constituting Ann Dickerson executrix. Said executrix was granted administration. Sureties: Ellis Slater, William Willmott. Date: 16 February 1744.
- bond of Barrington Pardo administrator of Liney Pardo. Sureties: Benjamin Hungerford, Benjamin Dixon. Date: 23 February

Court Session: 1744

1744.
- will of Ann Current.
- will of Dinah Hassett.
- inventory of John Phillips.
- accounts of Margaret Peirce executrix of Charles Somersett Smith.
- accounts of Caesar Jones acting executor of Peter Poore.

7 March. Exhibited from KE:
- LoD on estate of George Barber. Also, additional accounts of Richard Kennard administrator.

11 March. Exhibited from PG:
- inventory of William Hedge.

Court Session: 12 March 1744

31:564 Docket:
- Thomas Wilson administrator of Ann Davie (CH) vs. Arabella Hines wife of Joseph Hines (CH). Sheriff (CH) to summon defendant to testify regarding concealment of estate of dec'd.
- B.Y. for Richard Watts & John Carr executors of John Watts (PG) vs. S.B. for Andrew Scott administrator of John Watts. John Cooke (sheriff, PG) to summon defendant to render final accounts.

31:365 Ruling: plaintiff.
- Sheriff (PG) to render attachment to Lingan Wilson (PG) administrator of Joseph Willson (PG) to render inventory.
- Thomas Sligh & Henry Morgan sureties on estate of Buckler Partridge (BA) vs. Jane Partridge administratrix of said dec'd. John Risteau (sheriff, BA) to summon defendant to render accounts.
- Rev. John Lang vs. Richard Snowden (AA) administrator dbn of Thomas South (PG). Samuel Smith (sheriff, AA) to summon defendant to render accounts. N.E.
- Thomas Harrington (QA) son of Thomas Harrington (TA, dec'd) vs. James Slaughter (QA) & his wife Elisabeth

Court Session: 12 March 1744

   executrix of said dec'd. T. H.
   Wright (sheriff, QA) to summon
   defendants to show cause why they
   withhold legacy from plaintiff.

Court Session: 1744

31:566 13 March. Mr. William Tilghman (QA) to
   examine accounts of:
   • Mary Ann Powell executrix of James
     Powell executor of Thomas Powell
     (QA).

   Exhibited from DO:
   • inventory & additional inventory of
     Joseph Fisher. Also, accounts of
     Richard Harrington administrator
     dbn.

   Thomas Aisquith (g, SM) exhibited:
   • will of Edward APrice, constituting
     Ann APrice executrix. Also, widow's
     election. Said executrix was
     granted administration. Sureties:
     Anthony Browne, James Browne. Date:
     8 November 1744.
   • bond of Elisabeth Williams
     administratrix of William Williams.
     Sureties: Philip Key, William
     Browne. Date: 8 November 1744.
   • bond of Jane Fielder administratrix
     of Williams Fielder. Sureties:
     Thomas Wellman, James Tarlton.
     Date: 12 November 1744.
   • will of John Redman. Also, widow's
     election. Also, bond of Sarah
     Redman administratrix. Sureties:
     Robert Mosley, Thomas Cook. Date:
     12 November 1744.
   • bond of Jean West administratrix of
     William West. Sureties: James
     Swann, John Maddox. Date: 28
     November 1744.
   • bond of Thomas Coode & James Dunbar
     administrators dbn of Joshua
     Guibert. Surety: John Greaves.
     Date: 19 December 1744.
   • bond of John Gibbens administrator
     of Martha Gibbens. Sureties: John
     Wiseman, John Woodward. Date: 31
     December 1744.
   • bond of Mary Fardery administratrix

of Nicholas Fardery. Sureties: Luke Merrill, Daniel Clocker, Jr. Date: 28 January 1744.

- bond of Thomas Pearce administrator of Elinor Pearce. Sureties: Henry Riley, Basil Cooper. Date: 28 January 1744.
- will of John Johnson Sothoron, constituting Samuel Sothoron & Richard Sothoron executors. Said executors were granted administration. Sureties: Leonard Clark, John Briscoe. Date: 30 January 1744.
- will of William Cissell.
- inventory of John Steuart.
- additional inventory of George Knott.
- inventory of Richard Griffen.
- inventory of John Redman.
- accounts of James Howard & his wife Henrietta administratrix of James Clark.
- accounts of Sarah Cissell administratrix of John Cissell.
- accounts of Elisabeth Clark administratrix of Robert Clark.
- accounts of Luke Mattingly & his wife Priscilla administratrix of George Knott.
- accounts of James Thompson, Sr. & James Thompson, Jr. administrators of William Barnes.
- accounts of William Field & his wife Mary executrix of John Alvey.
- accounts of Thomas APrice & his wife Eliza administratrix of Nicholas Power.
- accounts of Thomas Wimsett administrator of Dorothy Smith.

Exhibited from AA:
- LoD on estate of John Watkins.
- LoD on estate of John Andrews.
- LoD on estate of Thomas South.

Exhibited from BA:
- inventory of James Tolley.

31:567 15 March. Exhibited from CH:
- additional accounts of Andrew Scott administrator of Capt. John Watts.

Court Session: 1744

Exhibited from PG:
- additional accounts of Andrew Scott & his wife Mary executrix of John Abington.

Exhibited from BA:
- will of Samuel Gover. Also, bond of Isaac Webster administrator. Sureties: Michael Webster (BA), John Talbot (AA). Date: 15 March 1744.
- inventory of Edward Evans.

Exhibited from DO:
- inventory of Robert Ritchie.

16 March. William Rogers (g, AA) exhibited:
- bond of Ann Edwards administratrix of Cadwallader Edwards. Surety: Jonas Green (Annapolis, AA). Date: 28 December 1744.
- bond of Samuel Smith & Francis Mapp executors of Alice Andrews. Sureties: Ashbury Sutton, Thomas Rutland. Date: 15 January 1744.
- bond of Richard Snowden administrator of John Rickets. Sureties: John Lomas (AA), Robert North (BA). Date: 23 January 1744. Also, renunciation of Elisabeth Rickets (widow), recommending Richard Snowden (greatest creditor). Date: 21 January 1744/5 at Fork of Pattuxent. Witness: James Brooke.
- bond of Ephraim & Philip Gover surviving executors of Samuel Gover. Sureties: Ephraim Gover (AA), Samuel Austin (CV). Date: 5 February 1744.
- bond of William Thornton administrator of Samuel Owens. Sureties: Patrick Creagh, Samuel Smith. Date: 7 February 1744.
- bond of Sarah Joyce administratrix of John Joyce. Sureties: William Forrest, Thomas Rowles. Date: 14 February 1744.
- will of Charles Cheney, constituting Agnes Cheney executrix. Said executrix was granted administration. Sureties: Thomas Cheney, Otho French. Date: 22 February 1744.

- bond of Jean Reynolds administratrix of John Reynolds. Sureties: William Reynolds, John Brewer. Date: 23 February 1744.
- bond of Barton Rodgett administrator of Jonas Ventstone. Sureties: Thomas Richardson, Thomas Williamson. Date: 26 February 1744.
- bond of Thomas King executor of James Wilson. Sureties: Richard Wilkins, Thomas Williamson. Date: 12 March 1744.
- bond of Ephraim Gover administrator of John Weden. Sureties: John Browne, Philip Gover. Date: 14 March 1744.

31:568 Also, renunciation of Lawrence Wilson (widow) [!], recommending Ephraim Gover (greatest creditor). Date: 7 March 1744.

- bond of William Ford administrator of Ambrose Warsebury. Sureties: Thomas Metcalfe, Thomas Norris. Date: 15 March 1744.
- will of Abraham Woodward.
- inventory of Cadwallader Edwards.
- inventory of Joshua Dorsey (son of Caleb).
- inventory & LoD of Samuel Burman.
- inventory of James English.
- inventory of Nicholas Hammond.
- inventory of Francis Crandall.
- additional inventory of Richard Richardson.

18 March. Col. Gabriel Parker (CV) to examine accounts of:
- William Milles, Jr. executor of John Richards (CV).

19 March. Peter Dent (g, PG) exhibited:
- will of Edward Willett, constituting William Willett executor. Said executor was granted administration. Sureties: William Harper, Edward Riston. Date: 11 February 1744.
- bond of John Haymond administrator of John Baldwin Adamson. Sureties: John Letton, John Jones. Date: 22 February 1744. Also, renunciation of Lucy Adamson (daughter), recommending John Haymond.

- bond of Christopher Edelin administrator of Thomas Smith. Sureties: William Thomas, William Dyer. Date: 26 February 1744.
- will of James Riggs.
- inventory of James Bowie.

20 March. Exhibited from CV:
- inventory of Rev. Mr. Richard Chase.

Court Session: 1745

26 March. Mr. Thomas Aisquith (SM) to examine accounts of:
- John McKellvie executor of James Taylor (SM).
- Thomas Greenwell & his wife Mary executrix of John Riley (SM).
- Monica Jarboe & Ignatius Jarboe executors of Peter Jarboe (SM).
- Peter Johnson & his wife Grace administratrix of John Mattingly (SM).
- John Norriss executor of Mary Gough (SM).
- John Temple surviving executor of Monica Monark (SM).

Thomas Bullen (g, TA) exhibited:
- bond of Elisabeth Williams administratrix of James Williams. Sureties: John Batcheldor, John Anderson. Date: 22 February 1744.
- bond of Eleanor Wrightson administratrix of Francis Wrightson. Sureties: John Carslake, Nathaniel Saintee. Date: 5 March 1744.
- will of Lewis Jones. Also, renunciation of 1 executor.
- inventory of Thomas Snelling.
- inventory & LoD of Charles Baning.
- inventory of James Webster.
- accounts of Peter Harwood & his wife Susannah administratrix of John Steuart.
- accounts of Philemon Hambleton executor of William Hambleton.

30 March. Peter Dent (g, PG) exhibited:
- will of John Atcheson. Also, widow's election.

31:569

Court Session: 1745

Mr. Peter Dent (PG) to examine accounts of:
- Mary Brawner administratrix of John Brawner (PG).
- Priscilla Wilson executrix of Thomas Wilson (PG).
- Priscilla Wilson administratrix of Nathan Masters (PG).

2 April. Exhibited from AA:
- accounts of Sarah Stewart executrix of John Stewart.

4 April. Peter Dent (g, PG) exhibited:
- will of Nathan Selby.
- bond of Charles Drury administrator of Nathan Selby. Sureties (AA):: Abraham Simmons, Jr., Walter Gott. Date: 4 April 1745.

Exhibited from BA:
- additional accounts of Matthew Beck & his wife Ann administratrix of Nicholas Horner.

5 April. Charles Hynson (g, KE) exhibited:
- bond of Issabella Wethered executrix of Richard Wethered. Sureties: Cornelius Comegys, Edward Comegys. Date: 17 November 1744.
- bond of Henry Spencer executor of Lawrence ONeil. Sureties: Matthias Day, Thomas Lynch. Date: 27 January 1744.
- will of Stephen Knight.
- LoD on estate of Dr. Thomas Williams, in KE, CE, QA, & in PA currency.
- LoD on estate of William Thomas.
- additional inventory & LoD of John Perkins.
- accounts of Matthias Harris acting executor of James Harris.
- accounts of John Read & his wife Mary executrix of Thomas Mahone.

Col. Thomas White (BA) exhibited:
- bond of Thomas Harrison administrator of John Chambers. Sureties: Philip Jones (BA), James Walker (AA). Date: 2 February 1744.

- bond of Francis Holland administratrix of Susanna Holland. Sureties: John Matthews, James Phillips. Date: 15 March 1744.

31:570
- inventory of George Baley, Jr.
- inventory of H. Wells Stokes.
- inventory of William Low.
- additional accounts of Robert Bishop & his wife Elisabeth executrix of Nicholas Day.

6 April. Mr. Thomas Bullen (TA) to examine accounts of:
- William Sharp executor of Solomon Birckhead (TA).
- Mary Snelling administratrix of Thomas Snelling (TA).
- Tristram Thomas & Adam Browne executor of James Webster (TA).

Exhibited from CV:
- inventory of Walter Smith, in CV & BA.

8 April. Exhibited from CV:
- accounts of Alexander Lawson executor of Walter Smith.

Exhibited from QA:
- 2nd additional accounts of Matthew Griffith one of executors & Edward Browne who married Rachel Griffith executrix of John Griffith other executor of Ann Price.

Walter Hanson (g, CH) exhibited:
- will of Thomas Coleman, constituting Thomas Coleman & Martha Coleman executors. Said executors were granted administration. Sureties: Henry Lyon, Luke Adams. Date: 11 February 1744.
- bond of William Carter administrator of William Carter. Sureties: Robert Hurdle, Basil Spalding. Date: 5 March 1744.
- bond of Mary Hamersley administratrix of Francis Hamersley. Sureties: Basil Brooke (CV), William Neale (CH), William Hamersley (CH). Date: 6 March 1744.
- bond of George Godfrey & John Clark,

Jr. administrators of John West.
Sureties: Joseph Palluffus, Hugh
McCoy. Date: 9 March 1744.

- will of Ann Howard, constituting
Joseph Lamaster executor. Said
executor was granted administration.
Sureties: John Lamaster, William
Neale. Date: 13 March 1744.
- bond of Ann Brent administratrix of
Randolph Brent. Sureties: Richard
Lee, John Courts. Date: 19 March
1744.
- inventory of Thomas Hall.
- inventory of Andrew Simpson.
- inventory of John Clubb.
- accounts of Katherine Bell
administratrix of Moses Bell.
- accounts of Thomas Reeves
administrator o Samuel Reeves.
- 2nd additional accounts of Barbara
Mugleston on estate of Thomas
Mugleston.
- 2nd additional accounts of Ann
Jenkins administratrix of Thomas
Jenkins.
- accounts of Matthew Breeding
executor of Henry Blanchett.

9 April. Exhibited from QA:
- accounts of Edward Browne & his wife
Rachel executrix of John Griffith.

31:571 Thomas Aisquith (g, SM) exhibited:
- will of Thomas Gosling. Also,
widow's election. Also, bond of
William Fowler administrator.
Sureties: Thomas Hall, Abraham Hall.
Date: 21 February 1744.
- will of Samuel Bagley, constituting
Drayden Bagley executrix. Also,
widow's election. Said executrix
was granted administration.
Sureties: William Mills, James
Connell. Date: 5 March 1744.
- bond of Winefred Burch
administratrix of Benjamin Burch.
Sureties: John Tipett, James Taylor.
Date: 5 March 1744.
- bond of Kenelm Truman Greenfield
administrator of Thomas Truman
Greenfield. Sureties: Zachariah
Bond, Thomas Hungerford. Date: 5

March 1744.

- will of Charles Ganyott, constituting Elisabeth Ganyott executrix. Also, widow's election. Said executrix was granted administration. Sureties: Enock Fenwick, John Fenwick. Date: 6 March 1744.
- bond of Susannah Lorton administratrix of John Lorton. Sureties: Joseph Owen, William Gerrard Coode. Date: 7 March 1744.
- will of Thomas Hebb, constituting Elisabeth Rule, Edward Hilliard Hebb, & William Hebb, Jr. executors. Said executors were granted administration. Sureties: William Hebb, Thomas Perrin. Date: 13 March 1744.
- nuncupative will of George Wallis. Also, bond of Mev. Lock administrator. Sureties: Stourton Edwards, Hugh Hopewell, Jr. Date: 28 March 1745.
- will of Elisabeth Aisquith.
- will of James Blumfied.
- inventory of Joseph Mitchell.
- inventory & LoD of Thomas Gosling.
- inventory of William West.
- inventory of Martha Gibbens.
- inventory & LoD of Daniel Duggins.
- inventory & LoD of Anthony Evans.
- inventory & LoD of William Fielder.
- inventory of Edward APrice.
- accounts of Ann Batson administratrix of John Batson.

Humphry Boone (AA) vs. John Burle surviving executor of John Burle (AA). Sheriff (AA) to summon defendant to render inventory.

10 April. Ennalls Hooper (g, DO) exhibited, taken by Edward Trippe (late Deputy Commissary [!]):
- bond of Adam Muir administrator of Lawrence Mason, during minority of William Mason. Surety: Thomas Muir. Date: 15 June 1744.
- bond of Hannah Reed administratrix of Ezekiel Reed. Sureties: John Anderton, Solomon Turpin. Date: 28

November 1744.
- accounts of Thomas Clarke executor of Thomas Clarke.

31:572   Ennalls Hooper (g, DO) exhibited:
- will of Benjamin Ball, constituting Elisabeth Ball executrix. Said executrix was granted administration. Sureties: Thomas Hicks, Charles Hodson. Date: 2 January 1744.
- bond of Rachel Owens administratrix of Edward Owens. Sureties: Moses Nicolls, Matthew Hardekin. Date: 12 January 1744.
- bond of Elisabeth Trippe administratrix of Henry Trippe. Sureties: Thomas Nevett, Esq., Jacob Hindman (g), Philip Emerson (g). Date: 2 February 1744.
- bond of Jean Harris administratrix of James Harris. Sureties: John Smith, Thomas Cawsey. Date: 10 February 1744.
- will of Edward Ross, constituting Mary Ross executrix. Said executrix was granted administration. Sureties: David Melvil, Sr., William Taylor. Date: 18 February 1744.
- bond of Sarah Morris administratrix of George Morris. Sureties: Benjamin Wheland, Thomas Brahon. Date: 22 February 1744.
- bond of Alice Covington administratrix of Jacob Covington. Sureties: James Langnall, George Langnall. Date: 7 March 1744.
- will of Thomas Brannock, constituting Frances Brannock & John Brannock executors. Said executors were granted administration. Sureties: William Byus, Arthur Whitely. Date: 14 March 1744.
- bond of Sarah Sulivane administratrix of William Sulivane. Sureties: James Jones, Daniel Jones. Date: 23 March 1744.
- bond of Richard Kendall Foxwell administrator of Robert Ross. Sureties: Edward Pritchett, Richard Wallis. Date: 27 March 1745.
- bond of Mary Carawon administratrix

of John Carawon. Sureties: Matthew
Carawon, Thomas Whitley. Date: 27
March 1745.
- inventory & LoD of Benjamin Ball.
- inventory of Henry Edgar.
- inventory & LoD of Edward Ross.
- inventory & LoD of William Adams.
- inventory & LoD of Edmond Owens.
- inventory & LoD of Ezekiel Reed.

Mr. Ennalls Hooper (DO) to examine
accounts of:
- Mary Williams executrix of William
  Williams (DO).
- Rachel Jones administratrix of
  Walter Hunter (DO).
- William Galloway executor of James
  Galloway (DO).
- Monica Williams executrix of William
  Williams (DO).
- Sarah Hayward acting executrix of
  John Hayward (DO).
- Elinor Lister administratrix of
  William Lister (DO).
- Elisabeth Cock administratrix of
  Edward Cock (DO).
- Elisabeth Jones executrix of Leonard
  Jones (DO).
- Elisabeth Ball executrix of Benjamin
  Ball (DO).
- Hannah Reed administratrix of
  Ezekiel Reed (DO).
- Sarah Stinson administratrix of
  Alexander Stinson (DO).
- Ruth Edger executrix of Henry Edger
  (DO).
- John Hudson administrator of Owen
  Ward (DO).
- William Cullens executor of Mark
  Fisher (DO). Additional accounts.

31:573 William Knight (g, CE) exhibited:
- bond of James Stevenson
  administrator of John Wiley.
  Sureties: John Smith, Patrick
  Kelley. Date: 15 October 1744.
- bond of Richard Price administrator
  of Alexander Duff. Sureties: Peter
  Bayard, Thomas Benston. Date: 13
  November 1744.
- bond of John Cockran & James Ogleby
  executors of John Ogleby. Sureties:

Peter Bouchell, James Boyle.   Date:
4 February 1744.

- bond of Rebecca Wye administratrix
  of William Wye. Sureties: Nicholas
  Hyland, John Currier. Date: 6 March
  1744.
- will of Hugh Walker, constituting
  Samuel Walker & William Mackey
  executors. Said executors were
  granted administration. Sureties:
  George Lawson, Andrew Hall. Date:
  11 March 1744.
- bond of George Lawson administrator
  of Joseph Redach. Sureties: Andrew
  Barry, John Reed. Date: 12 March
  1744.
- will of John Blake.
- inventory of Elisabeth Hogins
- inventory of John Knight.
- inventory of Alexander Duff.
- inventory of John Wiley.
- inventory of Thomas Walker.
- additional inventory of Rosamond
  Terry.
- inventory of James Wade.
- accounts of Edward Armstrong & his
  wife Ann administratrix of William
  Craig.
- accounts of Martha Wood
  administratrix of Joseph Wood.
- accounts of James Knox & his wife
  Jane administratrix of Edward Usher.
- accounts of John McWhorter
  administrator of Hugh McWhorter.
- accounts of James Redus & his wife
  Catherine administrators of William
  Parsons.
- accounts of Hermana Vanbebber
  executrix of Matthias Vanbebber.
- accounts of Mary Holton
  administratrix of George Holton.
- accounts of Hugh Terry administrator
  of Rosamond Terry.
- accounts of Adam Vanbebber & his
  wife Mary executrix of John Knight.
- additional accounts of John Harper
  administrator dbn of Robert Withers.
- accounts of John Harper & Cornelius
  Wolliston administrators of William
  Cook.

Mr. Thomas Bullen (TA) to examine accounts of:
- Mary Russell administratrix of Thomas Russell (TA).

Benton Harris (g, WO) exhibited:
- bond of Alexander Buncle administrator of William Thomas. Sureties: Thomas Lambden, William Nelson. Date: 8 January 1744.
- bond of Dunken Murray administrator of Isaac Brittingham, Jr. Sureties: Patrick Glasgow, John Martin. Date: 22 February 1744.
- will of John Wildman, constituting Catherine Wildman executrix. Said executrix was granted administration. Sureties: Alexander Buncle, Dunken Murray. Date: 22 February 1744.
- bond of Mary Harper administratrix of Isaac Wheeler. Sureties: Thomas Lambden, Edward Harper. Date: 6 March 1744.
- bond of Rouse Fassitt executor of William Fassitt. Sureties: John Fassitt, Ebenezar Evans. Date: 7 March 1744.
- bond of John Aydelott, Sr. administrator of William Salmon. Sureties: Joshua Robinson, John Aydelott, Jr. Date: 29 March 1744.

31:574
- bond of John Taylor administrator of John Hopkins. Sureties: John Aydelott, William Derrickson. Date: 29 March 1745.
- will of William Burton, constituting John Burton & Joshua Burton executors. Said executors were granted administration. Sureties: Paul Waples, William Collins. Date: 30 March 1745.
- bond of Bridgett Kennet executrix of Martin Kennet. Sureties: John Turvile, William Kennet, Jr. Date: 1 April 1745.
- bond of Joseph Quillen administrator of Benjamin Quillen. Sureties: Paul Alexander, Elias Evans. Date: 2 April 1745.
- bond of Ephraim Heather administrator of Ephraim Heather,

Sr. Sureties: Richard Blyzard, Henry Smock. Date: 3 April 1745.
- bond of William Toadvine administrator of John Blewett. Sureties: William Laws, Moses Driskell. Date: 5 April 1745.
- will of Isaac Adkins.
- will of Peter Claywell.
- inventory of John Dennis.
- inventory of James Townsend.
- inventory & LoD of John Watson.
- inventory of William Thomas.
- accounts of Alexander Buncle administrator of William Thomas.
- accounts of Catherine Breeman administratrix of James Breeman.
- accounts of Rachel Wheeler executrix of William Wheeler.
- accounts of Margery Morris administratrix of William Morris.
- accounts of Matthew Wise administrator of Thomas Wise.
- accounts of Joshua Burton executor of William Burton administrator of Christopher Topham.

11 April. Mr. Ennalls Hooper (DO) to examine accounts of:
- William Byus & his wife Elisabeth & Joseph Ennalls executors of Henry Ennalls (DO).

12 April. Nehemiah King (g, SO) exhibited:
- bond of Charles Dean administrator of Charles Dean. Sureties: John Badley, Samuel Badley. Date: 15 February 1744. Also, renunciation of Elisabeth Dean, recommending her son (son of dec'd). Date: 14 February 1745.
- will of William Collins. Also, widow's renunciation. Also, bond of Robert King, Sr. administrator. Surety: John Williams. Date: 8 March 1744.
- bond of Mary Moore administratrix of Francis Moore. Sureties: Jacob Moore, Nathaniel Horsey, Jr. Date: 8 March 1744.
- bond of Alice Dunn administratrix of Richard Dunn. Sureties: Robert

Court Session: 1745

Henderson, Teague Dickeson. Date:
12 March 1744.
- bond of Elisabeth Nicholson
  administratrix of Levin Nicholson.
  Sureties: Mitchell Dashiell, Joseph
  Dashiell. Date: 20 March 1744.
- will of Mary Hampton.
- inventory of Thomas Walker.
- additional inventory of Thomas
  Parker. Also, accounts of George
  Parker administrator.
- inventory of James Jones.
- inventory of Philip Harris.
- inventory of John Richardson. Also,
  accounts of Joseph Bounds
  administrator.

31:575 Bond of Ennalls Hooper (g, DO) as Deputy
Commissary (DO). Sureties (DO): Henry
Hooper, Levin Hicks. Date: 17 December
1744.

Thomas White (g, BA) exhibited:
- bond of Thomas White administrator
  of Isaac Milner. Sureties:
  Alexander Lawson, Thomas Franklin.
  Date: 6 April 1745.

16 April. Exhibited from AA:
- inventory of Elinor Herbert.

Mr. Nehemiah King (SO) to examine
accounts of:
- Tabitha Moore executrix of John
  Moore (SO).
- Sarah Howard administratrix of John
  Howard (SO).
- Joseph Cotman executor of John
  Robertson (SO).
- Martilda Horner administratrix of
  George Horner (SO).
- Richard Tulley administrator of
  Stephen Tulley, Jr. (SO).
- Edward Bennett & George Bennett
  sureties for Benjamin Tulley
  administrator of Stephen Tulley, Sr.
  (SO).
- George Hardy administrator of
  Christopher Nutter (SO).

Thomas Dyson (CH) who married Mary
daughter of George Whitter (SM, dec'd)

vs. Joseph Estep administrator of said dec'd. Sheriff (SM) to summon defendant to render accounts.

17 April. Mr. Nehemiah King (SO) to examine accounts of:
- Susannah Tulley administratrix of James Tulley (SO).
- William Hill & his wife Patience administratrix of William Powson (SO).

18 April. Exhibited from CV:
- will of William Jones, constituting Henry Darnall (Portland Mannor) executor. Said executor was granted administration. Sureties: Henry Darnall (PG), John Darnall (AA). Date: 18 April 1745.

Peter Dent (g, PG) exhibited:
- bond of Thomas Owen administrator of Robert Newstub. Sureties: Henry Massey, James Smith. Date: 28 March 1745.
- will of Virlinda Beall, constituting Josiah Beall & Lucy Beall executors. Said executors were granted administration. Sureties: James Edmundston, David Ross. Date: 29 March 1745.
- will of Thomas Brooke, constituting Lucy Brooke executrix. Said executrix was granted administration. Sureties: Samuel Beall, Jr., Richard Brooke, Isaac Brooke. Date: 29 March 1745.
- bond of Elisabeth Riggs executrix of James Riggs. Also, widow's election. Sureties: Michael Jones, John Riggs. Date: 2 April 1745.
- **31:576** will of Zachariah Wade, constituting Mary Wade & Zachariah Wade executors. Also, widow's election. Said executors were granted administration. Sureties: Butler Stonestreet, Nehemiah Wade. Date: 8 April 1745.
- bond of John Holly administrator of Humphry Deverson. Sureties: Thomas Holly, John Emerson. Date: 9 April 1745.

- inventory of Stephen Martin.
- inventory of John Baldwin Adamson.
- accounts of Jane Martin administratrix of Stephen Martin.
- accounts of Ann Hugoe executrix of Israel Hugoe.
- accounts of Mary Riley administratrix of Terrance Riley.

Thomas Wilson administrator of Ann Davie (CH) vs. Arabella Hine wife of Joseph Hine (CH). Sheriff (CH) to summon defendant to testify concerning concealment of estate of dec'd.

20 April. Mr. Thomas White (BA) to examine 3rd additional accounts of:
- Heathcoate Pickett & his wife Elisabeth executrix of William Wright (BA).

Mr. Peter Dent (PG) to examine accounts of:
- Priscilla Deakins executrix of John Deakins (PG).

Mr. William Knight (CE) to examine accounts of:
- Dorothy Patton administratrix of Robert Patton (CE).
- Thomas Severson administrator of Isaac Clements (CE).
- James Porter & Nathaniel Ewing acting executors of Alexander Ewing (CE).

Mr. Thomas Aisquith (SM) to examine accounts of:
- Matthias Nottingham & his wife Mary administratrix of Charles Griffen (SM).
- William Daft & his wife Elisabeth executrix of William Bold (SM).
- Thomas Ingalls executor of Benjamin Gale (SM).
- Elinor Read administratrix of John Read, Jr. (SM).

Mr. Walter Hanson (CH) to examine accounts of:
- Matthew Hennekin & his wife Eliza administratrix of JOhn Brayfield

(CH).

- Mary Robey administratrix of Benjamin Robey (CH).
- John Ashfield & his wife Eliza administratrix of William Monroe (CH).
- Henry Moore & his wife Sarah & George Brett executors of Richard Brett (CH).
- William Williams & Sarah Rozar executors of George Johnson (CH).
- Sarah Hawkins administratrix of Thomas Hawkins (CH).
- John Gray & his wife Ann executrix of John Sutcliffe (CH).
- Dorothy St. Clare administratrix of George St. Clare (CH).
- Peter Wright & his wife Ann executrix of Rowland Evans (CH).
- James Plant administrator of Thomas Haile (CH). Additional accounts.
- James Dyson & his wife Abigail administratrix of Thomas Swann (CH). Additional accounts.

31:577 Mr. Charles Hynson (KE) to examine accounts of:
- Miles Mason Shehawn & his wife Sarah administratrix of Charles Griffith (KE).
- Peter Cole & his wife Francina administratrix of John Perkins (KE).
- Elisabeth Ringgold administratrix dbn of William Buckham (KE).
- Francis Spearman & his wife Hester administratrix of Thomas Wyate (KE). Additional accounts.
- Christopher Hall surviving executor of Matthias Day (KE). Additional accounts.

Exhibited from AA:
- bond of John Bullen administrator of William Timbrell. Sureties (Annapolis, AA): Richard Tootell, Simon Duff. Date: 20 April 1745.

22 April. Exhibited from BA:
- bond of Cooper Oram executor of John Wright. Sureties: John Highter (BA), Henry Oram (AA). Date: 21 April 1745.

24 April. Exhibited from AA:
* accounts of Johanna Birckhead administratrix of Eleazer Birckhead.

Peter Dent (g, PG) exhibited:
* inventory of Charles Perry.
* bond of Mary Ann Atchison executrix of John Atchison. Sureties: John Hamill (CH), Thomas Monroe (PG). Date: 17 April 1745.
* will of Mary Norris.
* 3rd additional accounts of David Cranfurd administrator of William Green.
* accounts of John Henward administrator of John Cooper.

27 April. Col. Gabriel Parker (CV) to examine accounts of:
* Young Parran & Easter Parran administrators of John Parran (CV).

Mr. Ennalls Hooper (DO) to examine accounts of:
* James Billings executor of Capt. Charles Rider (DO).

Exhibited from SM:
* accounts of Philip Key administrator of William Smith.

Mr. Peter Dent (PG) to examine accounts of:
* Mary Osburn administratrix of Benjamin Osburn (PG).

31:578 1 May. Richard Purnall one of sureties on estate of Col. Josias Towgood (AA) vs. Mary Towgood surviving executrix of said dec'd. Sheriff (AA) to summon defendant to render final accounts.

6 May. Peter Dent (g, PG) exhibited:
* accounts of Mary Osborne administratrix of Benjamin Osborn.

8 May. Exhibited from AA:
* inventory of Charles Cheney.

9 May. Warrant issued to appraisers of estate of John Taillor (London, dec'd).

Court Session: 1745

13 May. Exhibited from AA:
- additional accounts of Clare Norris executrix of John Norris, Jr.

Exhibited from DO:
- additional accounts of Richard Harrington administrator dbn of Joseph Fisher.

Court Session: 14 May 1745

Docket:
- Thomas Wilson administrator of Ann Davie (CH) vs. Arabella Hines wife of Joseph Hines (CH). Sheriff (CH) to render attachment to defendant to testify concerning concealment of estate of dec'd.
- Sheriff (PG) to render attachment to Lingan Wilson (PG) administrator of Joseph Wilson (PG) to render inventory.
- Thomas Sligh & Henry Morgan sureties on estate of Buckler Partridge (BA) vs. Jane Partridge administratrix of said dec'd. Sheriff (BA) to summon defendant to render accounts.

31:579
- Rev. John Lang vs. Richard Snowden (AA) administrator dbn of Thomas South (PG). Sheriff (AA) to summon defendant to render accounts.
- Humphry Boone (AA) vs. John Burle surviving executor of John Burle (AA). Samuel Smith (sheriff, AA) to summon defendant to render additional inventory.
- Thomas Dyson (CH) who married Mary daughter of George Whitter (SM) vs. Joseph Estep administrator of said dec'd. Philip Key (sheriff, SM) to summon defendant to render accounts. Accounts exhibited. Discontinued.
- Richard Purnell one of sureties on estate of Col. Josias Towgood (AA) vs. Mary Towgood surviving executrix of said dec'd. Samuel Smith (sheriff, AA) to summon defendant to render final accounts. Said Mary exhibited by letter her indisposition & inability to attend the Office. Deputy Commissary (SM) to examine said accounts.

Court Session: 14 May 1745

Discontinued.
- Thomas Wilson administrator of Ann Davie (CH) vs. Arabella Hines wife of Joseph Hines (CH). Sheriff (CH) to summon defendant to testify concerning concealment of estate of dec'd.

Court Session: 1745

31:580 14 May. William Tilghman (g, QA) exhibited:
- bond of Amelia Walters administratrix of Robert Walters. Sureties: Nathaniel Wright, William Mayson. Date: 14 February 1744.
- will of Richard Buckley, constituting Thomas Lee executor. Said executor was granted administration. Sureties: John Young (son of William), William Young. Date: 14 February 1744.
- bond of Vincent Price administrator of Timothy Lane. Sureties: William Banning, William Robinson (Tuckahoe). Date: 16 February 1744.
- will of Benjamin Elliott, constituting Mary Elliott executrix. Also, widow's election. Said executrix was granted administration. Sureties: Edward Browne, Jr., Valentine Carter. Date: 21 March 1744.
- bond of Michael Atkinson administrator of Thomas Atkinson. Sureties: John Hays, Jr., John Weeks. Date: 4 April 1745.
- bond of Ambrose Wright administrator of John Sanders. Sureties: John Jackson, Thomas Dockery. Date: 2 May 1745.
- will of John Weeks, constituting Stephen Weeks & Matthew Weeks executors. Said executors were granted administration. Sureties: Daniel Swift, John Parsons. Date: 4 May 1745.
- will of James Powell.
- will of William Dulany
- inventory of Vincent Hollingworth.
- inventory of Fairclough Wright.
- additional inventory of Thomas

Powell. Also, accounts of Mary Ann Powell executrix of James Powell executor.
- LoD on estate of John Tucker. Also, accounts of Nathaniel Tucker administrator.
- inventory of Bartholomew Jenings.
- accounts of Nathaniel Tucker administrator of Edward Tucker.
- accounts of John Kearney & his wife Rachel executrix of John Primrose.
- accounts of Eleanor Murphy administratrix of William Murphy.

Exhibited from BA:
- LoD on estate of Dr. George Walker. Also, accounts of Mary Walker executrix.

Exhibited from AA:
- additional accounts of Dr. James Walker administrator of John Gardner.

15 May. Exhibited from AA:
- Additional accounts of Mark Guichard & his wife Diana executrix of Roger Crudgenton.

Exhibited from SM:
- accounts of Joseph Estep administrator of George Whitter.

17 May. Exhibited from PG:
- additional accounts of Col. Edward Sprigg & his wife Mary executrix of Edward Hall.

18 May. Exhibited from PG:
- inventory of Abraham Laking. Also, accounts of Martha Laking executrix.

31:581 Mrs. Araminta Alexander vs. Mr. Richard Young surviving executor of Col. Samuel Young (AA). Petition for full accounts.

Exhibited from AA & BA:
- inventory of Richard Galloway, Sr., in AA & BA. Also, receipts for filial portions.

Court Session: 1745

Exhibited from AA:
- additional inventory of Edmund Purdey.
- inventory of William Richardson.
- additional accounts of Catherine Minskie administratrix of John Samuel Minskie.

20 May. Thomas Bullen (g, TA) exhibited:
- will of John Harrison, constituting Mary Harrison & William Hebb Haddaway executors. Also, widow's election. Said executors were granted administration. Sureties: Ralph Dawson, Impey Dawson. Date: 19 March.
- will of Henry Oldfield, constituting Sarah Oldfield executrix. Also, widow's election. Said executrix was granted administration. Sureties: Isaac Falkner, John Small, Barber Oldfield. Date: 29 March 1745.
- bond of Christopher Wise administrator of John Sprignal. Sureties: John Tibbels, Thomas Kelld. Date: 30 April 1745.
- will of Samuel Martin, constituting Grace Martin & William Martin executors. Said executors were granted administration. Sureties: Morris Giddens, Philip Martin. Date: 23 April 1745.
- bond of Mary Merchant administratrix of James Merchant. Sureties: Henry Buckinham, John Walker. Date: 7 May 1745.
- bond of Thomas Dudley administrator of John Batcheldor. Sureties: Thomas Powell, Richard Dudley. Date: 10 May 1745.
- will of Samuel Dudley, constituting Mary Dudley & Richard Dudley executors. Also, widow's election. Said executors were granted administration. Sureties: Edward Nedels, Thomas Dudley. Date: 10 May 1745.
- bond of Francis Jones administrator of Lewis Jones. Sureties: Samuel Kininmont. Solomon Warner. Date:

Page 104

Court Session: 1745

10 May 1745.
- will of Thomas Trayman.
- will of John Dulin.
- nuncupative will of Ann Neall.
- will of Elisabeth Batchelder.
- will of Francis Neall.
- inventory of Richard Giles.
- additional inventory of John Sanckston, Jr.
- inventory of Jacob Williams.
- inventory of Varty Sweat.
- accounts of Rebecca Stacey administratrix of William Stacey.
- accounts of Margaret Jordon administratrix of Alexander Jordon.

Exhibited from AA:
- inventory of John Alston.

21 May. Exhibited from CE:
- will of William Alexander.

31:582   22 May. Thomas Lee executor of Philip Lee, Esq. deposed. Mentions: "Majors", "Barton's Hope", Richard Lee, Arthur Lee, Hancock Lee. Said Arthur Lee, Lettice Lee, Elisabeth Lee, & Hancock Lee were present at the appraisal. Also, said Arthur, Hancock Lee, & Elisabeth Fendall were present at the appraisal at Naval Office Plantation. Date: 18 December 1744.

24 May. Exhibited from CE:
- bond of Araminta Alexander executrix of William Alexander. Sureties (AA): Robert Gordon, Richard Young, William Cumming. Date: 23 May 1745.

Col. Gabriel Parker (CV) exhibited:
- bond of Gerrard Dixon & Thomas Shephard administrators of Ann Currant. Surety: James Kirshaw. Date: 22 March 1744.
- bond of Roseman Wilkinson administratrix of Thomas Wilkinson. Sureties: Martin Driver, Ellis Dixon. Date: 23 March 1744.
- will of Daniel Fraizer, constituting James Fraizer executor. Said executor was granted administration. Sureties: John Millis, Thomas Gray.

Date: 20 April 1745.
- bond of John Skinner administrator of Benjamin King. Date: 23 April 1745.
- will of John Armstrong.
- will of Mary Maners.
- inventory of Abraham Clark.
- inventory of John Williams.
- inventory of Thomas Stallings.
- inventory of James Hungerford.
- inventory of Henry Newton.
- inventory of William Skinner.
- inventory of John Dorumple
- accounts of Eliza Young administratrix of John Gough.
- accounts of William Hardie administrator of Thomas Stallings.
- accounts of William Mouett administrator of Ann Morgan.
- accounts of William Miller, Jr. executor of John Richards.

25 May. Exhibited:
- distribution of estate of Ishmael Devenish to: widow (1/3rd), Rachel daughter & wife of Richard Deford (1/3rd), Rebecca daughter & wife of John Mumford (1/3rd).

31:583 28 May. Maj. Thomas White (BA) exhibited:
- will of Capt. Daniel Bowley, constituting Elisabeth Bowley executrix. Said executrix was granted administration. Sureties: Darby Lux, Robert Sanders. Date: 9 April 1745.
- will of Daniel Scott, Sr.
- will of Thomas Coale.
- inventory & additional inventory of Col. Edward Hall. Also, accounts of Avarilla Hall executrix.
- inventory & LoD of Ephraim Standiford.
- inventory of Thomas Johnson.
- accounts of Lewis Lafee & his wife Sarah executrix of William Lowe.

Sheriff (AA) to summon Thomas Richardson (AA) surviving executor of Richard Richardson (AA) to render final accounts.

Court Session: 1745

29 May. Mr. Thomas Bullen (TA) to
examine accounts of:
• Robert Spencer administrator of
James Spencer, Jr. (TA).

30 May. Petition of George McKean (SO)
& Patrick McKean (SO). Jane Donaldson
executrix of Patrick Donaldson (SO) was
granted LoA on his estate on 1 November
1725. There is a residue of the estate
for distribution. The petitioners are
representatives of said dec'd. Bond on
said estate assigned to petitioners &
delivered to Col. Adam Muir.

5 June. Mr. Charles Hynson (KE) to
examine accounts of:
• John White & his wife Elisabeth
administratrix of THomas Rouse (KE).
• Jonathan Turner administrator of
Mary Forbush (KE). Additional
accounts.
• Sarah Kennard administratrix of John
Kennard (KE). Additional accounts.

8 June. Exhibited from AA:
• accounts of Elisabeth Burgess
administratrix of Samuel Burgess.
• 2nd additional accounts of Thomas
Richardson surviving executor of
Richard Richardson.

Samuel Smith (sheriff, AA) to summon
Thomas Richardson (AA) surviving
executor of Richard Richardson (AA) to
render final accounts. Accounts
exhibited. Discontinued.

31:584 Exhibited from AA:
• receipts for their filial portions.
Will of Richard Galloway (g, AA)
constituted his wife Sarah, now
Sarah Hill, & his son Richard
(dec'd) executors. Said Richard
(son) constituted by his will his
wife Sophia executrix. Said estates
were distributed. Witnesses: Joseph
Hill, Joseph Richardson, Edward
Edwards. Date: 25 May 1745.

10 June. Thomas Taney one of sureties &
Michael Taney & Sarah Taney executors of

Michael Taney other surety on estate of
Dorothy Smith (SM) vs. Basil Smith (SM)
surviving executor of said dec'd.
Sheriff (SM) to summon defendant to
render full accounts.

Mr. Thomas Aisquith (SM) to examine
accounts of:
- Sarah Taney & Michael Taney
  executors of Michael Taney (CV).

Thomas Aisquith (g, SM) exhibited:
- bond of Elisabeth Nelson
  administratrix of Joshua Nelson.
  Sureties: Thomas Greaves, George
  Greaves. Date: 26 March 1745.
- will of John Redman, Sr.,
  constituting Rebecca Redman
  executrix. Also, widow's election.
  Said executrix was granted
  administration. Sureties: Thomas
  Russell, Luke Russell. Date: 28
  March 1745.
- bond of Ann McKellvie administratrix
  of Andrew McKellvie. Sureties: John
  McKellvie, John Hammett. Date: 8
  April 1745.
- will of Clement Cheiverell,
  constituting Jane Cheiverell
  executrix. Also, widow's election.
  Said executrix was granted
  administration. Sureties: William
  Orr, James McCleland. Date: 29
  April 1745.
- will of Jeremiah Pickeils,
  constituting John Haddock executor.
  Said executor was granted
  administration. Sureties: John
  Wilkinson, Cuthbert Able. Date: 6
  May 1745.
- will of Stephen Notingham,
  constituting Athanasius Notingham
  executor. Said executor was granted
  administration. Sureties: Matthew
  Daft, John Cole. Date: 7 May 1745.
- bond of George Tolle administrator
  of Timothy Tolle. Sureties: John
  Carlett, Henry Really. Date: 11 May
  1745.
- will of John Bean, constituting Mary
  Bean & John Bean executors. Said
  executors were granted

administration. Sureties: John
Morgan, William Askings. Date: 16
May 1745.

- will of James Mattingly. Also, bond
of Henry Sheircliffe administrator.
Sureties: Peter Ford, Henry Bryon.
Date: 29 May 1745.
- will of John Carmichael. Also,
widow's election.

31:585
- inventory & LoD of Elinor Pearce.
- inventory of John Redman, Sr.
- accounts of John Noble & his wife
Elisabeth administratrix of William
Flower.

12 June. Exhibited from BA:
- bond of Samuel Richardson executor
of Thomas Coale. Sureties: Joseph
Richardson (PG), Joseph Richardson
(AA). Date: 12 June 1745.

Nehemiah King (g, SO) exhibited:
- bond of John Taylor administrator of
Abraham Taylor. Sureties: William
Taylor, Sr., John Hufington, Jr.
Date: 22 March 1744. Also,
renunciation of Rebecca Taylor
(widow), recommending John Taylor.
Date: 17 March 1745. Witness:
Robert Twilley.
- will of John Horsey. Also, bond of
Rachel Horsey acting executrix.
Sureties: Solomon Long, William
Dreaden. Also, renunciation of Jos.
Mitchell. Date: 22 March 1744.
- bond of Patience Hix administratrix
of William Hix. Sureties: John
Hufington, Woney McClamey. Date: 6
April 1745.
- will of Thomas Pryor. Also, widow's
election. Also, bond of Ann Pryor
administratrix. Sureties: Archibald
White, John Scott, Jr. Date: 19
April 1745.
- bond of Abraham Outten administrator
of Sarah Collam. Sureties: Purnall
Outten, Bell Maddux. Also,
renunciation of Purnell Outten
(son), recommending his elder
brother Abraham Outten. Date: 1
June 1745.
- will of John Connor, constituting

Elisabeth Connor executrix. Also, widow's election. Said executrix was granted administration. Sureties: Thomas Moore, Bell Maddux. Date: 27 April 1745.

- will of John Handy, constituting Jane Handy executrix. Said executrix was granted administration. Sureties: George Dashiell, Isaac Handy. Date: 28 May 1745.
- will of Matthias Dashiell.
- will of Giles Bashaw.
- will of Patrick Matthews.
- inventory of William Matthews.
- inventory & LoD of Richard Dunn.
- inventory of Robert Dashiell.
- inventory of Charles Dean.
- inventory of William Copsey.
- inventory of Francis Moore.
- additional inventory & LoD of Teague Riggen. Also, accounts of Mary & James Riggen executors.
- inventory of Nicholas Fountain.
- accounts of Joseph Riggen administrator of Ambrose Riggen.

31:586 12 June. Joseph Wilson (CV) vs. James Weems (g, CV) & Gabriel Parker (g, CV) subscribing witnesses to will of Edward Reynolds (CV). Sheriff (CV) to summon defendants to prove said will.

13 June. Exhibited from AA:
- additional accounts of Richard Fowler & his wife Elisabeth administrators of Stephen Stewart.

14 June. Exhibited from AA:
- accounts of James Dick administrator of Richard Goodman.
- accounts of Mary Watkins administratrix of John Watkins.

Mr. Nehemiah King (g, SO) to examine accounts of:
- Esther Dashiell executrix of Robert Dashiell (SO).
- Abraham Outten administrator of Sarah Kellam executrix of John Kellam (SO).
- Patience Mister executrix of William

Court Session: 1745

Mister (SO).

William Rogers (g, AA) exhibited:
- bond of William Thornton administrator of William Lloyd. Sureties: Nicholas Maccubbin, William Thomas. Date: 22 March 1744.
- bond of John Hall administrator of George Macquire. Sureties: William Hall, John Franklin. Date: 9 April 1745.
- will of Samuel Edgar, constituting Dr. George Steuart executor. Said executor was granted administration. Surety: James Dick, Date: 29 April 1745.
- will of Ferdinando Battee, constituting Elisabeth Battee & Samuel Battee executors. Said executors were granted administration. Sureties: Samuel Smith, Thomas Sparrow. Date: 29 April 1745.
- will of Thomas Mills, constituting Benjamin Gardner executor. Said executor was granted administration. Sureties: William Govane, John Gardner. Date: 29 April 1745.
- bond of Priscilla Woodward acting executrix of Abraham Woodward. Sureties: Alexander Gaither, William Woodward. Also, renunciation of R. Woodard (son & executor). Date: 1 May 1745. Witness: William Woodward.
- bond of Richard Smith administrator of Thomas Wooden. Sureties: John Burgess, James Deale. Date: 15 June 1745.
- will of Samuel Maccubbin.
- additional inventory & 2nd additional inventory of John Norris, Jr.
- inventory of James Wilson.
- inventory of Alice Andrews.
- inventory of Benjamin Prickyard.
- inventory of Dennis Ryan.
- inventory of John Reynolds.
- inventory of Samuel Simmons.
- inventory of Richard Goodman.
- additional accounts of Mark Geary

administrator of Thomas Lusby (son
of Robert).
- accounts of Isabella Alsworth
administratrix of Michael Alsworth.
- accounts of Mark Geary administrator
of Thomas Lusby administrator of
Laurence Geary.

31:587 21 June. Gabriel Parker (g, CV)
exhibited:
- bond of William Coster administrator
of John Coster. Sureties: William
Allnutt, Thomas Morgan. Date: 8
June 1745.
- will of Absalom Kent, constituting
Elisabeth Kent & Absalom Kent
executors. Also, widow's election.
Said executors were granted
administration. Sureties: Benjamin
Mackall, Jr., John Gray. Date: 15
June 1745.
- inventory of Stephen Dickenson.
- inventory of William Leach.
- inventory of Maj. Thomas Compton.

Mr. William Tilghman (QA) to examine
accounts of:
- Ann Carradine administratrix of John
Carradine (QA).

Exhibited from QA:
- inventory & LoD of Esther Williams.

22 June. Exhibited:
- order to pay to Daniel Dunaly money
due to Friend Ungle as executrix of
Robert Ungle, Esq. Date: 15 June
1739. Witness: Richard Snowden.

Exhibited from QA:
- accounts of Christopher Williams
executor of Esther Williams.

Mr. Charles Hynson (KE) to examine
additional accounts of:
- Katherine Smithers administratrix of
John Smithers (KE).

27 June. Walter Hanson (g, CH)
exhibited:
- will of George Medway, constituting
John Hatch & Edward Kellet

Court Session: 1745

executors. Said executors were
granted administration. Sureties:
Thomas Leftwich, George Waple.
Date: 5 April 1745.
- will of James Stewart, constituting
John Hanson executor. Said executor
was granted administration.
Sureties: John Cunningham, George
Godfrey. Date: 8 May 1745.
- bond of Winifred Mastin
administratrix of Francis Mastin.
Sureties: Thomas Wright, Richard
Wright. Date: 8 May 1745.
- will of Thomas Davis.
- inventory of Barton Smoot.
- accounts of John Gray & his wife Ann
executrix of John Sutcliffe.

Peter Dent (g, PG) exhibited:
- will of Bryant Kelley. Also, bond
of Mary Kelley administratrix.
Sureties (SM): Joseph Kelley, Thomas
Wilson. Date: 3 May 1745.
- bond of Jane McClash administratrix
of William McClash. Surety: Thomas
Munroe. Date: 18 June 1745.

31:588
- inventory of Thomas Jane.
- inventory of Edward Willett.
- inventory of Zachariah Wade.
- inventory of Robert Cloyd.
- accounts of Elisabeth White
administratrix of Joseph White.
- accounts of Priscilla Wilson
administratrix of Nathan Masters.
- accounts of Priscilla Deakins
executrix of John Deakins.

29 June. Exhibited from CV:
- inventory of Martha Lingan.

Exhibited from AA:
- inventory of William Wootton.
- accounts of Sarah Warfield &
Absolute Warfield executors of
Alexander Warfield.
- additional accounts of Charles
Griffith who married Mary Mercer
executrix of Jacob Mercer.

Exhibited from BA:
- inventory of James Powell.

Page 113

Court Session: 1745

Exhibited from DO:
- 2nd additional accounts of William Cullens executor of Mark Fisher.

Maj. Ennalls Hooper (DO) to examine 3rd additional accounts of:
- Joseph Cox Gray & his wife Rosannah executrix of Jacob Loockerman (DO).

Col. Gabriel Parker (CV) to examine accounts of:
- John James & his wife Margaret executrix of Edward Wood (CV).
- James Heighe surviving administrator of Arthur Jones (CV). Additional accounts.

8 July. MM John Elder (AA) & Robert Shipley (AA) to appraise estate of John Taillor at plantation of John Johnson.

Court Session: 9 July 1745

Docket:
- Sheriff (PG) to render attachment to Lingan Wilson (PG) administrator of Joseph Wilson (PG) to render inventory.
- 31:589 • Thomas Sligh & Henry Morgan sureties on estate of Buckler Partridge (BA) vs. Jane Partridge administratrix of said dec'd. Sheriff (BA) to summon defendant to render accounts.
- Rev. John Lang vs. Richard Snowden (AA) administrator dbn of Thomas South (PG). Samuel Smith (sheriff, AA) to summon defendant to render accounts.
- Humphry Boone (AA) vs. John Burle surviving executor of John Burle (AA). Samuel Smith (sheriff, AA) to summon defendant to render additional inventory. Additional inventory exhibited. Discontinued.
- Thomas Wilson administrator of Ann Davie (CH) vs. Arabella Hines wife of Joseph Hines (CH). Sheriff (CH) to summon defendant to testify concerning concealment of estate of dec'd. Struck off.
- Thomas Taney one of sureties & Michael & Sarah Taney executors of

Court Session: 9 July 1745

Michael Taney the other surety on
estate of Dorothy Smith vs. Basil
Smith (SM) surviving executor of
dec'd. Sheriff (SM) to summon
defendant to render final accounts.
Accounts exhibited. Discontinued.

- Joseph Wilson (CV) vs. James Weems
  (g, CV) & Gabriel Parker (g, CV)
  subscribing witnesses to will of
  Edward Reynolds (CV). James
  Somervell (sheriff, CV) to summon
  defendants to prove said will.
  James Weems is cited as NEI. Said
  Weems proved the will.
  Discontinued.

Court Session: 1745

31:590 9 July. Thomas Bullen (g, TA)
exhibited:
- bond of Robert Stapleford & his wife
  Mary executrix of Thomas Trayman.
  Sureties: Daniel Stapleford, Daniel
  Marshall, Barnaby Stapleford. Date:
  17 May 1745.
- bond of Mary Dulin executrix of John
  Dulin. Sureties: Henry Harris,
  William Anderson. Date: 17 May
  1745.
- bond of Samuel Neall administrator
  of Francis Neall. Sureties: Edward
  Neall, Jonathan Neall, Francis
  Neall. Date: 20 May 1745.
- bond of Judith Harrison
  administratrix of John Harrison.
  Sureties: David Robinson, William
  Harrison. Date: 24 May 1745.
- will of Thomas Wilson, constituting
  William Wilson executor. Said
  executor was granted administration.
  Sureties: James Wilson, Henry
  Buckingham. Date: 24 May 1745.
- will of Loton West. Also, widow's
  election. Also, renunciation of 1
  executor. Also, bond of Hannah West
  acting executrix. Sureties: Morris
  Giddens, William Alexander. Date:
  14 June 1745.
- will of Ann Neall. Also,
  renunciation of 1 executor.
- inventory of William Welsh.
- inventory of James Williams.

Page 115

- accounts of Francis Parrott administrator of William Welsh.
- accounts of Mary Snelling administratrix of Thomas Snelling.
- accounts of William Sharp executor of Solomon Birckhead.
- accounts of Tristram Thomas & Adam Brown executors of James Webster.

Exhibited from CV:
- additional accounts of Basil Smith surviving executor of Dorothy Smith.

At the request of Joseph Wilson (CV), Mr. James Weems, one of subscribing witnesses to will of Edward Reynolds (CV), proved said will.

15 July. Exhibited from AA:
- accounts of Elisabeth Ward administratrix of John Ward.

Exhibited from BA:
- inventory of Susannah Holland.

Sarah Rowles executrix of Thomas Rowles (AA) was granted continuance. She has not received accounts from ENG.

Baptist Barber & his wife Elisabeth (late Elisabeth Southorn (widow)) vs. Samuel Southorn & Richard Southorn executors of John Johnson Southorn (SM). Sheriff (SM) to summon defendants to render inventory.

31:591 17 July. Mr. Thomas Aisquith (SM) to examine accounts of:
- Elisabeth Briscoe administratrix of Philip Briscoe (SM).

Exhibited from AA:
- 3rd additional accounts of Mary Towgood surviving executrix of Col. Josias Towgood.

18 July. William Tilghman (g, QA) exhibited:
- bond of John Walker administrator of James Walker. Sureties: Thomas Price, John Knowles. Date: 9 May 1745.

- bond of William Dulany executor of William Dulany. Sureties: John Sullivant, John Higgens. Date: 30 May 1745.
- will of Christopher Yewell. Also, widow's election.
- will of William Vanderford. Also, widow's election.
- inventory & LoD of Thomas Atkinson.
- inventory of Richard Buckley.
- inventory & LoD of Benjamin Elliott.
- inventory & LoD of Robert Walters.
- inventory of Timothy Lane.
- additional inventory & LoD of Joshua Clarke. Also, accounts of John Baynard & his wife Elisabeth administratrix.

Joseph Milburn Simmes & his wife Rachel (CH) vs. John Smith Prather, Thomas Prather, & Thomas Williams executors of Martha Yoakley (CH). Sheriff (CH) to summon said John Smith Prather & sheriff (PG) to summon said Thomas Prather & Thomas Williams to render answer.

19 July. Ann Hall administratrix of Isaac Stevens (SO) vs. Matthew Kemp (SO) & his wife Rachel. Sheriff (SO) to summon defendants to render answer.

20 July. Exhibited from AA:
- additional accounts of John Burle, Jr. executor of Lancelott Todd.
- additional accounts of John Burle surviving executor of John Burle.

22 July. Col. Gabriel Parker (CV) exhibited:
- bond of James Richason executor of Mary Maners. Sureties: Alexander Parran, Daniel Rawlings. Date: 19 June 1745.
- bond of Susannah Armstrong executrix of John Armstrong. Sureties: John Hall, Robert Gardner. Date: 19 June 1745.
- will of John Baker. Also, renunciation of 1 executor. Also, bond of Grace Baker acting executrix. Sureties: Benjamin Dixon, Martin Driver. Date: 6 July

1745.
- will of James Chapple. Also, renunciation of 1 executor.
- inventory of Lucy Pardo.
- inventory of Sarah Malden.
- accounts of Sarah & Michael Taney executors of Michael Taney.

31:592 Col. Gabriel Parker (CV) to examine accounts of:
- Elisabeth Hungerford executrix of James Hungerford (CV).

Exhibited from AA:
- inventory of Charles Cheney. Also, accounts of John Deal & his wife Agnes executrix.

23 July. Mr. Thomas Bullen (TA) to examine accounts of:
- William Skinner executor of William Skinner, Jr. (TA).
- Frances Wiles administratrix of Thomas Wiles (TA).
- Margaret Neighbours acting executrix of John Neighbours (TA).

24 July. Exhibited from SM:
- inventory of John Johnson Sothoron.

Exhibited from AA:
- additional accounts of Elisabeth Browne executrix of John Elliott Browne.
- exemplifications of will & LoA on estate of Benjamin Richardson (London), by Capt. Darby Lux.

Mr. Peter Dent (PG) to examine accounts of:
- Margaret Markland administratrix of Matthew Markland (PG).
- James Bolton & his wife Elisabeth executrix of Robert Lloyd (PG).
- William Bright & his wife Mary executrix of Nathaniel Magruder (PG). 2nd additional accounts.

Mr. Walter Hanson (CH) to examine additional accounts of:
- Francis Ware & John Doncastle executors of Ann Ebernathy (CH).

25 July. Mr. Charles Hynson (KE) to examine additional accounts of:
- Simon Wilmer administrator dbn of Patrick Fitzgarril (KE).

Exhibited from AA:
- additional accounts of William Reynolds & his wife Deborah administratrix of John Syng.

27 July. Petition of Richard Cooper (DO). In 1732/3, petitioner & Gabriel Saile (TA) were bound for Mary Saile widow of George Saile (TA) for administration of his estate. Said Mary has since married William Matthews (TA). **31:593** Estate has not been completed. Children are of age. Sheriff (TA) to summon said Matthews to complete the administration.

30 July. Charles Hynson (g, KE) exhibited:
- bond of Richard Gresham & Sarah Thomas executors of William Thomas. Sureties: Thomas Bordley, Morgan Browne. Date: 20 April 1745.
- bond of Daniel Bryant administrator of Isaac Riley. Sureties: William Woodland, James Woodland. Date: 4 May 1745.
- bond of Elisabeth Quiney administratrix of Sutton Quiney. Sureties: Jacob Goodwin, James Smith. Date: 7 May 1745.
- renunciation of Hannah Riley widow of Isaac Riley, recommending Daniel Bryant (Georgetown, creditor). Witnesses: Daniel Long, Eliza Welch. Date: 24 April 1745.
- bond of James Woodland & Katherine Woodland administrators of William Woodland. Sureties: Daniel Perkins, Daniel Bryant. Date: 20 May 1745.
- bond of Beartine Pearce executor of Gideon Pearce, Jr. Sureties: Jervis Williams, Andrew Pearce. Date: 25 May 1745.
- will of Nicholas Riley, constituting Mary Riley & Nicholas Riley executors. Said executors were granted administration. Sureties: Benjamin Palmer, Daniel Cunningham.

Date: 25 May 1745.
- bond of Elisabeth Miller administratrix of Nathaniel Miller. Sureties: Ralph Page, Samuel Miller. Date: 8 May 1745.
- bond of Sarah Manley administratrix of Peter Manley. Sureties: Robert Meeks, John Thornton. Date: 12 June 1745.
- will of Robert Dew, constituting Collin Ferguson executor. Said executor was granted administration. Sureties: Anthony Camron, John Gale. Date: 6 July 1745.
- will of William Usler.
- will of Thomas Clay.
- inventory of Richard Wethered.
- inventory of Lawrence ONeall.
- inventory of Bowles Green.
- additional inventory of John Kennard.
- inventory & LoD of Francis Wetheral.
- accounts of James Smith administrator of Richard Reading.

31:594
- additional accounts of Christopher Hall surviving executor of Matthias Day.
- accounts of Nicholas Lynch executor of John Lynch.
- accounts of Peter Cole & his wife Francina administratrix of John Perkins.
- accounts of Francis Spearman & his wife Hester administratrix of Thomas Wyate.
- additional accounts of Jonathan Turner administrator of Mary Forbush.
- accounts of Elisabeth White administratrix of Thomas Rouse.
- accounts of Elisabeth Ringgold administratrix dbn of William Buckham.
- accounts of Elisabeth Ringgold administratrix of James Ringgold.

31 July. Elinor Hill late widow of John Durbin (BA) vs. John Durbin (BA) acting executor of said dec'd. Sheriff (BA) to summon defendant to render inventory.

Court Session: 1745

Sheriff (BA) to summon Judith Crow (BA) widow of John Crow (BA) to render inventory.

5 August. William Tilghman (g, QA) exhibited:
- bond of Edward Gregory administrator of John Gregory. Sureties: Thomas Nelson, John Lloyd. Date: 11 July 1745.
- bond of Ann Lambdin administratrix of John Lambdin. Sureties: Edward Roe, John Roe. Date: 16 July 1745.
- will of James Boone, constituting Phebe Boone executrix. Also, widow's election. Said executrix was granted administration. Sureties: Jacob Boone, Benjamin Boone. Date: 16 September 1745.
- bond of Ann Jackerman administratrix of John Jackerman. Sureties: William Barwick, Edward Barwick. Date: 18 July 1745.
- will of Patrick Robertson, constituting Patrick Robertson & Alexander Robertson executors. Also, widow's election. Said executors were granted administration. Sureties: Richard Harrington, Henry Burt. Date: 25 July 1745.
- will of Elisabeth Ricketts.
- additional inventory & LoD of Henry Coventon.
- inventory of John Saunders.
- LoD on estate of John Carradine.
- accounts of Dr. John Smith administrator of Thomas Smith.
- accounts of Ann Carradine administratrix of John Carradine.

Ennalls Hooper (g, DO) exhibited:
- bond of Ann Canner administratrix of Edward Canner. Sureties: Francis Carr, Thomas Canner, Jr. Date: 15 April 1745.
- bond of Modling Winstandly administratrix of Thomas Winstandly. Sureties: Capt. Levin Hicks, Capt. Henry Hooper. Date: 22 April 1745.
- will of Thomas Hayward, constituting Margaret Hayward executrix. Said

Page 121

executrix was granted administration. Sureties: Theophilus Hackett, William Whitely. Date: 22 April 1745.

31:595 • bond of Ann Trippe administratrix of John Trippe. Sureties: Capt. Bartholomew Ennalls, Thomas Ennalls. Date: 1 May 1745.

• bond of Thomas Williams administrator of William Stevens, during minority of Edward Stevens. Sureties: Charles Stanford, Thomas Brohon. Date: 11 May 1745.

• bond of Grace Stogdell administratrix of Michael Stogdell. Sureties: John Hodson IV, Roger Hodson. Date: 10 May 1745.

• will of John Rumbly, constituting Priscilla Rumbly executrix. Said executrix was granted administration. Sureties: Thomas Walters, William Rumbly. Date: 14 May 1745.

• bond of Katherine White administratrix of Charles White. Sureties: John Gorslyn, James Vinson. Date: 16 May 1745.

• bond of Ann Coburn administratrix of Samuel Coburn. Sureties: John Nicolls, Andrew Gray, Abraham Gambell. Date: 17 May 1745.

• will of William Harper, constituting Margaret Harper executrix. Said executrix was granted administration. Sureties: John Anderton, Solomon Turpin. Date: 24 May 1745.

• bond of Ann Coburn administratrix of Hannah Hill. Sureties: Joseph Alford, Jacob Low. Date: 2 June 1745.

• will of Daniel Murphy. Also, bond of Ann Coburn administratrix. Sureties: John Nicholls, Jr., Edward Hardikin. Date: 2 June 1745.

• bond of Mary Rimmer administratrix o Hugh Rimmer. Sureties: Edward Newton, William Newton. Date: 5 June 1745.

• bond of Sarah Cannon administratrix of James Cannon. Sureties: Henry Cannon, William Cannon, Sr. Date:

10 June 1745.

- bond of Francis Bickam administrator of Nehemiah Williams, during minority of Billy Williams. Sureties: Edward Palle, Jacob Gray. Date: 12 June 1745.
- will of John Rumbly, Jr., constituting Ann Rumbly executrix. Also, widow's election. Said executrix was granted administration. Sureties: John Pritchet Fisher, James Vaux, Jr. Date: 12 June 1745.
- bond of James Stafford administrator of Abraham Stafford. Sureties: William Dean, John Brawhan. Also, renunciation of Mary Stafford (widow), recommending his brother James Stafford. Date: 12 June 1745.
- bond of Alice McKeel administratrix of Charles McKeel. Sureties: Richard Dawson, William Twyford. Date: 12 June 1745.
- nuncupative will of William MacDaniel. Also, bond of Elisabeth MacDaniel administratrix. Sureties: George Williams, John Williams. Date: 12 June 1745.
- will of St. Leeger Pattison, constituting John Pattison & Mary Pattison executors. Said executors were granted administration. Sureties: Noah Pearson, Jacob Pattison. Date: 12 June 1745.
- bond of Elisabeth Proctor administratrix of Hugh Proctor. Sureties: Charles Powell, Stephen Ross. Date: 12 June 1745.
- bond of Roger Adams administrator of William Oston. Sureties: Thomas Clifton, Jacob Gray. Date: 13 June 1745.

31:596   Also, renunciation of widow Oston, recommending Roger Adams (biggest creditor). Date: 18 June 1745.

- bond of Thomas Veach administrator of John Griffin, during minority of John Griffin, Jr. Sureties: Edward Poole, Thomas Hackett. Date: 3 August 1745.
- bond of Rosannah Manning administratrix of Nathaniel Manning.

Court Session: 1745

Sureties: Arthur Wheatley, Matthew Driver. Date: 14 June 1745.
- will of William Adams. Also, bond of Roger Adams administrator. Sureties: Thomas Nutter, James Newton. Date: 20 June 1745.
- bond of Alice Warren administratrix of John Warren. Sureties: Henry Wheeler, John Wheeler. Date: 20 July 1745.
- will of John Creek, constituting Sarah Creek executrix. Said executrix was granted administration. Sureties: Richard Badley, Sr., Thomas Walker. Date: 24 July 1745.
- bond of James Billings administrator of Robert Thornwell. Surety: John Hodson. Date: 26 July 1745. Also, renunciation of Elisabeth Thornwell (widow), recommending Maj. James Billings. Date: 17 July 1745.
- bond of Rebecca Watkins administratrix of William Watkins. Sureties: William Draper, Robert Titus. Date: 30 July 1745.
- will of Thomas Royall, constituting Mary Royall executrix. Also, widow's election. Said executrix was granted administration. Sureties: Thomas Royall, Samuel Royall. Date: 2 August.
- will of William Stevens.
- inventory & LoD of Michael Stogdell.
- inventory of John Carawon.
- inventory of Edward Canner.
- inventory of Morgan Adams.
- inventory & LoD of Robert Ross.
- inventory & LoD of James Harris.
- inventory & LoD of Jacob Coventon.
- additional inventory of William Cannon.
- inventory & LoD of George Morris.
- inventory of Lawrence Mason.
- inventory & LoD of Thomas Brannock.
- inventory & LoD of William Stevens.
- inventory & LoD of Thomas Hayward.
- inventory & LoD of William Sulivant.
- inventory of John Trippe.
- inventory & LoD of Thomas Winstandly.
- inventory & LoD of James Cannon.

- accounts of Monica Williams executrix of William Williams.
- accounts of William Galloway executor of James Galloway.
- accounts of Elinor Lister administratrix of William Lister.
- accounts of William Cullens executor of Mark Fisher.
- accounts of Grace Hooper administratrix of William Cooper.
- accounts of Elisabeth Cock administratrix of Edward Cock.
- accounts of Sumner Adams administrator of Morgan Adams.
- accounts of Rachel Jones administratrix of Walter Hunter.
- accounts of John Hodson III administrator of Owen Ward.
- accounts of Ruth Edgar executrix of Henry Edgar.
- accounts of Elisabeth Ball executrix of Benjamin Ball.

31:597
- accounts of Sarah Stinson administratrix of Alexander Stinson.
- accounts of Mary Williams executrix of William Williams.
- accounts of Elisabeth Jones executrix of Leonard Jones.
- accounts of Sarah Hayward acting executrix of John Hayward.

Walter Hanson (g, CH) exhibited:
- inventory of William Carter.
- inventory of Thomas Coleman.
- inventory of John West.
- inventory of Randolph Brandt.
- inventory of Francis Hamersley.
- inventory of Ann Howard.
- accounts of George Brett & Henry Moore & his wife Sarah executors of Richard Brett.
- accounts of John Ashfield & his wife Elisabeth administratrix of William Munroe.
- additional accounts of James Dyson & his wife Abigail administratrix of Thomas Swann.
- accounts of Matthew Hennekin & his wife Elisabeth administratrix of John Brayfield.
- accounts of William Williams & Sarah Rozier executors of George Johnson.

- accounts of Sarah Hawkins administratrix of Thomas Hawkins.

Mr. Walter Hanson (CH) to examine accounts of:
- Mary Neale executrix of Raphael Neale (CH).
- John Mcferson & his wife Sarah administratrix of Jacob Miller (CH). Additional accounts.
- Alexander McLaran & his wife Janet executrix of Peter Mitchell (CH). Additional accounts.

6 August. Thomas Williamse (g, SM) exhibited:
- bond of Mary Mollihone administratrix of John Mollihone. Sureties: John Bond, William Bond. Date: 4 April 1745.
- bond of Agnes Pembrooke administratrix of John Pembrooke. Sureties: Edward Abell, John Aulthors. Date: 22 July 1745.
- will of John Green, constituting Rachel Green executrix. Also, widow's election. Said executrix was granted administration. Sureties: William Jones, John Thomas. Date: 22 July 1745.
- will of Mary Slye.
- will of Thomas Warren.
- inventory of Andrew McKellvie.
- inventory of Timothy Toles.
- inventory & LoD of William Watts.
- inventory of Thomas Hobbs.
- inventory of Samuel Bagley.
- inventory & LoD of George Wallis.
- inventory & LoD of Thomas Truman Greenfield.
- inventory & LoD of William Williams.
- inventory & LoD of Benjamin Burch.
- inventory & LoD of Clement Cheverell.
- inventory & LoD of Charles Ganyott.
- inventory & LoD of Stephen Notingham.
- accounts of John McKellvie executor of James Taylor.
- accounts of John Norris executor of Mary Gough.
- accounts of Matthias Nottingham &

Court Session: 1745

his wife Mary administratrix of
Charles Griffin.
- accounts of Mary Tennison
administratrix of Samuel Tennison.
- accounts of Henry Fowler & his wife
Elisabeth administratrix of Benjamin
Stephens.
- accounts of Monica Jarboe & Ignatius
Jarboe executors of Peter Jarboe.
- accounts of Thomas Greenwell & his
wife Mary executrix of John Realey.
- accounts of John Temple surviving
executor of Monica Monark.

31:598
- accounts of Peter Johnson & his wife
Grace administratrix of John
Mattingly.
- accounts of Elinor Read
administratrix of John Read.
- accounts of William Daft & his wife
Elisabeth executrix of William Bold.
- accounts of Thomas Ingalls executor
of Benjamin Gale.

William Knight (g, CE) exhibited:
- bond of Augustina Ward
administratrix of John Ward.
Sureties: James Paul Heath, John
Thompson. Date: 9 May 1745.
- bond of Thomas Colvill executor of
Solomon Hodgson. Sureties: John
Veazey, Peter Bayard. Date: 30 May
1745.
- bond of John Kankey administrator of
Johannes Sluyter. Sureties: William
Bristow, Michael Linn. Date: 2 July
1745.
- will of Terrance OBryan.
- will of Howell James.
- will of John Ryland.
- inventory of William Wye.
- inventory of Joseph Rodoch.
- inventory of Solomon Hodgson.
- inventory of John Ogleby.
- accounts of John Gibbony
administrator of John Archibald.
- accounts of Elisabeth Beazley
administratrix of Jeffry Beazley.
- accounts of Elisabeth Alricks
administratrix of Sigfredus Alricks.
- accounts of Rachel Piggot
administratrix of John Piggot.
- accounts of Elisabeth Frisby

administratrix of Peregrine Frisby.
- accounts of Robert Patton administrator of Dorothy Patton.
- accounts of Thomas Severson administrator of Isaac Clements.

Exhibited from DO:
- inventory of Maj. Henry Trippe.

Benton Harris (g, WO) exhibited:
- bond of Mary Taylor administratrix of William Taylor. Sureties: William Holston, William Johnson. Date: 12 April 1745.
- will of Francis Allen, constituting Mary Allen executrix. Also, widow's election. Said executrix was granted administration. Sureties: Alexander Buncle, Abraham Outten. Date: 17 May 1745.
- bond of Ann Jarman administratrix of William Jarman. Sureties: Abraham Outten, Samuel Parker. Date: 26 April 1745.
- bond of Catherine Wildman administratrix of John Dennin. Sureties: Dunken Murray, Arthur Mackallen. Date: 3 May 1745.
- bond of Levin Disharoon administrator of John Disharoon. Sureties: Thomas Davis, George Smith. Date: 5 June 1745.
- bond of Joseph Robinson administrator of John Robinson. Sureties: Alexander Linch, Race Clark. Date: 27 June 1745.
- will of Lewis Disharoone.
- will of Martin Kennett.
- will of Ephraim Heather.
- will of Joseph Taylor.
- inventory & LoD of William Salmon.
- inventory of Richard Badard.
- inventory & LoD of John Harvey.
- inventory of William Smith.
- inventory of Absolom Bessicks.
- inventory & LoD of Joseph Schoolfield.
- inventory & LoD of John Hopkins.
- inventory of John Blewitt.
- accounts of Littleton Townsend executor of Job Shery.
- accounts of Alexander Massey

administrator of William Massey.
31:599 • accounts of Henry Ayres
administrator of John Ayres.

8 August. Exhibited from PG:
• accounts of Robert Pottenger & his
wife Rachel executrix of Charles
Perry.

9 August. Exhibited from DO:
• additional accounts of Joseph Cox
Gray & his wife Rosannah executrix
of Jacob Loockerman executor of
Elisabeth Holland.

12 August. Exhibited from BA:
• bond of Darby Lux administrator of
Benjamin Richardson (mariner,
London). Sureties: George Buchanan
(BA), Thomas Jennings (AA). Date:
12 August 1745.

13 August. Exhibited from AA:
• accounts of Nehemiah & John Birkhead
executors of Nehemiah Birkhead.

Col. Gabriel Parker (CV) to examine
accounts of:
• Claranna Winall administratrix of
William Winall (CV).
• John Ogleby & John Sedwick executors
of Sarah Ogleby (CV).
• Ann Dickenson executrix of Stephen
Dickenson (CV).
• Robert Freeland & his wife Sarah
executrix of Thomas Holland (CV).
Additional accounts.

14 August. Exhibited from BA:
• inventory of John Lloyd. Also,
accounts of Elisabeth Lloyd
executrix.
• Mrs. Elisabeth Lloyd widow of John
Lloyd chose her thirds. Date: 1
April 1743.

Mr. Benton Harris (WO) to examine
accounts of:
• William Wale executor of Nathaniel
Wale (SO now WO).

20 August. Mr. Peter Dent (PG) to examine accounts of:
- Mary Waring acting executrix of Martha Greenfield (PG).
- Mary Ashcom Brooke executrix of Walter Brooke (PG).

21 August. Exhibited from PG:
- LoD on estate of Col. Leonard Hollyday.

22 August. Exhibited from PG:
- 2nd additional accounts of Dr. William Murray & his wife Elinor executrix & Thomas Hollyday executor of Col. Leonard Hollyday.

31:600 23 August. Col. Gabriel Parker (CV) exhibited:
- will of Benjamin Sedwick, constituting Betty Sedwick executrix. Said executrix was granted administration. Sureties: John Skinner, Leonard Skinner. Date: 5 August 1745
- inventory of Benjamin King.
- additional accounts of James Heighe surviving administrator of Arthur Jones.
- accounts of John James & his wife Margaret executrix of Edward Wood.
- accounts of John Ogleby & John Sedwick executors of Sarah Ogleby.

26 August. Exhibited from AA:
- will of Thomas Blackstone. Also, exemplification from London. Also, bond of Richard Blackstone administrator. Sureties: Thomas Sheredine (BA), Jacob Holland (AA). Date: 26 August 1745.

27 August. Col. Charles Hynson (KE) exhibited:
- bond of Charles Hynson as Deputy Commissary (KE). Sureties: John Williamson, Lambert Wilmer. Date: 8 November 1742.

Mr. Ennalls Hooper (DO) to examine accounts of:
- William Byus & his wife Eliza &

Joseph Ennalls executors of Henry Ennalls (DO).
- Maj. James Billings executor of Capt. Charles Rider (DO).
- Grace Stogdell administratrix of Michael Stogdell (DO).
- Mary Carawon administratrix of John Carawon (DO).
- Alice Covington administratrix of Jacob Covington (DO).
- Jane Harris administratrix of James Harris (DO).
- Margaret Hayward executrix of Thomas Hayward (DO).
- James Baker executor of Jane Baker (DO).
- John Robson & Joseph Shenton executors of Josias Mace (DO).
- Hannah Reed administratrix of Ezekiel Reed (DO).
- Sarah Cannon administratrix of James Cannon (DO).
- Sarah Morris administratrix of George Morris (DO).
- Adling Cannon administratrix of William Cannon (DO).
- Richard Kendall Foxwell administrator of Robert Ross (DO).
- Rosannah Manning administratrix of Nathaniel Manning executor of Richard Manning (DO).
- Ann Wing administratrix of Robert Wing executor of Gary Warner (DO). Additional accounts.

29 August. Peter Dent (g, PG) exhibited:
- will of Benjamin West, constituting John West executor. Said executor was granted administration. Sureties: Nathaniel Wickham, Jr., Luke Bernard. Date: 9 July 1745.
- will of Owen Ellis. Also, renunciation of executors.
- inventory of James Rigg.
- accounts of Mary Osburn administratrix of Benjamin Osburn.

Mr. Benton Harris (WO) to examine accounts of:
- Rouse Fassitt executor of Mary Fassitt (WO).

Page 131

Court Session: 1745

- John Rickards & Isaac Bell executors of Elisabeth Smith (WO).
- Hutton Hill executor of Samuel Tarr (WO).

31:601 30 August. Thomas Bullen (g, TA) exhibited:
- bond of Robert Hall administrator of Robert Dodson, Jr. Sureties: Thomas Bruff, Francis Armstrong. Date: 9 July 1745.
- bond of Alice Nowland administratrix of Augustin Nowland. Sureties: Nicholas Lowe, Vincent Paddison. Date: 10 July 1745.
- bond of Mary Ann Robotham administratrix of Ralph Robotham. Sureties: Robert Noble, Solomon Warner. Date: 19 July 1745.
- will of Nathaniel Santee, constituting Sarah Santee executrix. Also, widow's election. Said executrix was granted administration. Sureties: Francis Pickerin, Thomas Ray. Date: 26 July 1745.
- bond of Elisabeth Louther administratrix of Robert Louther. Sureties: Isaac Dobson, George Eubanks. Date: 2 August 1745.
- bond of Fiddeman Rolle administrator of Francis Rolle. Sureties: John Auld, Daniel Sherwood. Date: 6 August 1745.
- inventory of Francis Wrightson.
- accounts of William Skinner executor of William Skinner, Jr.
- accounts of Robert Spencer administrator of James Spencer, Jr.

Mr. Thomas Bullen (TA) to examine accounts of:
- Richard Warner executor of Charles Warner (TA).

4 September. Exhibited from DO:
- 2nd additional accounts of Richard Harrington administrator dbn of Joseph Fisher.

5 September. Exhibited from QA:
- 2nd additional accounts of

Court Session: 1745

Christopher Wilkinson & his wife
Eliza executrix of Joseph Earle.

Exhibited from PG:
• 2nd additional accounts of William
  Smith executor of Mary Demall.

6 September. Exhibited from QA:
• additional accounts of Edmond Kelley
  & his wife Ann executrix of John
  Dailey.

William Rogers (g, AA) exhibited:
• bond of John Tayman administrator of
  Joseph Tayman. Sureties: William
  Tayman, Robert Connant. Date: 9
  July 1745.
• bond of Mary Henderson executrix of
  Thomas Henderson. Sureties: James
  Walker (AA), Peregrine Frisby (BA).
  Date: 22 July 1745.
• bond of Thomas Wasson, Jr.
  administrator of Francis Sutor.
  Sureties: James Deale, Thomas
  Metcalfe. Date: 22 July 1745.
• will of John Powell, constituting
  Rebecca Powell executrix. Said
  executrix was granted
  administration. Sureties: John
  Trott, Samuel Scott. Date: 19
  August 1745.
• inventory of William Jones.
• inventory of Joseph Tayman.
• inventory of Nathan Selby.
• inventory of Abraham Woodward.
• inventory of John Wooden.
• inventory of Ferdinando Battee.
• additional inventory of John Burle.
• additional inventory of Nehemiah
  Birckhead.

31:602 14 August. Henry Darnall executor of
William Jones (CV) vs. Martha Griffith
(CV). Sheriff (CV) to summon defendant
to show cause why she conceals estate of
dec'd.

Court Session: 10 September 1745

Docket:
• Sheriff (PG) to render attachment to
  Lingan Wilson (PG) administrator of

Joseph Wilson (PG) to render inventory.

- Thomas Sligh & Henry Morgan vs. Jane Partridge administratrix of Buckler Partridge (BA). John Risteau (sheriff, BA) to summon defendant to render accounts.
- Baptist Barber & his wife Eliza (late Elisabeth Southoron, widow of John Johnson Southoron (SM)) vs. Samuel Southoron & Richard Southoron executors of said dec'd. Philip Key (sheriff, SM) to summon defendants to render inventory. Inventory exhibited. Discontinued.
- S.B. for Joseph Milburn Semmes & his wife (CH) vs. William Cumming, Esq. for executors of Martha Yoakley. Libel. Samuel Hanson (sheriff, CH) to summon John Smith Prather executor. John Cooke (sheriff, PG) to summon Thomas Williams & Thomas Prather executors. Thomas Prather is cited as NE.

31:603
- Stephen Bordley for Ann Hall administratrix of Isaac Stevens (SO) vs. Edward Dorsey for Matthew Kemp & his wife. Libel. John Dennis, Jr. (sheriff, SO) to summon defendant.
- Richard Cooper one of sureties on estate of George Saile (TA) vs. William Matthews (TA) & his wife Mary (formerly Mary Saile) administratrix of said dec'd. Richard Porter (sheriff, TA) to summon defendants to render accounts. Continuance granted. Discontinued.
- Elinor Hill late widow of John Durbin (BA) vs. John Durbin acting executor of said dec'd. John Risteau (sheriff, BA) to summon defendant to render inventory. Continuance was granted.
- John Risteau (sheriff, BA) to summon Judith Crow (BA) widow of John Crow to show cause why the inventory should not be recorded. James Crow has LoA on estate of his father John Crow. Right to LoA belongs to said Judith.

Court Session: 10 September 1745

- Henry Darnall executor of William
  Jones (CV) vs. Martha Griffith
  (CV). James Somervell (sheriff, CV)
  to summon defendant to show cause
  why she conceals estate of dec'd.
  31:604   Said Griffith deposed.
  Discontinued.

Court Session: 1745

10 September. Nehemiah King (g, SO)
exhibited:
- will of Thomas Winder, constituting
  Alice Winder executrix. Also,
  widow's election. Said executrix
  was granted administration.
  Sureties: Matthew Kemp, William
  Giles. Date: 19 June 1745.
- bond of Teague Dickeson
  administrator of David Wallace.
  Sureties: Jessey Dashiell, Lewis
  Beard. Date: 19 June 1745. Also,
  renunciation of Martha Wallace
  (widow, Stepney Parish),
  recommending Teague Dickeson. Date:
  21 June 1745. Witnesses: Jesse
  McCabe, William Stephens.
- bond of Joshua Caldwell
  administrator of John Price.
  Sureties: John Dennis, Sr., Thomas
  Moore. Date: 20 June 1745.
- will of John Reckords, constituting
  Thomas Reckords executor. Said
  executor was granted administration.
  Sureties: Thomas Jackson, James
  Nicholson. Date: 21 June 1745.
- bond of Susanna Phillips
  administratrix of John Phillips.
  Sureties: Richard Phillips, Thomas
  Phillips. Date: 9 August 1745.
- bond of William Dashiell executor of
  Matthias Dashiel. Sureties: Joshua
  Jackson, Mitchel Jones. Date: 21
  August 1745.
- will of Christopher Piper,
  constituting Rachel Piper &
  Christopher Piper executors. Said
  executors were granted
  administration. Sureties: Henry
  Lowes, Thomas Gillis. Date: 21
  August 1745.
- 31:605 • will of James Goslee. Also, widow's

election. Also, bond of Mary Goslee administratrix. Sureties: Willson Rider, Joshua Jackson. Date: 21 August 1745.

- bond of George Dashiell, Sr. administrator of Peter Burnett. Sureties: Henry Ballard, Sr., John Handy. Date: 24 August 1745.
- will of John Gunby, constituting Sarah Gunby & James Gunby executors. Said executors were granted administration. Sureties: John Horsey, Michael Roach. Date: 29 August 1745.
- inventory & LoD of Abraham Taylor.
- inventory of Levin Nicholson.
- inventory & LoD of James Train, Jr.
- inventory of John Connor.
- inventory & LoD of William Hicks.
- inventory of Thomas Pryor.
- inventory & LoD of David Wallace.
- LoD on estate of Nathaniel Cottman.
- accounts of Richard Tulley administrator of Stephen Tulley, Jr.
- accounts of Edward Bennett & George Bennett sureties for Benjamin Tulley administrator of Stephen Tulley, Sr.
- accounts of Martilda Horner administratrix of George Horner.
- accounts of Patience Hix surviving administratrix of William Powson.
- accounts of Sarah Howard administratrix of John Howard.
- accounts of Tabitha More executrix of John More.
- accounts of Joseph Cottman executor of John Roberts.
- accounts of Susannah Tulley administratrix of James Tulley.
- accounts of Esther Dashiell executrix of Robert Dashiell.

12 September. Exhibited from QA:
- inventory of Jacob Winchester. Also, accounts of Mary Winchester executrix.

13 September. Mr. Benton Harris (WO) to examine accounts of:
- Elisabeth Dennis executrix of John Dennis, Sr. (WO).

Court Session: 1745

14 September. Notice sent to Mr.
Daniel Steel administrator of James
Steel, that he has omitted items from
the appraisal, as informed by Charles
Hinderson who married one of the
children of said dec'd.

Mr. Thomas Bullen (TA) to examine
accounts of:
- Mary Russell administratrix of
  Thomas Russell (TA).
- Sarah Reynolds executrix of John
  Reynolds (TA).

31:606 17 September. Notice sent to Mr.
Robert Norris Wright (QA), to take
testimony regarding chattel allowed in
2nd additional accounts of Christopher
Wilkinson & his wife Elisabeth executrix
of Joseph Earle (QA). Mentions:
depositions by William Uphill, Thomas
Wilkinson, & said Christopher Wilkinson.
Mentions: Col. Richard Tilghman.

19 September. Exhibited from CH:
- accounts of Richard Brooke surviving
  executor of Ignatius Boarman.

20 September. Exhibited from TA:
- 2nd additional accounts of John
  Carslake administrator dbn of
  Solomon Horney who married Jane
  Kersey executrix of John Kersey.

21 September. Exhibited from TA:
- 2nd additional accounts of John
  Carslake administrator dbn of
  Solomon Horney.

23 September. Thomas Bullen (g, TA)
exhibited:
- will of John Tibbels, constituting
  Ann Tibbels executrix. Also,
  widow's election. Said executrix
  was granted administration.
  Sureties: William Waring, Francis
  Armstrong. Date: 23 August 1745.
- will of Philemon Porter,
  constituting Eliza Porter executrix.
  Also, widow's election. Said
  executrix was granted
  administration. Sureties: Aaron

Higgs, Samuel Kininmont.   Date: 13
September 1745.
- inventory of Thomas Wilson.
- inventory of Samuel Martin.
- inventory of Thomas Trayman.
- additional inventory of John
  Neighbours. Also, accounts of Mary
  Neighbours acting executrix.

Walter Hanson (g, CH) exhibited:
- bond of Margaret Jenkins
  administratrix of William Jenkins.
  Sureties: Benjamin King, John
  Wakefield. Date: 26 August 1745.
- will of Daniel McDaniel.
- inventory of Raphael Neale.
- inventory of George Medway
- inventory of James Stewart.
- inventory of Francis Mastin.
- additional inventory of Richard
  Brett.
- accounts of Mary Robey
  administratrix of Benjamin Robey.
- accounts of Dorothy Saint Clare
  administratrix of George Saint
  Clare. accounts of Francis Ware &
  John Doncastle executors of Ann
  Ebernethy.

31:607 -   accounts of William Smallwood
Taylor
 administrator of Ann Taylor.
- accounts of William Butler
  administrator of John Butler.
- accounts of Mary Neale executrix of
  Raphael Neale.

Col. Gabriel Parker (CV) exhibited:
- bond of Thomas Cullinbur
  administrator of Thomas Cullinbur.
  Sureties: Obed Dixon, Ellis Dixon.
  Date: 7 September 1745.
- bond of Ann Wood administratrix of
  Edward Wood. Sureties: William
  Whittington, Roger Boyce. Date: 30
  August 1745.
- will of Henry Austin. Also, bond of
  Samuel Austin surviving executor.
  Sureties: Thomas Marshall, Henry
  Hardesty. Date: 31 August 1745.
- inventory of John Coster.
- inventory of Thomas Brittain.
- inventory of Mary Maners.

- inventory of Catherine Hollyday.
- accounts of Clarana Winall
  administratrix of William Winall.
- accounts of Ann Dickenson executrix
  of Stephen Dickenson.

Exhibited from TA:
- inventory of Francis Neall.

24 September. Exhibited from TA:
- accounts of Samuel Neall
  administrator of Francis Neall.

Mr. Thomas Bullen (TA) to examine
accounts of:
- William Cooper & his wife Frances
  administratrix of Thomas Wiles (TA).

26 September. Mr. Walter Hanson (CH)
to examine accounts of:
- Ann Brandt administratrix of
  Randolph Brandt (CH).
- Elisabeth Tarvin executrix of
  Richard Tarvin, Sr. (CH).
  Additional accounts.
- James Plant administrator of Thomas
  Haile (CH). Additional accounts.

27 September. Mr. Peter Dent (PG) to
examine additional accounts of:
- Priscilla Wilson administratrix of
  Nathan Masters (PG).
- Mary Browner administratrix of John
  Browner (PG).

Mr. William Knight (CE) to examine
accounts of:
- Henry Jackson executor of Edward
  Jackson (CE).
- Martha Wood administratrix of Joseph
  Wood (CE). Additional accounts.

31:608 Mr. Charles Hynson (KE) to examine
accounts of:
- Elisabeth Ricketts & Joseph Ricketts
  administrators of Nathaniel Ricketts
  (KE).

Col. Gabriel Parker (CV) to examine
accounts of:
- Archable Freeman administrator of
  Catherine Hollyday (CV).

Mr. William Tilghman (QA) to examine accounts of:

- John Coventon & Henry Coventon executors of Henry Coventon (QA).
- John Swift executor of William Swift (QA).

Mr. Thomas White (BA) to examine accounts of:

- Nicholas Day administrator dbn of Samuel Maxwell (BA).
- Susanna Stokes, Sr. executrix of Capt. John Stokes (BA). Additional accounts.
- Roger Bishop & his wife Eliza executrix of Nicholas Day (BA). Additional accounts.

2 October. Exhibited from CV:

- 2nd additional accounts of Basil Smith surviving executor of Dorothy Smith.

Thomas Aisquith (SM) exhibited:

- 2nd additional accounts of Ann Greenfield executrix of Col. Thomas Truman Greenfield.
- nuncupative will of Michael Burn. Also, bond of Priscilla Burn administratrix. Sureties: James Burn, T. Burne. Date: 11 August 1745.
- bond of Mazolin Furgoe administrator of Alexander Furgoe. Sureties: John Bean, William Askins. Date: 26 August 1745.
- will of John Johnson, constituting Peter Johnson executor. Said executor was granted administration. Sureties: Matthew Cartwright, William Howard. Date: 2 September 1745.
- will of Thomas Boult, constituting Kenelm Boult, Edward Hilliard Hebb, & Ann Boult executors. Also, widow's election. Said executors were granted administration. Sureties: Thomas Coode, Peter Mugg. Date: 3 September 1745.
- inventory & LoD of James Mattingly.
- inventory & LoD of John Beans.
- inventory & LoD of Jeremiah

Court Session: 1745

Pickerls.
- inventory & LoD of John Mollohone.
- inventory of John Loton.
- inventory & LoD of Joshua Guibert.
- inventory & LoD of Joshua Nelson (VA).
- accounts of Samuel Chunn administrator of Philemon Vadry.
- accounts of George Clarke administrator of James Crackson.
- accounts of Elisabeth Briscoe administratrix of Philip Briscoe.

31:609 3 October. Warrant issued for appraisers of estate of Thomas Blackston (BA).

4 October. Exhibited from QA:
- additional inventory & LoD of Joseph Wickes.
- accounts of Rev. John Bradford & his wife Eliza executrix of Joseph Wickes.

8 October. Exhibited from PG:
- 2nd additional accounts of William Young executor of Mary Young.

Ezekiel Millard vs. William Davis (AA). Sheriff (AA) to summon defendant to prove will of his father William Davis (AA) & to take LoA.

15 October. Exhibited from AA:
- additional accounts of Winifred Cutchin administratrix of Robert Cutchin.

21 October. William Beall, Ninian Beall, & John Jackson executors of Alexander Beall (PG) were granted continuance.

22 October. Exhibited from AA:
- 2nd additional accounts of John Burle executor of John Burle.

8 November. Exhibited from QA:
- accounts of Anthony Price & his wife Sarah administratrix of John Evans.

Court Session: 1745

9 November. Exhibited from BA:
* LoD on estate of Susannah Holland. Also, accounts of Francis Holland executor.

Thomas Aisquith (g, SM) exhibited:
* will of John Gibson, constituting Alice Gibson executrix. Said executrix was granted administration. Sureties: John Bond, Samuel Lee. Date: 6 August 1745.
* bond of Margaret Graves administratrix of John Graves. Sureties: George Graves, Anthony Alvey. Date: 17 October 1745.
* will of Hezekiah Bussey, constituting Rachel Bussey executrix. Also, widow's election. Said executrix was granted administration. Sureties: John Shurmadine (SM), William Taman (CV). Date: 21 October 1745.
* will of Thomas Waters, constituting Elisabeth Waters executrix. Said executrix was granted administration. Sureties: Thomas Fish, William Hall. Date: 5 November 1745.
* bond of Margaret Boyd & James Dickson administrators of George Boyd. Sureties: Capt. Gilbert Ireland, Capt. Richard Ward Key. Date: 5 November 1745.
* inventory & LoD of John Gibson.
* inventory & LoD of John Green.
* inventory & LoD of John Pembrooke.

31:610 Thomas Sligh vs. Joseph Lane (AA) executor of Samuel Maccubbin, Jr. (BA). Sheriff (AA) to summon defendant to render final accounts.

Thomas Brereton administrator of Richard Brereton (SO) vs. John Mullen (CE). Sheriff (CE) to summon defendant to show cause why he conceals estate of dec'd.

Mr. Thomas White (BA) to examine accounts of:
* Walter Tolley executor of James Tolley (BA).

Court Session: 1745

Exhibited from CH:
- inventory of Rowland Evans.

William Rogers (g, AA) exhibited:
- bond of Samuel Howard administrator of Philip Howard. Sureties: Samuel Soumaien, Thomas Lusby. Date: 17 September 1745.
- bond of Patrick Doran administrator of John Handling. Sureties: John Inch, Barton Rodgett. Date: 14 October 1745.
- will of Thomas Gassaway.
- inventory of Francis Suter.
- inventory of Samuel Gover.

Court Session: 12 November 1745

Docket:
- Sheriff (PG) to render attachment to Lingan Wilson (PG) administrator of Joseph Wilson (PG) to render inventory.
- Thomas Sligh & Henry Morgan vs. Jane Partridge administratrix of Buckler Partridge (BA). Sheriff (BA) to summon defendant to render accounts.
- S.B. for Joseph Milburn Semmes & his wife (CH) vs. W.C. for executors of Martha Yoakley. Libel, answer by John Smith Prather & Thomas Williams.
- S.B. for Ann Hall administratrix of Isaac Stevens (SO) vs. E.D. for Matthew Kemp & his wife. Libel.
- Richard Cooper one of sureties on estate of George Saile (TA) vs. William Matthews (TA) & his wife Mary (formerly Mary Saile) administratrix of said dec'd. Sheriff (TA) to summon defendants to render accounts. Accounts exhibited. Discontinued.
- Elinor Hill late widow of John Durbin (BA) vs. John Durbin (BA) executor of said dec'd. Sheriff (BA) to summon defendant to render inventory.
- Sheriff (BA) to summon Judith Crow (BA) widow of John Crow (BA) to render inventory.

31:611

Court Session: 12 November 1745

- Ezekiel Millard vs. William Davis
  (AA). Sheriff (AA) to summon
  defendant to prove will of his
  father William Davis (AA) & to take
  LoA.
- Thomas Sligh vs. Joseph Lane (AA)
  executor of Samuel Maccubbin, Jr.
  Sheriff (AA) to summon defendant to
  render final accounts.

Court Session: 1745

12 November. Exhibited from TA:
- accounts of William Matthews & his
  wife Mary administratrix of George
  Saile.

Peter Wright & his wife Ann executrix of
Rowland Evans (CH) vs. John Evans (AA).
Sheriff (AA) to summon defendant to show
cause why he refuses to sign inventory
of dec'd as next of kin.

31:612 15 November. Exhibited from BA:
- inventory of Benedict Bourdillon.

19 November. Mr. Charles Hynson (KE)
to examine accounts of:
- John Green administrator of Bowles
  Green (KE).
- George Hall executor of Benjamin
  Jones (KE).

Mr. William Tilghman (QA) to examine
accounts of:
- Mary Hollingsworth administratrix of
  Vincent Hollingsworth (QA).
- Henry Lisenby & his wife Amy
  administratrix of John Powell, Jr.
  (QA).

Exhibited from AA:
- additional accounts of David Weems
  administrator of Charles Barnard.

20 November. Charles Hynson (g, KE)
exhibited:
- bond of Ann Richardson
  administratrix of Thomas Richardson.
  Sureties: David Hull, William Rasin.
  Date: 12 July 1745.
- bond of Elisabeth Hickman & Henry

Truelock administrators of John Hickman. Sureties: William Truelock, Charles Millward. Date: 20 July 1745.

- bond of Katherine Simpson administratrix of Thomas Simpson. Sureties: Daniel Hull, William Mullett. Date: 27 July 1745.
- bond of Mary Massey administratrix of William Massey. Sureties: Zerobabel French, John Nicholson. Date: 3 August 1745.
- bond of William Butcher administrator of Robert Randall. Sureties: John Foreman, Robert Randall. Also, renunciation of Bethia Randall, recommending William Butcher. Date: 20 August 1745.
- bond of Cuthbert Hall & his wife Rosetta acting executrix of Edward Holman. Sureties: George Hall, William Smithers. Also, renunciation of George Vansandt, recommending Cuthbert Hall & his wife Rosetta. Date: 5 October 1745. Witness: Cornelius Vansandt.
- will of George Still.
- inventory of Isaac Riley.
- inventory of Robert Dew.
- inventory of William Woodland.
- inventory of Thomas Simpson.
- inventory of William Reading.
- inventory of Gideon Pearce.
- inventory of Nicholas Riley.
- inventory of Nathaniel Miller.
- accounts of Miles Mason Shehawn & his wife Sarah administratrix of Charles Griffith.
- accounts of Sarah Kennard administratrix of John Kennard.
- accounts of William Hynson executor of Mary Freestone.
- accounts of Thomas Hynson administrator of William Reading.

31:613 Petition of Stephen Glanville (KE), for self & Samuel Thomas to record will of Henry Staples, from a copy signed by William Taylard (late Register). Date: 13 November 1745.

Court Session: 1745

Mr. Charles Hynson (KE) to examine accounts of:
- Daniel Bryant administrator of John Riley (KE).

Thomas White (g, BA) exhibited:
- will of John Taylor, constituting Kezia Taylor executrix. Said executrix was granted administration. Sureties: Richard Robinson, William Dallam. Date: 5 June 1745.
- bond of John Morgan administrator of Joseph Peregoy. Sureties: Thomas Sligh, John Thrashier. Date: 5 June 1745.
- bond of John Frashier administrator of Matthew Fisher. Sureties: John Morgan, John Metcalfe. Date: 5 June 1745.
- bond of Jacob Giles administrator of William Pratt. Sureties: John Paca, Nicholas Ruxton Gay. Date: 11 June 1745. Also, renunciation of Ann Pratt (widow), recommending Jacob Giles (greatest creditor). Date: 14 May 1745. Witnesses: James Morgan, Moses Paries.
- bond of Sarah Brady administratrix of Terrance Brady. Sureties: Richard Denver, Ford Barnes. Date: 5 September 1745.
- bond of Richard Dallam administrator of Peter Farmer. Sureties: Gregory Farmer, Sr., Gregory Farmer, Jr. Also, renunciation of Mary Farmer (widow), recommending Richard Dallam (principle creditor). Date: 23 October 1745.
- will of Samuel Griffith.
- will of Edmond Howard.

31:614
- inventory & LoD of Joshua Starkey.
- inventory of John Taylor.
- 3rd additional accounts of Heathcoat Pickett & his wife Eliza executrix of William Wright.

25 November. Nehemiah King (g, SO) exhibited:
- will of Richard Wallace.
- inventory & LoD of John Phillips.
- inventory of Matthias Dashiell.

Court Session: 1745

- inventory of Christopher Piper.
- inventory of James Goslee.
- inventory of John Price.
- inventory of Isaac Costin.
- inventory of Solomon Mitchell.
- accounts of Richard Waller administrator of Nathaniel Cottman.
- accounts of Patience Mister acting executrix of William Mister.

Col. Gabriel Parker (CV) exhibited:
- inventory of Richard Peirce.
- inventory of Daniel Fraizer.
- inventory of Thomas Cullenbur.
- inventory of Thomas Wilkinson.
- inventory of Edward Reynolds.
- inventory of Michael Hassett.
- inventory of John Baker.
- accounts of Robert Freeland & his wife Sarah executrix of Thomas Holland.
- accounts of Young Parran & Easter Parran executors of John Parran.
- accounts of Elisabeth Hungerford executrix of James Hungerford.

26 November. Benton Harris (g, WO) exhibited:
- bond of Joshua Morss & his wife Mary administrators of John Burton. Sureties: Edward Franklin, Whittington Bowen. Date: 12 August 1745.
- accounts [!] of Lucretia Claywell & Peter Claywell executors of Peter Claywell. Sureties: Hutten Hill, John Atkinson. Date: 17 August 1745.
- will of Tabitha Parker.
- inventory of Nathaniel Rackliff.
- inventory of John Robinson.
- inventory of John Disharoon.
- inventory of Ephraim Heather.
- additional inventory of Rev. Thomas Fletcher.
- inventory of William Taylor.
- inventory & LoD of Francis Allen.
- inventory & LoD of William Burton.
- additional accounts of Hutton Hill executor of Samuel Tarr.
- accounts of Elisabeth Dennis executrix of John Dennis.

- accounts of Rous Fassitt executor of Mary Fassitt.
- accounts of John Rickards & Isaac Bell executors of John Smith.

27 November. Mr. Nehemiah King (SO) to examine accounts of:
- Elisabeth Tulley administratrix of Benjamin Tulley (SO).
- George Hardy administrator of Christopher Nutter (SO).
- Thomas Rickords executor of John Rickords, Sr. (SO).
- accounts of Ezekiel Reed & his wife Judah administratrix of William Langston (SO).
- James Richardson & Sarah Fletcher executors of Thomas Walker (SO).
- Rose Costin administratrix of Isaac Costin (SO).
- John Taylor administrator of Abraham Taylor (SO).
- James Train administrator of James Train, Jr. (SO).

31:615 insert Exhibited:
- bond of Joseph Dyson administrator of Andrew Chunn. Sureties: Justinian Burch, William Campton, Robert Horner. Date: 29 November 1756.

31:615 28 November. Exhibited from DO:
- accounts of Elisabeth Trippe administratrix of Maj. Henry Trippe.

24 November. Walter Hanson (g, CH) exhibited:
- bond of John Chunn administrator of Richard Chunn. Sureties: Andrew Chunn, Samuel Amery. Date: 4 October 1745.
- bond of Andrew Chunn administrator of John Chunn. Sureties: Thomas Burch, Sr., Samuel Amery. Date: 4 October 1745.
- bond of Penelope Browne administratrix of John Browne. Sureties: John Wilder, James Plant. Date: 14 October 1745.
- will of Vincent Askin, constituting

Ignatius Gardiner & James Middleton executors. Said executors were granted administration. Sureties: Philip Edelin, Holland Middleton. Date: 22 October 1745.

- will of George Lewis. Also, bond of John Courts administrator. Sureties: John Cunningham, William Hanson. Date: 4 November 1745.
- bond of Ann Scott administratrix of William Scott. Sureties: Robert Yates, Samuel Chunn. Date: 13 November 1745.
- bond of Henry Barnes, Jr. administrator of Thomas Barnes. Sureties: Henry Moore, James Carroll, Thomas Sanders, Samuel Lucket. Date: 15 November 1745.
- bond of Samuel Burgess administrator of John Craxon. Sureties: Patrick Burn, James Carroll. Date: 19 November 1745.
- bond of Ann McDaniel executrix of Daniel McDaniel. Sureties: William Middleton, Benjamin Downes. Date: 25 November 1745.
- inventory of Richard Chunn.
- inventory of William Jenkins.
- additional accounts of Alexander McLaran & his wife Jannet executrix of Peter Mitchell.
- additional accounts of John Mcferson & his wife Sarah administratrix of Jacob Miller.
- additional accounts of James Plant administrator of Thomas Haile.

Mr. Walter Hanson (CH) to examine accounts of:
- Thomas Coleman executor & James Greenfield Wood & his wife Martha executrix of Thomas Coleman (CH).
- Margaret Jenkins administratrix of William Jenkins (CH).
- William Carter administrator of William Carter (CH).
- Matthew Clubb surviving executor of John Clubb (CH).
- Prudence Green executrix of Leonard Green (CH). Additional accounts.

Court Session: 1745

Mr. Thomas Aisquith (SM) to examine
accounts of:
- Thomas Beale & his wife Mary
  executrix of Richard Griffen (SM).
- Thomas Kirkley administrator dbn of
  Rebecca Colter (SM).
- Dryden Forbes administratrix of
  Kenelm Greenfield Jowles (SM).

2 December. Col. Gabriel Parker (CV)
to examine accounts of:
- Jane Phillips executrix of John
  Phillips (CV).
- Dorcus Whinfield executrix of Jonah
  Whinfield (CV).
- William Holland & William Miller,
  Jr. executors of John Couran (CV).
  Additional accounts.

31:616 Peter Dent (g, PG) exhibited:
- bond of Ann Adkinson administratrix
  of John Adkinson. Sureties: John
  Evans, Edward Riston. Date: 9
  October 1745.
- will of John Orchard, constituting
  Joseph Ryon executor. Said executor
  was granted administration.
  Sureties: Gerard Truman Greenfield,
  Thomas Gibbens. Date: 14 October
  1745.
- will of Sarah Busey, constituting
  John Busey executor. Said executor
  was granted administration.
  Sureties: Samuel Busey, Henry Smith.
  Date: 15 October 1745.
- will of Samuel Waring.
- inventory of Thomas Smith.
- inventory of Humphry Deverson
- inventory of John Atchison.
- accounts of Margaret Markland
  administratrix of Matthew Markland.
- accounts of Martha Waring executrix
  of Martha Greenfield.
- accounts of William Bright & his
  wife Mary administratrix of
  Nathaniel Magruder.
- accounts of Priscilla Wilson
  administratrix of Nathan Masters.
- accounts of James Bolton & his wife
  Elisabeth executrix of Robert Cloyd.
- accounts of Mary Brawner
  administratrix of John Brawner.

6 December. Thomas Clark on behalf of Margaret & Susanna Clark orphans of Abraham Clark (CV, dec'd) vs. John Griffin (CV) administrator of said dec'd. Sheriff (CV) to summon defendant to show cause why he did not appraise certain chattel.

Exhibited:
* Allowance given to Christopher Wilkinson & his wife Elisabeth on the last accounts on estate of Joseph Earle for certain chattel, as contested by representatives of said dec'd. Mentions: James Buchanan, Mr. Charles Browne

31:617

9 December. Exhibited from BA:
* inventory of Joseph Peregoy. Also, accounts of John Morgan administrator.

16 December. William Tilghman (g, QA) exhibited:
* will of John Daley, constituting James Dailey executor. Also, widow's election. Said executor was granted administration. Sureties: Stephen Sweatnam, Edward Tippens. Date: 17 October 1745.
* bond of William Roberts administrator of Edward Jones, Jr. Sureties: Thomas Powell, John Davis, Jr. Date: 28 November 1745.
* will of Thomas Davis, constituting John Davis, Jr. executor. Also, widow's election. Said executor was granted administration. Sureties: George Smith, Thomas OBryan. Date: 2 December 1745.
* will of William Jumpe. Also, widow's election. Also, bond of Susannah Jumpe acting executrix. Sureties: Nathan Knotts, Solomon Kentin. Also, renunciation of Benjamin Jumpe (son). Witnesses: Nathaniel Knott, Solomon Kentin. Also, renunciation of Van Jump. Date: 10 December 1745. Witnesses: Nathaniel Knott, Solomon Kentin.
* will of Thomas Ruth.
* will of John Evans.

- will of William Merridith.
- inventory of John Powell.
- inventory & LoD of John Lambden.
- inventory of William Dulany.
- inventory of John Gregory.
- inventory & LoD of John Week.
- inventory of Patrick Robertson.

<u>20 December</u>. William Rogers (g, AA)
exhibited:
- bond of John Battson administrator
  of Richard Randell. Sureties:
  Francis Crandall, John Clavey.
  Date: 27 November 1745.
- will of Richard Tootell,
  constituting Helen Tootell & Richard
  Tootell executors. Said executors
  were granted administration.
  Sureties: Richard Chase (AA), John
  Tootell (DO). Date: 13 December
  1745.
- bond of John Gassaway administrator
  of Thomas Gassaway. Sureties:
  William Colter, Henry Gassaway.

31:618
  Also, renunciation of Sarah Gassaway
  (widow), recommending John Gassaway
  (gentleman). Date: 6 December 1745.
  Witnesses: George Lingan, Law.
  Maynard.
- inventory of Elisabeth Todd.
- inventory of John Powell.

<u>25 December</u>. Peter Dent (g, PG)
exhibited:
- inventory of John Adkinson.
- accounts of Mary Ashcom Brooke
  executrix of Walter Brooke.

Court Session: 14 January 1745

Docket:
- Sheriff (PG) to render attachment to
  Lingan Wilson (PG) administrator of
  Joseph Wilson (PG) to render
  inventory.
- Thomas Sligh & Henry Morgan sureties
  on estate of Buckler Partridge (BA)
  vs. Jane Partridge administratrix
  of said dec'd. Sheriff (BA) to
  render attachment to defendant to
  render accounts.
- S.B. for Joseph Milburn Semmes & his

Court Session: 14 January 1745

- wife (CH) vs. W.C. for executors of Martha Yoakley. Libel, answers.
- S.B. for Ann Hall administratrix of Isaac Stevens (SO) vs. E.D. for Matthew Kemp & his wife. Libel.

31:619
- Elinor Hill late widow of John Durbin (BA) vs. John Durbin (BA) acting executor of said dec'd. Sheriff (BA) to render attachment to defendant to render inventory.
- Sheriff (BA) to summon Judith Crow (BA) widow of John Crow (BA) to show cause why inventory should not be recorded. Struck off.
- Ezekiel Millard vs. William Davis (AA). William Thornton (sheriff, AA) to summon defendant to prove will of his father William Davis (AA) & to take LoA. Said son exhibited that his father made a will & he (son) refused to take LoA. Discontinued.
- Thomas Sligh vs. Joseph Lane (AA) executor of Samuel Maccubbin, Jr. (BA). Sheriff (AA) to summon defendant to render a full account. 2nd additional accounts exhibited. Discontinued.
- Thomas Brereton administrator of Richard Brereton (SO) vs. John Mullen (CE). Sheriff (CE) to summon defendant to show cause why he conceals estate of dec'd.
- Peter Wright & his wife Ann executrix of Rowland Evans vs. John Evans (AA). William Thornton (sheriff, AA) to summon defendant to show cause why he does not sign inventory as next of kin. NEI.
- Thomas Clark on behalf of Margaret & Susanna Clark minors & orphans of Abraham Clark (CV, dec'd) vs. John Griffen (CV) administrator of said dec'd. Sheriff (CV) to summon defendant to appraise chattel of said estate.

Court Session: 1745

31:620 15 January. Mr. Thomas Aisquith (SM) to examine accounts of:
- Dryden Forbes administratrix of

Court Session: 1745

Kenelm Greenfield Jowles (SM).

16 January. Exhibited from AA:
* additional accounts of William
  Sellman & his wife Charity executrix
  of Solomon Sparrow.

Exhibited from BA:
* 2nd additional accounts of Joseph
  Lane executor of Samuel Maccubbin,
  Jr.

23 January. Mr. Thomas Aisquith (SM)
to examine accounts of:
* Henry Sheircliffe administrator of
  James Mattenly (SM).

Thomas Bullen (g, TA) exhibited:
* will of Nicholas Lowe, constituting
  Margaret Lowe executrix. Also,
  widow's election. Said executrix
  was granted administration.
  Sureties: William Thomas, William
  Sharp, Edward Oldham, Trust. Thomas.
  Date: 7 December 1745.
* will of William White, constituting
  Cassandra White executrix. Said
  executrix was granted
  administration. Sureties: Adam
  Brown, James Chaplin, William
  Sanders, Edward Harrison, William
  White. Date: 14 December 1745.
* nuncupative will of Thomas Higgs.
* additional inventory of John
  Reynolds. Also, accounts of Sarah
  Reynolds executrix.
* inventory & LoD of John Dodson, Jr.
* inventory & LoD of Robert Louther.
* inventory of John Harrison.
* inventory & LoD of Henry Oldfield.
* accounts of Richard Warner executor
  of Charles Warner.
* accounts of John Sanckston, Jr.
  administrator of Jacob Gore.

30 January. Exhibited from AA:
* additional accounts of Elisabeth
  Burgess administratrix of Samuel
  Burgess.

31:621 Exhibited from PG:
* accounts of Charles Drury

Court Session: 1745

administrator of Nathan Selby.

4 February. Francis Noblitt who married
only child of Mark Fisher (DO, dec'd)
vs. William Cullens (DO) executor of
said dec'd. Sheriff (DO) to summon
defendant to show cause why the amount
for Negro Tom (who died within 12 months
of said dec'd) should not be disallowed.

6 February. Exhibited from TA:
* additional accounts of James
  Priestly administrator of John Hawk.

7 February. Mr. Thomas Bullen (TA) to
examine accounts of:
* Robert Hall administrator of Robert
  Dodson, Jr. (TA).
* William Cooper & his wife Frances
  administratrix of Thomas Wiles (TA).
* Rachel Williams acting executrix of
  Jacob Williams (TA).
* Robert Stapleford & his wife Mary
  executrix of Thomas Trayman (TA).
* Russell Armstrong & his wife Rebecca
  administratrix of Moses Clayland
  (TA).

Mr. William Tilghman (QA) to examine
accounts of:
* Thomas Cooper & his wife Amelia
  administratrix of Robert Walters
  (QA).

13 February. Samuel Blunt (QA) vs. Rev.
John Bradford (CE) & his wife Elisabeth
executrix of Joseph Wickes (QA). Libel.
Sheriff (CE) to summon defendants to
render answer.

Col. Gabriel Parker (CV) to examine
accounts of:
* Elisabeth Morris & Richard Johns
  executors of Randolph Morris (CV).

14 February. Exhibited from BA:
* release of Juda Crow to James Crow
  on estate of John Crow. Date: 12
  November 1745. Witnesses: John
  Adams, Jacob Giles.
* inventory of John Crow.

Court Session: 1745

15 February. Exhibited from BA:
* accounts of James Crow administrator of John Crow.
* 2nd additional accounts of Mark Guichard & his wife Diana executrix of Roger Crudgenton.

31:622 Exhibited from AA:
* will of Mary Jones.

17 February. Col. Gabriel Parker (CV) exhibited:
* bond of Sarah Scarff administratrix of William Scarff. Sureties: William Lyle, Benjamin Clayton. Date: 19 November 1745.
* will of Richard Fryer, constituting Elisabeth Fryer & John Fryer executors. Said executors were granted administration. Sureties: Richard Stallings, Richard Gibson. Date: 14 February 1745.
* will of William Wood. Also, bond of John Wood administrator. Sureties: John Miller, Thomas Gray. Date: 16 January 1745.
* will of James Freeman, constituting James Dotson executor. Said executor was granted administration. Sureties: John Young, James Bowen. Date: 22 January 1745.
* will of Richard Lock.
* inventory of Absolom Kent.
* accounts of Jane Phillips executrix of John Phillips.

21 February. William Tilghman (g, QA) exhibited:
* will of William Primrose (blacksmith). Also, bond of Bridget Primrose administratrix. Sureties: Charles Garford, John Railey. Date: 14 December 1745. Also, renunciation of John Nevil. Date: 13 December 1745.
* will of John Hawkins, constituting Deborah Hawkins executrix. Said executrix was granted administration. Sureties: Grundy Pemberton (g), William Banks (g). Date: 13 January 1745.
* bond of Edward Godwin administrator

Page 156

Court Session: 1745

of John Douglass. Surety: Thomas
Lee. Date: 24 January 1745. Also,
renunciation of Eliza Douglas
(widow), recommending Mr. Godwin.
Date: 15 January 1745.
- bond of Jonathan Evans surviving
executor of John Evans. Sureties:
William Emory, John Oldson (son of
Henry). Date: 30 January 1745.
- bond of Rebecca Costin
administratrix of Henry Costin.
Sureties: John Downs, Richard
Costin. Date: 6 February 1745.
- will of Edith Wilde.
- additional inventory of John Powell,
Jr. Also, accounts of Henry Lazenby
& his wife Amy administratrix.
- additional inventory of Fairclough
Wright.
- inventory of John Dailey.
- accounts of Mary Hollingsworth
administratrix of Vincent
Hollingsworth.

Mr. William Tilghman (QA) to examine
accounts of:
- Susanna & James Mayner executors of
Timothy Mayner (QA).

31:623 22 February. Sheriff (QA) to summon
Mary Ann Powell executrix of James
Powell (QA) to take LoA.

Thomas Bullen (g, TA) exhibited:
- bond of Elisabeth Storey
administratrix of Richard Storey.
Sureties: Thomas Ward, William
Whaley. Date: 30 January 1745.
- will of Thomas Armstrong,
constituting John Coward executor.
Said executor was granted
administration. Sureties: Risdon
Bozman, David Robinson. Date: 5
February 1745.
- will of John Sherwood, constituting
Philemon Hambleton & Lydia Sherwood
executors. Said executors were
granted administration. Sureties:
Richard Feddeman, David Robinson.
Date: 18 February 1745.
- inventory of Francis Rolle.
- inventory of John Dulen.

1 March.   Thomas Aisquith (g, SM)
exhibited:
* will of William Bradburne,
  constituting William Yates executor.
  Said executor was granted
  administration.   Sureties: John
  Baptist Carbery, George Thompson.
  Date: 6 November 1745.
* bond of Winefred Thomas
  administratrix of Mark Thomas.
  Sureties: Samuel Abell, John Abell.
  Date: 26 November 1745.
* bond of Isaac Pavatt administrator
  of Joseph Pavatt.   Sureties: Joseph
  White, James Griffen.   Date: 13
  January 1745.
* will of Richard Hopewell,
  constituting Elisabeth Hopewell
  executrix.   Also, widow's election.
  Said executrix was granted
  administration.   Sureties: George
  Aisquith, Charles King.   Date: 14
  January 1745.
* bond of Philip Key administrator of
  Joseph Owen Sureties: Abraham
  Barnes, Robert Chesley.   Date: 21
  January 1745.
* bond of Benjamin Fenwick
  administrator of Cuthbert Fenwick.
  Sureties: Robert Fenwick, Hugh
  Hopewell, Jr.   Date: 23 January
  1745.
* inventory & LoD of Thomas Waters.
* inventory & LoD of Michael Burn.
* inventory of John Johnson.
* inventory & LoD of Alexander Furgoe.
* accounts of Elisabeth Hull
  administratrix of Meverell Hull
* accounts of James Richardson
  administrator of Daniel Duggens.

Exhibited from AA:
* additional accounts of William
  Hollyday & his wife Mary
  administratrix of Mark Richardson.

Exhibited from BA:
* additional accounts of John Morgan
  administrator of Joseph Peregoy.

3 March.   Mr. Thomas Bullen (TA) to
examine accounts of:

Court Session: 1745

- Abraham Clark & his wife Elisabeth administratrix of James Williams (TA).
- Mary Dulin executrix of John Dulin (TA).
- Lawrence Calk & his wife Mary administratrix of John Camper (TA).

31:624 4 March. Sheriff (AA) to summon Rachel Welsh (AA) executrix of John Welsh (AA) to render final accounts.

Court Session: 11 March 1745

Docket:
- Sheriff (PG) to render attachment to Lingan Wilson (PG) administrator of Joseph Wilson (PG) to render inventory.
- Thomas Sligh & Henry Morgan sureties on estate of Buckler Partridge (BA) vs. Jane Partridge administratrix of said dec'd. Sheriff (BA) to render attachment to defendant to render accounts.
- S.B. for Joseph Milburn Semmes & his wife (CH) vs. W.C. for executors of Martha Yoakley. Libel, answers.
- S.B. for John Hall administrator of Isaac Stevens (SO) vs. Matthew Kemp & his wife. Libel, answer.
- Elinor Hill late widow of John Durbin (BA) vs. John Durbin (BA) acting executor of said dec'd. Sheriff (BA) to summon defendant to render inventory.
- Thomas Brereton administrator of Richard Brereton (SO) vs. John Mullen (CE). Sheriff (CE) to render attachment to defendant to show cause why he conceals estate of dec'd.
- Peter Wright & his wife Ann executrix of Rowland Evans (CH) vs. John Evans (AA). William Thornton (sheriff, AA) to summon defendant to show cause why he does not sign inventory of dec'd as next of kin.

31:625 Said Wright exhibited that said Evans has left the Province. Discontinued.
- Thomas Clark on behalf of Margaret &

Court Session: 11 March 1745

Susanna Clark minors & orphans of Abraham Clark (CV, dec'd) vs. John Griffen (CV) administrator of said dec'd. Sheriff (CV) to summon defendant to show cause why he did not appraise certain chattel.

- Francis Noblitt who married only child of Mark Fisher (DO, dec'd) vs. William Cullens (DO) executor of said dec'd. T. Muir (sheriff, DO) to summon defendant to show cause why the amount for Negro Tom (who died within 12 months of said dec'd) should not be disallowed. N.E.
- S.B. for Samuel Blunt (QA) vs. Rev. John Bradford & his wife Eliza executrix of Joseph Wickes. Libel. Sheriff (CE) to summon defendant.
- James Hollyday, (sheriff, QA) to summon Mary Ann Powell executrix of James Powell to take LoA. NEI.
- William Thornton (sheriff, AA) to summon Rachel Welsh (AA) executrix of John Welsh (AA) to render full accounts. 2nd additional accounts exhibited. Discontinued.

Court Session: 1745

31:626 11 March. Nehemiah King (g, SO) exhibited:
- will of Ann Walker. Also, bond of James Lucas administrator. Sureties: Samuel Wilson, Thomas Bleuett. Date: 11 December 1745.
- bond of Matthew Wallace acting executor of Richard Wallace. Sureties: Samuel Wilson, Panther Lawes. Date: 1 January 1745. Also, renunciation of Grace Wallace (executrix), recommending Matthew Wallace. Date: 16 October 1745.
- bond of Margaret Blewer executrix of James Blewer. Sureties: George Dashiell, Jr., George McClester. Date: 1 February 1745.
- will of William Jones, constituting Thomas Jones executor. Said executor was granted administration. Sureties: Samuel Wilson, Ephraim King. Date: 1 February 1745.
- will of Arabella Bird.

- inventory of John Gunbey.
- inventory of John Rickords.
- inventory of Thomas Winder.
- accounts of Sarah Richardson & Mary Richardson executrices of Thomas Walker.
- accounts of George Hardy administrator of Christopher Nutter.
- accounts of James Train, Sr. administrator of James Train, Jr.
- accounts of Thomas Rickords executor of John Rickords.
- accounts of Ezekiah Reed & Juda Reed administrators of William Langston.
- accounts of John Taylor administrator of Abraham Taylor.
- accounts of Elisabeth Tulley administratrix of Benjamin Tulley.

12 March. Mr. Nehemiah King (SO) to examine accounts of:
- Samuel Collins surviving executor of Richard Chambers (SO).

13 March. Thomas Bullen (g, TA) exhibited:
- will of William Barwick, constituting Rosannah Barwick executrix. Also, widow's election. Said executrix was granted administration. Sureties: Abner Dudley (TA), John Baynard (QA). Date: 17 February 1745.
- bond of William Alexander administrator of Thomas Alexander, during minority of John Alexander. Sureties: Thomas Jenkins, Matthew Hardekin. Date: 21 February 1745.
- bond of Barnaby Stapleford administrator of Barnaby Stapleford, Jr. Sureties: John Stapleford, Daniel Stapleford. Date: 22 February 1745.
- bond of David Jones administrator of John Jones. Sureties: William Dickinson, William Anderson. Date: 28 February 1745.
- will of Rev. Daniel Maynadier. Also, renunciation of executors. Also, bond of Daniel Maynadier administrator. Sureties: William Goldsborough, Jacob Hindman. Date:

7 March 1745.

31:627 Thomas Aisquith (g, SM) exhibited:
- bond of Ann Cutler administratrix of William Cutler. Sureties: John Curlott, Thomas Wenvier. Date: 27 January 1745.
- will of Henry Wharton, constituting John Parnham & Joseph Pile executors. Said executors were granted administration. Sureties: Richard Ward Key, John Llewellin. Date: 4 February 1745.
- will of John Fanning, constituting Mary Fanning executrix. Also, widow's election. Said executrix was granted administration. Sureties: John Tippett, Joseph Estep. Date: 4 February 1745.
- bond of Mary Sledmore administratrix of John Sledmore. Sureties: Edward Hilliard Hebb, William Baxter. Date: 11 February 1745.
- inventory & LoD of Hezekiah Busey.
- accounts of Rebecca Williams administratrix of William Williams.

14 March. Col. Charles Hynson (KE) to examine accounts of:
- George Hall executor of Benjamin Jones (KE).
- Elisabeth Quinney administratrix of Sutton Quinney (KE).
- Thomas Crow & his wife Sarah administratrix of George Skirven (KE).

Col. Charles Hynson (KE) exhibited:
- will of John Tharp. Also, widow's election. Also, bond of Elisabeth Tharp acting executrix. Sureties: John Gresham, Ralph Page. Date: 9 November 1745. Also, renunciation of Ra. Page. Date: 10 October 1745.
- bond of Isaac Freeman administrator of John Bennett. Sureties: Richard Wilson, John Read. Date: 29 November 1745. Also, renunciation of Eliza Bennett (widow), recommending Isaac Freeman (landlord & greatest creditor). Date: 26 November 1745. Witness: James

Christian.

- will of William Crow. Also, bond of
  Isaac Crow administrator. Sureties:
  Thomas Crow, John Smith. Date: 7
  January 1745. Also, renunciation of
  William Crow (son), recommending his
  next brother Isaac Crow. Date: 7
  December 1745.
- bond of Thomas Carwarden
  administrator dbn of Robert Key.
  Sureties: Abraham Carwarden, William
  Burk. Date: 18 January 1745.
- bond of Joseph Wickes & James Dunn
  administrators of Robert Dunn.
  Sureties: William Hynson, William
  Wilmer. Date: 22 February 1745.

31:628
- will of Katherine Thornton.
- will of William Salter.
- will of William Rue.
- will of Sarah Hatcheson.
- inventory of John Hickman.
- inventory of John Tharp.
- additional inventory of Nathaniel
  Miller.
- inventory of Peter Manley.
- inventory of Robert Randall, Jr.
- inventory of Sutton Quinney.
- inventory of William Massey.
- LoD on estate of John Kennard.
- LoD on estate of Richard Wethered.
- accounts of Joseph Ricketts
  administrator of Nathaniel Ricketts.

Walter Hanson (g, CH) exhibited:
- bond of John Alexander & Gerrard
  Fowke administrators of Sarah Fowke.
  Sureties: David Stone, John
  Cunninghame. Date: 26 November
  1745.
- bond of Alexander McLeod
  administrator of John Malony.
  Sureties: Thomas Wentworth, William
  Carpenter. Date: 29 November 1745.
- will of Robert Mchorne, Sr. Also,
  bond of Elisabeth Mchorne
  administratrix. Sureties: Thomas
  Burch, Sr., Samuel Amery. Date: 20
  December 1745.
- will of Richard King, constituting
  James Muncaster executor. Said
  executor was granted administration.
  Sureties: Thomas Keyberd, George

Waple. Date: 3 January 1745.

- will of William Brent, constituting Jane Brent executrix. Said executrix was granted administration. Sureties: Walter Pye, Jacob Clements. Date: 16 January 1745.
- will of Francis Goodrick, constituting Mary Goodrick, Edward Goodrick, & Francis Goodrick executors. Said executors were granted administration. Sureties: John Lawson (PG), John Courts (CH). Date: 22 January 1745.
- will of John Wathen constituting Hudson Wathen & John Wathen executors. Also, widow's election. Said executors were granted administration. Sureties: William Sympson, Ignatius Sympson. Date: 27 January 1745.
- will of Benjamin Neale, constituting Mary Neale executrix. Also, widow's election. Said executrix was granted administration. Sureties: William Neale, Jr., Edward Edelen. Date: 28 January 1745.
- will of Matthew Barnes. Also, widow's election. Also, bond of Henry Barnes acting executor. Sureties: Godshall Barnes, Matthew Barnes. Date: 20 February 1745.
- will of Richard Chapman.
- LoD on estate of Richard Davis.
- inventory of Vincent Askin.
- inventory of John Brown.
- inventory of John Craxon.
- accounts of Ann Brandt administratrix of Randolph Brandt.
- 2nd additional accounts of Eliza Tarvin executrix of Richard Tarvin.

Exhibited from AA:
- 2nd additional accounts of Rachel Welsh administratrix of John Welsh.
- accounts of Magdalen Cumming administratrix of Robert Cumming.

Mr. Thomas Bullen (TA) to examine accounts of:
- William Moore & his wife Rachel administratrix of Charles Baning

Court Session: 1745

(TA).
* Margaret Edmondson acting executrix of John Edmondson (TA).

31:629 Exhibited from AA:
* additional accounts of Ruth Davis executrix of Richard Davis.

<u>15 March</u>. Mr. Peter Dent (PG) to examine accounts of:
* Sarah Reading executrix of John Mawdesley (PG).

John Thompson (g, CE) exhibited:
* bond of Susanna Vandergrift administratrix of Nicholas Vandergrift. Sureties: Lawrence Lawrensin, Thomas Beastin. Date: 21 August 1745.
* will of Abraham Alman, constituting Margaret Alman executrix. Said executrix was granted administration. Sureties: Richard Thompson, Sr., Peter Bouchelle. Date: 6 August 1745.
* will of Samuel Savin, constituting John Savin executor. Said executor was granted administration. Sureties: Cornelius Augustine Savin, Thomas Savin. Date: 26 August 1745.
* will of John Watson, constituting James Calder executor. Said executor was granted administration. Sureties: Joshua George, John Thompson. Date: 22 October 1745.
* will of John Pennington, constituting Mary Pennington executrix. Said executrix was granted administration. Sureties: Francis Bonner, John Roberts, Jr. Date: 22 October 1745.
* bond of Margaret Reynolds administratrix of Thomas Reynolds. Sureties: Hugh Matthews, Jr., Edward Armstrong. Date: 3 February 1745.
* bond of John Tree administrator of John Urm. Sureties: David Ricketts, Joseph Roberts. Date: 18 February 1745.
* bond of Ann Steel administratrix of Archibald Steel. Sureties: John Kankey, William Bristow. Date: 10

Page 165

February 1745.
- will of Hermana Vanbebber.
- will of Sarah Duffey.
- will of Daniel Hukil.
- will of Jeremiah Larkin.
- inventory of William Alexander.
- inventory of Nicholas Vandergrift.
- additional inventory of Joseph Wood.
Administratrix: Martha Wood.

17 March. Mr. Benton Harris (WO) to examine accounts of:
- John Teague administrator dbn of John McCalley (WO).
- John Teague administrator of John Watson (WO).

Mr. Walter Hanson (CH) to examine accounts of:
- Ann Smoot & Thomas Smoot executors of Barton Smoot (CH).
- James Middleton & Ignatius Gardner executors of Vincent Askin (CH).
- Joseph Lancaster executor of Ann Howard (CH).

Benton Harris (g, WO) exhibited:
- bond of Ratclief Pointer administrator of Turville Pointer. Sureties: John Jenckins, Elias Pointer. Date: 24 January 1745.
- **31:630** bond of Mary Hudson administratrix of Richard Hudson, Jr. Sureties: Samuel Hudson, Arthur Lathbury. Date: 31 January 1745.
- bond of Isaac Tull administrator of Robert Caldwell. Sureties: James Smith, Henry Ayres. Date: 19 February 1745.
- bond of John Teague administrator dbn of John McCalley. Sureties: Abraham Outten, Peter Claywell. Date: 8 March 1745.
- inventory of William Fassitt.
- inventory of William Jarman.
- inventory & LoD of Martin Kennett.
- accounts of Solomon Townsend administrator of James Townsend.

Thomas White (g, BA) exhibited:
- bond of William Fell administrator of John Cole. Sureties: Robert

North, William Hammond. Date: 28 December 1745.

- bond of Jacob Giles administrator of Thomas Litton, Jr. Sureties: Jonathan Jones, John Kemp. Date: 15 February 1745. Also, renunciation of (N) Litton (widow), recommending Jacob Giles. Date: 15 January 1745.
- bond of Ruth Howard executrix of Edmund Howard. Sureties: John Metcalfe, Emanuel Teal. Date: 5 March 1745.
- will of Joseph Towson.
- will of Sarah Tayman.
- inventory of John Durbin.
- 2nd additional accounts of Robert Bishop & his wife Elisabeth executrix of Nicholas Day.
- accounts of Nicholas Ruxton Gay administrator dbn of Samuel Maxwell.
- accounts of Walter Tolley executor of Thomas Tolley.

Mr. Thomas White (BA) to examine accounts of:
- John Durbin acting executor of John Durbin (BA).
- Mary Stokes administratrix of Humphry Wells Stokes (BA).
- Kezia Taylor executrix of John Taylor (BA).
- Isaac Litton & his wife Mary executrix of Thomas Jones (BA).

19 March. Exhibited:
- depositions of John Hues, William Grantham, George Drury, & William Little. Mentions: Negro Tom who belonged to Mark Fisher (dec'd), William Cullen executor of said Fisher.

22 March. Exhibited from CV:
- inventory of Henry Austins.

31:631 Sheriff (PG) to render attachment to Lingan Wilson (PG, dec'd) to render inventory. [Ed. note: there is obviously something missing.]

24 March. Mr. William Knight (CE) to examine accounts of:

- John Cockran & James Ogleby
  executors of John Ogleby (CE).
- George Rock & his wife Mary
  administratrix of Robert Story (CE).
- Frances Yorkson administratrix of
  Thomas Yorkson (CE).
- Richard Thomas surviving executor of
  Margaret Nicholas (CE).
- John Stockton & his wife Elisabeth
  administratrix of Sickfredius
  Alricks (CE).
- Joseph Thomas & John Rickets
  executors of Roger Mirick (CE).
- John Rickets & Thomas Rickets
  executors of Samuel Jones (CE).
- James Foster & John Foster executors
  of William Foster (CE). Additional
  accounts.

Court Session: 1746

28 March. Mr. Thomas Aisquith (SM) to
examine accounts of:
- Thomas Pearce administrator of
  Elinor Pearce (SM).

At the request of Samuel Chamberlain,
Esq., transcript of will of Anthony
Mayle (TA) to be recorded from the
county records.

29 March. Mr. Nehemiah King (SO) to
examine accounts of:
- Mary Moore administratrix of Francis
  Moore (SO).
- Alice Dunn administratrix of Richard
  Dunn (SO).

4 April. Peter Dent (g, PG) exhibited:
- will of Margaret Holland. Also,
  bond of Richard Holland acting
  executor. Sureties: Samuel Plumer,
  John Waters, Jr. Date: 10 December
  1745.
- bond of Charles Hays administrator
  of Nathaniel Hays. Surety: John
  Brown (brazier). Date: 23 January
  1745.
- bond of William West administrator
  of John Magee. Surety: John
  Stoddert. Date: 19 February 1745.
- will of George Woodhead.

Court Session: 1746

- will of Joshua Wilson.
- will of Gabriel Parker.
- inventory of Margaret Holland.
- inventory of Sarah Busey.
- accounts of Christopher Edelen administrator of Thomas Smith.

7 April. Col. Gabriel Parker (CV) exhibited:
- will of Susannah Hellen. Also, bond of Peter Hellen administrator. Sureties: Moses Parran, Samuel Parran. Date: 20 March 1745.
- inventory of Nicholas Scarff.
- inventory of Richard Fryer.
- inventory of Edward Wood.
- inventory of Benjamin Sedwick.
- accounts of Dorcus Whinfield executrix of Jonah Whinfield.

31:632 8 April. Col. Gabriel Parker (CV) to examine accounts of:
- Barrington Pardo administrator of Liney Pardo (CV).
- William Coster administrator of John Coster (CV).
- Elisabeth Skinner administratrix of William Skinner (CV).

9 April. Thomas Aisquith (g, SM) exhibited:
- will of William Billingsly, constituting William Sumner Billingsly executor. Said executor was granted administration. Sureties: Joseph Edwards, Nathaniel Truman Greenfield. Date: 4 March 1745.
- will of William Phippard, constituting Mary Phippard executrix. Said executrix was granted administration. Sureties: John Bond, James Bissco. Date: 4 March 1745.
- bond of Mary Swann administratrix of James Swann. Sureties: Zachariah Bond, Peter Mugg. Date: 6 March 1745.
- bond of John Wherritt administrator of John Bronam. Sureties: Thomas Wherritt, Thomas Cook. Date: 7 March 1745.

Page 169

- inventory & LoD of Thomas Boult.
- inventory of Nicholas Fardery.
- inventory of Henry Wharton.
- inventory & LoD of John Greaves.
- inventory & LoD of William Bradburne.
- inventory of Mark Thomas.
- inventory & LoD of George Boyd.
- additional accounts of Thomas Wellman executor of Joseph Wellman.

12 April. Mr. Thomas Aisquith (SM) to examine accounts of:
- Winifred Burch administratrix of Benjamin Burch (SM).
- Winifred Trepe executrix of Anthony Evans (SM).
- Thomas Coode & James Dunbar administrators dbn of Joshua Guibert (SM).
- Alexander Farguson & his wife Rebecca executrix of John Redman, Sr. (SM).
- Thomas Beale & his wife Mary executrix of Richard Griffen (SM).
- Edward Castor & his wife Sarah administratrix of John Redman, Jr. (SM).
- Thomas Kirkley administrator dbn of Rebecca Colter (SM).

Mr. Charles Hynson (KE) to examine accounts of:
- Issabella Wethered executrix of Richard Wethered (KE).
- Daniel Bryant administrator of Isaac Riley (KE).
- Thomas Carwarden administrator dbn of Robert Keys (KE).
- Simon Wilmer administrator dbn of Patrick Fitzgerald (KE). Additional accounts.

14 April. Thomas Bullen (g, TA) exhibited:
- will of Henry Harding, constituting Elisabeth Harding executrix. Also, widow's election. Said executrix was granted administration. Sureties: Samuel Abbott, Evan Jones. Date: 14 March 1745.
- will of John Powell, constituting

Daniel Dickinson executor. Said
executor was granted administration.
Sureties: Henry Dickinson, Samuel
Sharp, Solomon Sharp. Date: 29
March 1746.
- bond of Daniel Dickenson
administrator of Susannah Powell.
Sureties: John Dickinson, William
Dickinson, William Harrison. Date:
29 March 1746.

31:633 • inventory of John Harrison.
- accounts of Lawrence Calk & his wife
Mary administratrix of John Camper.
- accounts of Abraham Clark & his wife
Elisabeth administratrix of James
Williams.
- accounts of Robert Stapleford & his
wife Mary administratrix of Thomas
Trayman.
- Robert Hall administrator of Robert
Dodson, Jr.

Ennalls Hooper (g, DO) exhibited:
- bond of Sarah Adams administratrix
of Thomas Adams. Sureties: William
Clifton, John Clifton. Date: 5
August 1745.
- bond of Elinor Johnson
administratrix of Henry Johnson.
Sureties: Richard Perry, Stephen
Ross. Date: 13 November 1745.
- will of Hugh Perry. Also, bond of
Richard Perry administrator.
Sureties: John Nicols, Jr., Abraham
Gamble. Date: 13 November 1745.
- will of Thomas Brawhorn. Also, bond
of Margaret Brawhorn administratrix.
Sureties: John Brawhorn, John
Stewart, Jr. Date: 14 November
1745.
- will of Thomas Eccleston,
constituting Elinor Eccleston & Hugh
Eccleston executors. Said executors
were granted administration.
Sureties: John Eccleston, John
McKeel, Walter Stevens. Date: 19
November 1745.
- will of Francis Willey. Also, bond
of Dianah Willey administratrix.
Sureties: Francis Willey, Job
Slacum. Date: 13 December 1745.
- bond of William Smith administrator

of John Hudson 2nd. Sureties:
Thomas Ennalls, Job Slacum. Also,
renunciation of Thomas Loockerman &
John Cannon, Jr. on estate of John
Hodson. Date: 13 December 1745.

- bond of Joanna Alcock administratrix
of Burton Wood Alcock. Sureties:
John Stevens, Walter Stevens. Date:
17 December 1745.
- bond of Col. Joseph Ennalls
administrator of John Noell.
Sureties: Thomas Ennalls, James
Hooper. Date: 16 January 1745.
Also, renunciation of Ann Noell
(widow). Date: 7 January 1745.
Witness: Betty Ennalls.
- will of Roger Mackimmy. Also, bond
of Col. Joseph Ennalls
administrator. Sureties: Thomas
Ennalls, James Hooper. Date: 16
January 1745. Also, renunciation of
Thomas Mackemy. Date: 13 January
1745. Witness: John Ennalls. Also,
renunciation of William Mackemmy
(brother). Date: 16 December 1745.

31:634
- will of Margaret Manning,
constituting John Phips executor.
Said executor was granted
administration. Sureties: James
Phillips, Thomas Vickars. Date: 24
January 1745.
- bond of Ann Hill administratrix of
Daniel Hill. Sureties: John King,
John Thompson. Date: 4 February
1745.
- will of James Vaulx, Sr.,
constituting Sarah Vaulx executrix.
Said executrix was granted
administration. Sureties: Ebenezar
Vaulx, John Vaulx. Date: 17
February 1745.
- bond of Josias Moore administrator
of John Jameson. Sureties: David
Melvill, Sr., William Smith, Sr.
Date: 17 February 1745.
- will of James Vaulx, Jr.,
constituting Catherine Vaulx
executrix. Said executrix was
granted administration. Sureties:
William Addams, Harman Johnson.
Date: 17 February 1745.
- bond of Abigail Scott administratrix

of William Scott. Sureties:
Benjamin Edgell, Edward Hargaton.
Date: 19 February 1745.

- bond of William Twyford
administrator of William Twyford.
Sureties: Isaac Brown, Jonathan
Twyford. Date: 19 February 1745.
- bond of Martha Connerly
administratrix of Owen Connerly.
Sureties: Thomas Connerly, Merida
Williams. Date: 19 February 1745.
- bond of Comfort Graham
administratrix of George Graham.
Surety: William Addams. Date: 19
February 1745.
- will of William Edmondson,
constituting Elisabeth Edmondson &
William Edmondson executors. Said
executors were granted
administration. Sureties: Daniel
Sulivane, William Perry. Date: 19
February 1745.
- bond of Jane Brown administratrix of
John Brown (son of John). Sureties:
Joseph Brown, Jonathan Twyford.
Date: 19 February 1745.
- bond of Margaret Arnatt & Andrew
Arnatt administrators of William
Arnatt. Sureties: John Nuner,
Edward Trippe. Date: 20 February
1745.
- bond of Betty Cole administratrix of
Samuel Cole. Sureties: Edward
Trippe, Charles Eccleston. Date: 20
February 1745.
- will of Grace Hupper, constituting
John Hupper executor. Said executor
was granted administration.
Sureties: Henry Hupper, Joseph
Ricords. Date: 20 February 1745.
- will of Elisabeth Taylor,
constituting Raymond Stapleford,
Charles Stapleford, & Thomas
Stapleford executors. Said
executors were granted
administration. Sureties: Richard
Tubman, Charles Powell. Date: 20
February 1745.
- will of John Standford, constituting
Thomas Standford executor. Said
executor was granted administration.
Sureties: Charles Standford, John

Nuner. Date: 20 February 1745.
- bond of William Harvey administrator of Richard Harvey. Sureties: Isaac Partridge, Patrick Stock. Date: 20 February 1745.
- will of Charles Standford, constituting Rosannah Standford & Thomas Standford executors. Also, widow's election. Said executors were granted administration. Sureties: Charles Standford, Jr., Henry Hooper. Date: 20 February 1745.
- bond of Thomas Jones executor of William Jones. Sureties: John Jones, Thomas Loockerman. Date: 21 February 1745.
- will of William Standford, constituting Samuel Standford executor. Said executor was granted administration. Sureties: Isaac Partridge, Abraham Broadess. Date: 21 February 1745.

31:635
- bond of Capt. Thomas Nevett administrator of Thomas Moore. Surety: Thomas Stewart. Date: 23 February 1745.
- bond of Capt. Thomas Nevett administrator of Edward Chamberlain. Surety: Thomas Stewart. Date: 23 February 1745.
- bond of Col. Joseph Ennalls administrator of Francis Sanders. Sureties: Benjamin Wheland, George Slacum. Date: 24 February 1745. Also, renunciation of Elisabeth Sanders (widow). Date: 21 January 1745. Witness: J. Ennalls.
- bond of Col. Joseph Ennalls administrator of Samuel Stinson. Sureties: Benjamin Wheland, George Slacum. Date: 24 February 1745.
- bond of Col. Joseph Ennalls administrator of Joseph Argoe. Sureties: Benjamin Wheland, George Slacum. Date: 25 February 1745.
- bond of Philemon LeCompte administrator of John Ogden. Sureties: Edward Newton, James Sewers. Date: 26 February 1746.
- bond of Mary Whiteacre administratrix of Joseph Whiteacre.

Sureties: Patrick Reed, John Snelson. Date: 3 March 1745.

- bond of George Williams administrator of Jonathan Arnatt. Surety: Henry Campling. Date: 11 March 1745.
- bond of Ann Tregoe & William Tregoe administrators of William Tregoe. Sureties: Stephen Ross, George Williams. Date: 11 March 1745.
- bond of Elinor Phillips administratrix of Thomas Phillips. Sureties: Henry Fisher, William Standford, Jr. Date: 12 March 1745.
- will of Charles Stapleford, constituting Rebecca Wall executrix. Said executrix was granted administration. Sureties: William Standford, Sr., Thomas Stapleford. Date: 12 March 1745.
- will of John Pitt. Also, bond of Thomas Airey administrator. Sureties: Thomas Howell, John Stewart. Date: 12 March 1745.
- will of John Turpin. Also, bond of Clarada Turpin acting executrix. Sureties: Nehemiah Lecompte, Charles Lecompte. Date: 23 March 1745. Also, renunciation of (N). Date: 5 March 1745.
- bond of Mary Nuttawell administratrix of Richard Nuttawell. Surety: Nehemiah Lecompte. Date: 23 March 1745.
- bond of Thomas Woolford administrator of John Monday. Surety: Henry Traverse. Date: 24 March 1745.
- bond of Henry Hooper, Jr. administrator of Rosannah Reed. Surety: Thomas Hicks. Date: 24 March 1745.
- will of Sarah Langrill, constituting James Langrill executor. Said executor was granted administration. Sureties: Thomas Thompson, Andrew Lord. Date: 24 March 1745.

31:636 • bond of William Woodland administrator of William Shockneshire. Sureties: John Langrill, Thomas Hutchings. Date: 24 March 1745.

- bond of Hannah Trotter (alias Hannah Hutchings) executrix of Ephraim Trotter. Sureties: Thomas Hutchings, John Layton, Anthony Chillcutt. Date: 24 March 1745.
- will of George Chillcutt, constituting Sarah Chillcutt executrix. Said executrix was granted administration. Sureties: John Layton, Anthony Chillcutt. Date: 26 March 1746.
- bond of Elisabeth Cole administratrix of John Cole. Sureties: Patrick Stack, Richard Cole. Date: 26 March 1746.
- bond of Catharine Hendrick administratrix of William Hendrick. Sureties: Patrick Stack, Richard Cole. Date: 26 March 1746.
- will of Lewis Griffith, constituting Frances Griffith executrix. Said executrix was granted administration. Sureties: Raymond Stapleford, William Standford. Date: 12 April 1746.
- will of Turpin Beauchamp. Also, renunciation of executors.
- inventory of William McDaniel.
- inventory & LoD of Hugh Procter.
- inventory of Hannah Hill.
- inventory of John Creek.
- inventory & LoD of Thomas Brawhorn.
- inventory & LoD of William Adams.
- inventory of Francis Willey.
- inventory of Abraham Stafford.
- inventory & LoD of Thomas Adams.
- inventory & LoD of William Austin.
- inventory & LoD of Thomas Royall.
- inventory of John Rumbly, Sr.
- inventory of William Watkins.
- inventory of Nathaniel Manning.
- inventory of Charles McKeel.
- inventory of John Rumbly, Jr.
- inventory of John Warren.
- inventory & LoD of Daniel Murphy.
- inventory & LoD of Henry Johnson.
- inventory of Robert Thornell.
- inventory of John Griffin.
- inventory & LoD of John Brown.
- inventory & LoD of Charles White.
- inventory of Nehemiah Williams.
- additional inventory of George

Morris. Also, accounts of Sarah
Morris administratrix.
- inventory & LoD of William Harper.
- inventory & LoD of Hugh Perry.
- inventory & LoD of St. Leegar
Pattison.
- inventory & LoD of Hugh Rimmer.
- inventory & LoD of John Hodson 2nd.
- inventory & LoD of Samuel Coburn.
- accounts of Ann Canner
administratrix of Edward Canner.
- accounts of Jacob Gray & his wife
Rachel administratrix of Edmond
Owens.
- accounts of William Byus & his wife
Eliza & Col. Joseph Ennalls
executors of Henry Ennalls.
- accounts of Rosannah Manning
administratrix of Nathaniel Manning
executor of Richard Manning.
- accounts of Grace Stogdell
administratrix of Michael Stogdell.
- accounts of Sarah Cannon
administratrix of James Cannon.
- accounts of Alice Covington
administratrix of Jacob Covington.
- accounts of Francis Bickham
administrator of Nehemiah Williams.
- 3rd additional accounts of Joseph
Cox Gray & his wife Rosannah
executrix of Jacob Loockerman.
- accounts of Mary Carawon
administratrix of John Carawon.
- accounts of Jane Harris
administratrix of James Harris.
- accounts of Sarah Sulivane
administratrix of William Sulivane.
- accounts of Ann Wing administratrix
of Robert Wing executor of Garey
Warner.
- accounts of Margaret Hayward
executrix of Thomas Hayward.
31:637 • accounts of Alice McKeel
administratrix of Charles McKeel.
- accounts of Adling Cannon
administratrix of William Cannon.
- accounts of Mary Ross executrix of
Edward Ross.
- accounts of James Baker executor of
Jane Baker.
- accounts of Hannah Reed
administratrix of Ezekiel Reed.

Court Session: 1746

Thomas Bullen (g, TA) exhibited:
- 3rd additional accounts of Frances Ungle administratrix of Robert Ungle, Esq.

William Knight (g, CE) exhibited:
- bond of George Rock administrator of William Cox. Sureties: Edward Johnson, John Kankey. Date: 14 March 1745.
- bond of Mary Bellarmin administratrix of John Bellarmin. Sureties: John Tree, Robert Mong, Jr. Date: 8 April 1746.
- inventory of John Ward.
- inventory of John Pennington.

16 April. Mr. Ennalls Hooper (DO) to examine accounts of:
- Edward Trippe & his wife Ann administratrix of John Trippe (DO).
- Frances Brannock & John Brannock executors of Thomas Brannock (DO).
- Richard Kendall Foxwell administrator of Robert Ross (DO).
- Priscilla Rumbly executrix of John Rumbly (DO).
- Margaret Harper executrix of William Harper (DO).
- Ann Coburn administratrix of Samuel Coburn (DO).
- Catherine White administratrix of Charles White (DO).
- Rosannah Manning administratrix of Nathaniel Manning (DO).
- Elisabeth Procter administratrix of Hugh Procter (DO).
- Mary Royall executrix of Thomas Royall (DO).
- Elisabeth McDaniel administratrix of William McDaniel (DO).
- John Pattison & Mary Pattison executors of St. Leeger Pattison (DO).
- Ann Rumbly executrix of John Rumbly, Jr. (DO).
- Thomas Williams administrator of William Stevens (DO), during minority of Edward Stevens.
- Diana Willey administratrix of Francis Willey (DO).
- John Robson & Joseph Shenton

executors of Josias Mace (DO).
- Richard Perry administrator of Hugh Perry (DO).
- Elinor Johnson administratrix of Henry Johnson (DO).
- Roger Addams administrator of William Addams (DO).
- Ann Coburn administratrix of Daniel Murphy (DO).
- Mary Rimmer administratrix of Hugh Rimmer (DO).
- Margaret Brawhorn administratrix of Thomas Brawhorn (DO).
- James Peterkin executor of Mary Peterkin (DO).

19 April. Exhibited from CE:
- accounts of Araminta Alexander executrix of William Alexander.

31:638   Exhibited from TA:
- receipt of Thomas Love for his filial portion from William Martin executor of Loftus Bowdle, due of said Bowdle as a bondsman for Thomas Ranhill & his wife Ann. Date: 11 April 1746. Witnesses: Tristram Thomas, James Roe.

Mr. Thomas Bullen (TA) to examine accounts of:
- Sarah Oldfield executrix of Henry Oldfield (TA).

21 April. Col. Gabriel Parker (CV) exhibited:
- bond of Thomas Ireland, Jr. administrator of William Summers. Surety: Thomas Ireland. Date: 9 April 1746.
- inventory of Francis Spencer.
- inventory of James Freeman.
- additional accounts of Elisabeth Morris & Richard Johns executors of Randolph Morris.

Nicholas Gassaway (g, AA) or Alexander Warfield (g, AA) to administer oath to Ruth Howard executrix of John Howard (AA).

22 April. Mr. Peter Dent (PG) to
examine accounts of:
• Mary Ann Atchison executrix of John
  Atchison (PG).

Peter Dent (g, PG) exhibited:
• bond of Gabriel Parker & Sarah
  Parker executors of Gabriel Parker.
  Surety: George Parker. Date: 18
  March 1745.
• bond of Duncan Fargason executor of
  George Woodhead. Sureties: Thomas
  Marshall, George Scott. Date: 31
  March 1746.
• bond of Elisabeth Davison
  administratrix of John Davison.
  Sureties: William Marbury, John
  Dawson. Date: 12 April 1746.

26 April. Exhibited from CE:
• bond of John Thompson as Deputy
  Commissary (CE). Sureties: John
  Baldwin (CE), James Calder (KE).
  Date: 22 April 1746.

31:639 23 April. Col. Gabriel Parker (CV) to
examine accounts of:
• William Hardisty executor of Thomas
  Hardisty (CV).
• William Tayman & his wife Elisabeth
  executrix of Thomas Morsell (CV).

24 April. Mary Walker executrix of Dr.
George Walker (BA) was granted
continuance.

26 April. Exhibited from TA:
• inventory of William White. Also,
  accounts of Cassandra White
  executrix.

Exhibited from CE:
• accounts of Augustina Ward
  administratrix of John Ward.

29 March. William Cullens executor of
Mark Fisher (DO) vs. Elisabeth
Brickhill (DO), Margaret wife of John
Woollford (DO), & Sarah Almsby (DO).
Sheriff (DO) to summon defendants to
testify concerning Negro Tom (dec'd) as
an allowance.

Francis Noblitt who married the only child of Mark Fisher (dec'd) vs. William Grantham & his wife (DO), John Hughs (DO), William Little (DO), & George Drury (DO). Sheriff (DO) to summon defendants to testify concerning Negro Tom (dec'd) as an allowance.

Francis Noblitt who married the only child of Mark Fisher (dec'd) vs. James Mulany (DO), Amos Bunt (DO), John Steward, Sr. (DO), & Patrick Reed (DO). Sheriff (DO) to summon defendants to testify concerning Negro Tom (dec'd) as an allowance.

29 April. Mr. Benton Harris (WO) to examine accounts of:
* Ann Badard executrix of Richard Badard (WO).
* William Lathinghouse & his wife Mary administratrix of William Smith (WO).

3 May. Exhibited from CE:
* 2nd additional accounts of Araminta Alexander executrix of Col. Joseph Young.

5 May. Henry Hooper, Jr. administrator of Rosannah Reed vs. Sarah Dodd (DO). Sheriff (DO) to summon defendant to show cause why she conceals estate of dec'd.

Raymond Stapleford, Charles Stapleford, & Thomas Stapleford executors of Elisabeth Taylor (DO) vs. Dorothy Gollothon (DO) & Dorothy Loockerman (DO). Sheriff (DO) to summon defendants to show cause why they conceal estate of dec'd.

31:640   Sheriff (SO) to summon Thomas Morrisson who married widow of Philip Ellis (DO) to take LoA on his estate.

12 May. John Hartshorn & his wife Elisabeth daughter of Francis Spry (QA, dec'd) vs. John Spry executor, William Spry executor, & Robert Worton & his wife Rebecca executrix of said dec'd. Sheriff (QA) to summon defendants to

show cause why they don't pay plaintiff her legacy.

William Rogers (g, **AA**) exhibited:
- bond of Susanna Jones administratrix of Morgan Jones. Sureties: David Weems, Thomas Metcalfe. Date: 10 April 1746.
- will of Abraham Simmons, constituting Sarah Simmons executrix. Said executrix was granted administration. Sureties: Charles Drury, William Tillard. Date: 16 April 1746.
- will of John Howard, constituting Ruth Howard & John Grinef Howard executors. Said executors were granted administration. Sureties: John Dorsey, Jr., Edward Dorsey. Date: 21 April 1746.
- will of John Young, constituting Margaret Young executrix. Also, widow's election. Said executrix was granted administration. Surety: John Ross, Esq. Date: 29 April 1746.
- inventory of John Mills.
- inventory of Richard Randell.
- accounts of Joseph Crouch & his wife Mary administratrix of John Rockhold.

21 October 1743. [Omitted from f. 416.] Walter Harris (Deputy Commissary, CH) exhibited testimony of Joseph Milburn Simmes & his wife Rachel concerning estate of Martha Yoakley (CH, dec'd):
- Rachel Simmes deposed. Mentions: her mother Martha Yoakley.
- Joseph Milburn Simmes deposed.

Court Session: 13 May 1746

31:641 Docket:
- John Cooke (sheriff, PG) to render attachment to Lingan Wilson (PG) administrator of Joseph Wilson (PG) to render inventory. Inventory exhibited. Mentions: James Wilson (brother of dec'd) who refused to sign, Henry Wright Wilson (nephew of dec'd) who refused to sign. Said

Cooke to summon said James Wilson &
said Henry Wright Wilson to show
cause why they refuse to sign
inventory.

31:642 • Thomas Sligh & Henry Morgan sureties
on estate of Buckler Partridge (BA)
vs. Jane Partridge administratrix
of said dec'd. Sheriff (BA) to
render attachment to defendant to
render accounts.

• S.B. for Joseph Milburn Simms & his
wife (CH) vs. W.C. for executors of
Martha Yoakley. Libel, answers.

• S.B. for Ann Hill administratrix of
Isaac Stevens (SO) vs. E.D. for
Matthew Kemp & his wife. Libel,
answer.

• Elenor Hill late widow of John
Durbin (BA) vs. John Durbin (BA)
acting executor of said dec'd.
Sheriff (BA) to render attachment to
defendant to render inventory.
Inventory exhibited. Discontinued.

• Thomas Brereton administrator of
Richard Brereton (SO) vs. John
Mullen (CE). Sheriff (CE) to render
attachment to defendant to show
cause why he conceals estate of
dec'd.

• Thomas Clark on behalf of Margaret &
Susanna Clark orphans of Abraham
Clark (CV, dec'd) vs. John Griffin
(CV) administrator of said dec'd.
James Somervell (sheriff, CV) to
summon defendant to show cause why
certain chattel was not appraised in
estate of dec'd. NEI.

31:643 • Francis Noblitt who married only
child of Mark Fisher (DO, dec'd) vs.
William Cullens (DO) executor of
said dec'd. Sheriff (DO) to summon
defendant to show cause why
allowance for Negro Tom (dec'd)
should not be disallowed.

• J.B. for Samuel Blunt (QA) vs. Rev.
John Bradford & his wife Elisabeth
executrix of Joseph Wickes. Libel.
Abated by death of Mr. Bradford.

• Ja. Hollyday, Jr. (sheriff, QA) to
summon Mary Ann Powell executrix of
James Powell (QA) to take LoA on his
estate.

Court Session: 13 May 1746

- William Cullens executor of Mark
  Fisher vs. Elisabeth Brickhill,
  Margaret wife of John Woollford, &
  Sarah Almsley. Sheriff (DO) to
  summon defendants to testify
  regarding Negro Tom (dec'd).
- Francis Noblitt who married only
  child of Mark Fisher (DO, dec'd) vs.
  William Grantham (DO) & his wife,
  John Hughs (DO), William Little
  (DO), & George Drury (DO). Sheriff
  (DO) to summon defendants to testify
  regarding Negro Tom (dec'd).

31:644
- Francis Noblitt who married only
  child of Mark Fisher (DO, dec'd) vs.
  James Mulany (DO), Amos Bunt (DO),
  John Steward, Sr. (DO), & Patrick
  Read (DO). Sheriff (DO) to summon
  defendants to testify regarding
  Negro Tom (dec'd).
- Henry Hooper administrator of
  Rosannah Reed (DO) vs. Sarah Dodd.
  Sheriff (DO) to summon defendant to
  show cause why she conceals estate
  of dec'd.
- Raymond Stapleford, Charles
  Stapleford, & Thomas Stapleford
  executors of Elisabeth Taylor (DO)
  vs. Dorothy Gollothon (DO) &
  Dorothy Loockerman (DO). Sheriff
  (DO) to summon defendants to show
  cause why they conceal estate of
  dec'd.

31:645
- Sheriff (SO) to summon Thomas
  Morrisson & his wife widow of Philip
  Ellis (DO) to take LoA on his
  estate.

Court Session: 1746

15 May. Charles Drury administrator of
Nathan Selby (PG) was granted
continuance.

16 May. Exhibited from AA:
- accounts of Thomas Howard & his wife
  Ann administratrix of Cadwallader
  Edwards.

Exhibited from QA:
- accounts of Susanna Elliott
  executrix of John Elliott.

Page 184

Exhibited from PG:
* additional inventory of Edward Willett. Also, accounts of William Willett executor.

17 May. Col. Gabriel Parker (CV) exhibited:
* inventory of John Armstrong.

Exhibited from DO:
* additional accounts of Elisabeth Trippe administratrix of Henry Trippe.

22 May. Nicholas Goldsborough attorney in fact for William Gale executor of Margaret Connor executrix of Arthur Connor (TA) vs. Elijah Skillington (TA) administrator of said Arthur Connor. Sheriff (TA) to summon defendant to show cause why he conceals estate of said Arthur.

23 May. Peter Dent (g, PG) exhibited:
* will of Alexander Magruder.
* inventory of William McClash.
* inventory of Thomas Brooke.
* additional inventory of John Atcheson.
* additional accounts of John Orme executor of Amy Groome.

31:646 24 May. George Gordon vs. John Smith (PG) surviving executor of Thomas Smith (CV). Sheriff (PG) to summon defendant to show cause why he doesn't pay the wife of plaintiff her portion of estate of her sister Mary's share of estate of dec'd.

26 May. William Tilghman (g, QA) exhibited:
* will of James Hicks. Also, widow's election.
* will of Margaret Boon.
* will of James Hamilton.
* will of Charles ONeal.
* will of Trustram Thomas. Also, widow's election.
* will of John Carman.
* inventory of Thomas Davis.
* inventory of Edward Jones, Jr.

Court Session: 1746

- inventory of William Jumpe.
- inventory of James Walker.
- inventory & LoD of Henry Costin.

27 May. Mr. Charles Hynson (KE) to examine accounts of:
- Mary Massey administratrix of William Massey (KE).
- James Woodland & Katherine Woodland administrators of William Woodland (KE).
- Katherine Simpson administratrix of Thomas Simpson (KE).

30 May. Mr. Thomas White (BA) to examine additional accounts of:
- Lewis Lafee & his wife Sarah executrix of William Lowe (BA).

Col. Gabriel Parker (CV) to examine accounts of:
- Isaac Monett & his wife Elisabeth administratrix of John Williams (CV).
- Joseph Tanner & his wife Susannah executrix of John Armstrong (CV).
- Capel King administrator of Sarah Malden (CV).
- Sarah & Michael Taney executors of Michael Taney (CV). Additional accounts.
- Elisabeth Kent & Absolam Kent executors of Absolam Kent (CV).

13 June. Exhibited from AA:
- additional inventory of Abraham Woodward.

31:647 Mr. William Tilghman (QA) to examine accounts of:
- Robert Basnet & his wife Suanna executrix & James Maynor executor of Timothy Maynor (QA).
- Ambrose Wright administrator of John Saunders (QA).

23 May. Peter Dent (g, PG) exhibited:
- bond of Susanna Magruder executrix of Alexander Magruder. Sureties: Henry Trueman, John Hawkins, Jr. Date: 20 May 1746.

26 May. William Tilghman (g, QA)
exhibited:

- bond of Richard Reading & his wife Mary executrix of James Powell. Sureties: Thomas Tate, James Sutton. Date: 8 May 1746.
- bond of Richard Leech & his wife Rebecca administrators of Thomas Civil. Sureties: John Roe, James Berwick. Date: 27 February 1745.
- bond of Anne & Giles Hicks executors of James Hicks. Sureties: Henry Clift, Vincent Price. Date: 27 February 1745.
- bond of Sarah Hays administratrix of John Hays, Jr. Sureties: George Elliott, William Robinson. Date: 3 March 1745.
- bond of Nathan Wright, Jr. administrator of Michael Serjeant. Sureties: William Coursey, Edward Clayton. Date: 10 April 1746.
- bond of Rebecca Williams administratrix of John White. Sureties: Daniel Newman, Thomas Ford. Date: 24 April 1746.
- bond of Rebecca Williams administratrix of Thomas Williams. Sureties: Daniel Newman, Thomas Ford. Date: 24 April 1746.
- bond of Benjamin Boone executor of Margaret Boon. Sureties: William Starkey, Nathaniel Clough. Date: 8 May 1746.
- bond of Jane McClean administratrix of Daniel McClean. Sureties: John Hamilton, William Carman. Date: 16 May 1746.
- bond of William Hamilton (Lancaster Co. PA, shoemaker) executor of James Hamilton. Sureties: William Carman, Samuel McCosh. Date: 19 May 1746.

31:648 6 June. Walter Hanson (g, CH)
exhibited:

- will of Benjamin Sothoron.
- will of Thomas Reed.
- bond of Margaret Chapman administratrix of John Chapman. Sureties: Patrick Byrn, Matthew Breeding. Date: 5 March 1745.
- bond of Mary Chapman executrix of

Richard Chapman. Sureties: Thomas
Rayley, William Muncaster. Date: 19
March 1745.
- inventory of Daniel McDaniel.
- inventory of Robert Mahone.
- inventory of William Scott.
- inventory of Sarah Fowkes.
- inventory of John Mahoney.
- inventory of Thomas Barnes.
- inventory of Benjamin Neale.
- inventory of Richard King.
- inventory of William Brent.
- additional accounts of William
  Hunter & his wife Mary
  administratrix of Dennis Nalley.
- accounts of Matthew Barnes
  administrator of Murdoc Baton.
- accounts of George Godfrey & John
  Clark, Jr. administrator of John
  West.

9 June. Mr. Walter Hanson (CH) to
examine accounts of:
- Richard Nalley & his wife Elisabeth
  administratrix of Thomas Goley (CH).
- Winfred Mastin administratrix of
  Francis Mastin (CH).

Thomas Aisquith (g, SM) exhibited:
- will of Eleanor Asten, constituting
  John Smoot executor. Said executor
  was granted administration.
  Sureties: Thomas Guythers, George
  Jenkins. Date: 14 April 1746.
- will of Mary Jones, constituting
  Joseph Jones executor. Said
  executor was granted administration.
  Sureties: William Thomas, James
  Granan. Date: 12 May 1746.
- bond of Elenor Gardiner
  administratrix of Clement Gardiner.
  Sureties: Richard Brooke, Baker
  Brooke. Date: 26 May 1746.
- bond of Mary Watts administratrix of
  Thomas Watts. Sureties: Thomas
  Breeden, James Breeden. Date: 1 May
  1746.
- bond of James Watts administrator
  dbn of Timothy Tole. Sureties: Hugh
  Hopewell, Basil Cooper. Date: 8 May
  1746.
- inventory & LoD of Joseph Prevatt.

31:649

- inventory & LoD of William Cutler.
- inventory of John Sledmore.
- inventory & LoD of John Fanning.
- accounts of Dryden Forbes administratrix of Kenelem Greenfield Jowles.
- accounts of Henry Sheircliffe administrator of James Mattenly.
- accounts of Ann McKelvey administratrix of Andrew McKelvey.

16 June. Mr. Thomas Bullen (TA) to examine additional accounts of:
- Elisabeth Stevens administratrix of John Stevens (TA).

E.D. for Richard Watts & John Carr executors of John Watts vs. Andrew Scott administrator of John Watts. Attachment issued on a decree to the defendant.

17 June. John Thompson (g, CE) exhibited:
- bond of James Bayard administrator of William Richison. Sureties: Adam Vanbebber (g), Joshua George (g). Date: 10 May 1746.
- bond of Jacob Vanbebber & Adam Vanbebber administrators of Harmana Vanbebber. Sureties: John Baldwin, Michael Earle. Date: 12 May 1746.
- inventory & LoD of John Watson.

18 June. Thomas Bullen (g, TA) exhibited:
- will of James Berry, constituting Sarah Berry executrix. Also, widow's election. Said executrix was granted administration. Sureties: John Goldsborough, Peter Commerford. Date: 4 May 1746.
- will of Richard Skinner, constituting Katharine Skinner executrix. Said executrix was granted administration. Sureties: Joseph Hopkins, Richard Bruff, Robert Spencer. Date: 20 May 1746.
- bond of Jane Studham executrix of John Studham. Sureties: John Lloyd, John Hutchinson. Date: 9 May 1746.
- will of Thomas Spry. Also, bond of

Christopher acting executor.
Sureties: Samuel Hopkins, Henry
Robson. Date: 18 April 1746.

31:650 • will of Michael Ryan. Also, bond of
Samuel Jenkins administrator.
Sureties: James Walker, William
Moor. Date: 14 April 1746.

• bond of Lambert Robson administrator
of James Robson. Sureties: William
Price, Thomas Neighbours. Date: 30
May 1746.

• bond of Mary Ward administratrix of
Daniel Ward. Sureties: Andrew Orem,
John Barrock. Date: 9 May 1746.

• bond of Rigby Foster administrator
of Elisabeth Lawes. Sureties: David
Robinson, Peter Goff. Date: 16
April 1746.

• bond of William Buckley
administrator of Alexander Mecotter.
Sureties: Bryan Seeney, Erasmus
Hallaran. Date: 5 May 1746.

• bond of Thomas Greenhough & John
Davis administrator of Thomas
Greenhough. Sureties: Lemmon John
Catrop, James Merrick. Date: 18
April 1746.

• bond of Jacob Hindman administrator
of Robert Bettice. Sureties: Josias
Moore (DO), James Johnson (DO).
Date: 17 April 1746.

• bond of Ann Tipler administratrix of
William Tipler. Sureties: William
Higgins, Robert Harding. Date: 1
April 1746.

• additional inventory of Jacob
Williams.

• inventory & LoD of Augustine
Nowland.

• inventory of Henry Harding.

• inventory of John Jones.

• inventory of James Merchant.

• inventory of John Batcheldor.

• inventory of William Barwick.

• additional inventory of John
Edmondson.

• accounts of Margaret Edmondson
acting executrix of John Edmondson.

• accounts of Mary Dulen executrix of
John Dulen.

• accounts of Alice Nowland
administratrix of Augustine Nowland.

- accounts of William Cooper & his wife Frances administratrix of Thomas Wiles.

Mr. Thomas Bullen (g) to examine accounts of:
- Rachel Williams acting executrix of Jacob Williams (TA).
- Mary Merchant administratrix of James Merchant (TA).
- Richard Dove & his wife Rachel administratrix of William Ardery (TA).

19 June. Nehemiah King (g, TA) exhibited:
- will of William Dashiell, constituting Isabell Dashiell executrix. Said executrix was granted administration. Sureties: Joseph Dashiell, Jessey Dashiell. Date: 20 March 1745.
- will of William Miles. Also, bond of Stacey Miles acting executor. Sureties: John Turpin, Barnaby Willis.

31:651
Also, renunciation of Mary Miles (widow), recommending her son Stacy. Date: 19 April 1746.
- will of Robert Boyer, constituting Sarah Boyer executrix. Said executrix was granted administration. Sureties: John Williams (Pocomoke), John Clifton. Date: 27 May 1746.
- bond of Purnall Newbold administrator of Thomas Newbold. Sureties: Edward Waters, David Dreddon. Date: 4 March 1745.
- bond of Isaac Moore administrator of Mary Sterling. Sureties: David Bird, William Williams. Date: 10 May 1746.
- bond of John Dennis, Sr. administrator dbn of James Longo. Sureties: Samuel Wilson, Samuel Long. Date: 1 May 1746.
- inventory of Richard Chambers.
- accounts of Charles Dean administrator of Charles Dean.
- accounts of Mary Moore administratrix of Francis Moore.

- accounts of Samuel Collins surviving executor of Richard Chambers.

21 June. Col. Gabriel Parker (CV) exhibited:
- will of Elisabeth Young, constituting William Williams & John Howerton executors. Said executors were granted administration. Sureties: Philip Dossey, James Bowen. Date: 10 May 1746.
- bond of Elisabeth Griffin administratrix of John Griffin. Sureties: Isaac Stallings, Kent Stallings. Date: 22 May 1746.
- accounts of Barrington Pardo administrator of Lucey Pardo.
- accounts of William Coster administrator of John Coster.
- accounts of Elisabeth Skinner administratrix of William Skinner.
- accounts of Elisabeth Newton administratrix of Henry Newton.

23 June. Exhibited from WO:
- accounts of Rous Fassitt executor of William Fassitt administrator of Francis Hamblin.

24 June. Mr. Walter Hanson (CH) to examine additional accounts of:
- Walter Scott administrator of James Scott (CH).

31:652 25 June. Exhibited from CV:
- additional accounts of Jane Wells administratrix of Martin Wells.

Mr. Thomas White (BA) to examine accounts of:
- Ruth Howard executrix of Edmond Howard (BA).
- William Standiford & his wife Christiana administratrix of Thomas Wright (BA). 2nd additional accounts.

Mr. John Thompson (CE) to examine accounts of:
- John Harper administrator dbn of Robert Withers (CE). 2nd additional accounts.

- George Lawson administrator of Joseph Rodach (CE).
- John Stockton & his wife Elisabeth administratrix of Sigefredus Aldrecks (CE). Additional accounts.

26 June. Exhibited from KE:
- additional inventory of James Harris, Esq. Also, additional accounts of Matthias Harris acting executor.

Mr. Nehemiah King (SO) to examine accounts of:
- Elisabeth Connor executrix of John Connor (SO).
- Rose Costin administratrix of Isaac Costin (SO).
- Sarah Jones executrix of James Jones (SO).
- Teague Dickeson administrator of David Wallace (SO).
- John Caldwell & his wife Mary acting executrix of William Vaughan (SO).
- Mary Gosle administratrix of James Goslee (SO).
- Ann Pryor administratrix of Thomas Pryor (SO).
- Marsey Fountain administrator of William Copsey (SO).
- Mary Fountain & Marsey Fountain executors of Nicholas Fountain (SO).

2 July. Mr. Charles Hynson (KE) to examine accounts of:
- Colin Farguson executor of Robert Dew (KE).
- Elisabeth Ringgold administratrix of James Ringgold (KE). Additional accounts.
- Elisabeth Ringgold administratrix dbn of William Buckham (KE). Additional accounts.

4 July. Col. Gabriel Parker (CV) to examine accounts of:
- Elinor Dorrumple & John Dorrumple executors of John Dorrumple (CV).
- James Rickason executor of Mary Maners (CV).
- Grace Baker acting executrix of John Baker (CV).

Court Session: 1746

- Ann Wood administratrix of Edward Wood (CV).

31:653 Mr. Thomas Bullen (BA) to examine accounts of:
- Hannah West acting executrix of Loton West (TA).
- Russel Armstrong & his wife Rebecca administratrix of Moses Clayland (TA).

Exhibited from KE:
- LoD on estate of James Harris, Esq.

Exhibited:
- depositions of Mary Kelly (sister, PG) & William West (brother, PG) that they have refused to sign inventory of Benjamin West (dec'd). Appraisers: Maj. Jeremiah Belt, Mr. Thomas Gant.

Exhibited from PG:
- inventory of John Magee.
- inventory of Bryant Kelley.

Elisabeth Gosling widow & executrix of Thomas Gosling (SM) vs. William Fowler (SM) administrator of said dec'd. Sheriff (SM) to summon defendant to render accounts & to pay plaintiff.

5 July. Mr. Nehemiah King (SO) to examine accounts of:
- James Gunby surviving executor of John Gunby (SO).

7 July. Mr. Thomas Aisquith (SM) to examine accounts of:
- Alice Gibson executrix of John Gibson (SM).
- Thomas Alstone & his wife Drayden executrix of Samuel Bagley (SM).
- Jane Watts executrix of William Watts (SM).
- Mary Bean & John Bean executors of John Bean (SM).
- Gustavus Brown & his wife Margaret administratrix of John Dickson administrator of George Boyd (SM).
- Rachel Billingsly administratrix of Bowles Billingsly (SM).

31:654 Exhibited:
- deposition of George Dashiell (SO), age over 55, that he was a security on estate of Isaac Stevens (SO). Mentions: Negroes left said Isaac by his father, deponent as a friend of the widow & child, Negro Moll (girl), Richard Stevens administrator of his mother Abigail. Said Richard said he would keep the girl, several years before filing the libel against Mathew Kemp & his wife.
- deposition of John Mullen (p, CE), age 31, that he received from Richard Brereton (SO, dec'd) chattel.

Court Session: 8 July 1746

31:655 Docket:
- Sheriff (PG) to render attachment to Lingan Wilson (PG) administrator of Joseph Wilson (PG) to render inventory.
- John Cooke (sheriff, PG) to summon James Wilson (brother) & Henry Wright Wilson (nephew) to show cause why they refuse to sign inventory of Joseph Wilson (PG) as next of kin. Said Henry Wright Wilson appeared; said Capt. James Wilson did not.
- Thomas Sligh & Henry Morgan sureties on estate of Buckler Partridge (BA) vs. Jane Partridge administratrix of said dec'd. Sheriff (BA) to summon defendant to render accounts.
- S.B. for Joseph Milburn Semmes & his wife (CH) vs. W.C. for executors of Martha Yoakley. Libel, answers.

31:656 • Stephen Bordley procurator for Ann Hall widow & administratrix of Isaac Stevens (SO) vs. Edward Dorsey procurator for Mathew Kemp & his wife Rachel.
Text of libel. Mentions: Richard Stevens (SO, d. October/November 1713) made will, constituting his wife Abigail executrix. Legatees: wife Abigail Negro Jacob & Negro Jeffer & Negro Bess and then to 3 sons John Stevens, Richard Stevens,

31:657

& Isaack Stevens. Negro Bess had a child Negro Moll (girl). Said Richard delivered to said John Negro Bess & retained Negro Jeffer & Negro Moll, & paid plaintiff Negro Jack (very aged). Said Richard died, leaving a widow Rachel. Said Rachel has Negro Moll & her 3 children. Plaintiff married Phenix Hall who is now runaway 7 years ago. Said Rachel married Matthew Kemp (p, SO).

31:658

Mentions: John Dennis, Jr. (sheriff, SO).

31:659

Text of answer.

31:660

Mentions: Mitchell Dashiell (justice of peace, SO).
Ruling: Negroes bequeathed by Richard Stevens to be appraised by William Stoughton, Esq., Capt. David Wilson, & Mr.

31:661

John Dennis. Estate is to be divided into 3 parts. Plaintiff to receive 1 part.

- Thomas Brereton administrator of Richard Brereton (SO) vs. John Mullen (CE). Sheriff (CE) to summon defendant to show cause why he conceals estate of dec'd. Said Mullen deposed. Discontinued.

- Thomas Clark on behalf of Margaret & Susannah Clark minors & orphans of Abraham Clark (CV) vs. John Griffin (CV) administrator of said dec'd. James Somervell (sheriff, CV) to summon defendant to show cause why certain chattel was not appraised.

- Francis Noblitt who married only child of Mark Fisher (DO, dec'd) vs. William Cullens (DO) executor of said dec'd. Sheriff (DO) to summon defendant to show cause why allowance for Negro Tom (now dec'd) should not be allowed. Said Cullens is dead; abated.

- James Hollyday, Jr. (sheriff, QA) to render attachment to Mary Ann Powell executrix of James Powell (QA) to take LoA on his estate. Said Mary Ann has taken LoA. Discontinued.

31:662

- William Cullens executor of Mark Fisher (DO) vs. Elisabeth Brickhill

Court Session: 8 July 1746

(DO), Margaret wife of John
Woollford (DO), & Sarah Almesby
(DO). Sheriff (DO) to summon
defendants to testify concerning the
allowance of Negro Tom (now dec'd).
Said Cullens is dead; abated.

- Francis Noblitt who married only
child of Mark Fisher (DO) vs.
William Grantham & his wife (DO),
John Hughs (DO), William Little
(DO), & George Drury (DO). Sheriff
(DO) to summon defendants to testify
concerning the allowance of Negro
Tom (now dec'd). William Cullens
executor of said Fisher is now dead;
abated.

- Francis Noblitt who married only
child of Mark Fisher (DO) vs. James
Mulony (DO), Amos Bunt (DO), John
Steward, Sr. (DO), & Patrick Read
(DO). Sheriff (DO) to summon
defendants to testify concerning the
allowance of Negro Tom (now dec'd).
William Cullens executor of said
Fisher is now dead; abated.

- Henry Hooper, Jr. administrator of
Rosannah Reed (DO) vs. Sarah Dodd
(DO). T. Muir (sheriff, DO) to
summon defendant to show cause why
she conceals estate of dec'd. NE.

- Raymond Stapleford, Charles
Stapleford, & Thomas Stapleford
executors of Elisabeth Taylor (DO)
vs. Dorothy Gollothon (DO) &
Dorothy Loockerman (DO). Sheriff
(DO) to summon defendants to show
cause why they conceal estate of
dec'd.

31:663 - Sheriff (SO) to summon Thomas
Morrisson & his wife widow of Philip
Ellis (DO) to take LoA on his
estate.

- Nicholas Goldsborough attorney in
fact for William Gale executor of
Margaret Connor executrix of Arthur
Connor (TA) vs. Elijah Skillington
(TA) administrator of said Arthur.
Ja. Henderson (sheriff, TA) to
summon defendant to show cause why
he conceals effects of said Arthur.
  - Said Skillington deposed. Dec'd
  had a pew in White Marsh Church

Page 197

Court Session: 8 July 1746

in St. Peter's Parish.

31:664
Discontinued.
- George Gordon vs. John Smith (PG) surviving executor of Thomas Smith (CV). Sheriff (PG) to summon defendant to show cause why he doesn't pay plaintiff his wife's portion of estate of her sister Mary's portion of said estate.
- John Hartshorn who married Elisabeth Spry daughter of Francis Spry (QA, dec'd) vs. John Spry & William Spry executors & Robert Worton & his wife Mary executrix of said dec'd. Ja. Hollyday, Jr. to summon defendants to show cause why they don't pay plaintiff her legacy.
- E.D. for Richard Watts & John Carr executors of John Watts (PG) vs. Andrew Scott administrator of John Watts. John Cooke rendered attachment to defendant until he was discharged by Mr. Henry Massey attorney in fact for plaintiffs.

Court Session: 1746

31:665 9 July. Mr. William Tilghman (QA) to examine accounts of:
- Abraham Williams & his wife Rebecca executrix of Peter Hand (QA).
- Stephen Weeks & Matthew Weeks executors of John Weeks (QA).
- Vincent Price administrator of Timothy Lane (QA).
- Phineas Wilson & his wife Ann administratrix of John Jackerman (QA).

Exhibited from QA:
- additional accounts of Robert Worton & his wife Rebecca executrix of Francis Spry.

10 July. Exhibited from AA:
- will of Gassaway Watkins.

14 July. Peter Dent (g, PG) exhibited:
- will of John Riddle.
- will of Samuel Waring.
- will of Middleton Bell.

16 July. Walter Hanson (g, CH)
exhibited:
- will of Samuel Burgess, constituting
  Elisabeth Burgess executrix. Said
  executrix was granted
  administration. Sureties: John
  Burgess, James Gray. Date: 18 June
  1746.
- bond of Andrew Chunn administrator
  dbn of John Chunn. Sureties: Samuel
  Amery, Edward Swann. Date: 21 May
  1746.
- bond of Susannah Waters
  administratrix of William Waters.
  Sureties: Matthew Marten, Benjamin
  Thomas. Date: 18 June 1746.
- bond of Anne Ross administratrix of
  James Ross. Sureties: James
  Carroll, Thomas Raley. Date: 18
  June 1746.
- inventory of Matthew Barnes.
- inventory of John Wathen.
- inventory of Francis Goodrick.
- inventory of Richard Chapman.
- inventory of John Chapman.
- accounts of Joseph Lancaster
  executor of Anne Howard.
- accounts of Winifred Mastin
  administratrix of Francis Mastin.
- accounts of John Hanson, Jr.
  executor of James Stewart.
- accounts of Charles Spaulding
  administrator of James Hamblin.
- accounts of John Rigg administrator
  of Anne Howison.
- accounts of John Hatch & Edward
  Kellet executors of George Medway.

31:666 14 July. Exhibited from PG:
- accounts of Eleanor Jones
  administratrix of Edward Jones.

11 July. Lawrence Macnemara (CH) & his
wife Elisabeth vs. Mary Ann Atcherson
(PG) executrix of John Atcherson (PG).
Sheriff (PG) to summon defendant to
render answer.

14 July. Mr. Peter Dent (PG) to
examine additional accounts of:
- William Robinson & his wife Dianah
  administratrix of John Williams

(PG).

Exhibited:
- deposition of Susannah Davis (CV), age 75, regarding concealment of estate of Abraham Clark (CV) by his administrator John Griffen.

16 July. Mr. Walter Hanson (CH) to examine accounts of:
- Mary Hamersley administratrix of Francis Hamersley (CH).
- Thomas Coleman executor & James Greenfield & his wife Martha executrix of Thomas Coleman (CH).
- Matthew Clubb surviving executor of John Clubb (CH).
- William Carter administrator of William Carter (CH).
- Andrew Chunn administrator dbn of John Chunn (CH).
- Anne Scott administratrix of William Scott (CH).
- Margaret Jenkins administratrix of Willianm Jenkins (CH).
- Joseph Lancaster executor of Anne Howard (CH). Additional accounts.
- Prudence Green administratrix of Leonard Green (CH). Additional accounts.

31:667 18 July. Exhibited from BA:
- inventory & LoD of John Mahone. Also, accounts of Mary Mahone executrix.

19 July. William Tilghman (g, QA) exhibited:
- will of Trustram Thomas, constituting Anne Thomas executrix. Said executrix was granted administration. Sureties: Christopher Thomas, William Prior. Date: 29 May 1746.
- will of Peter Countiss, constituting Rebecca Countiss executrix. Said executrix was granted administration. Sureties: John Alley, William Wrench, Jr. Date: 30 May 1746.
- bond of Rachael Carman executrix of John Carman. Sureties: William

Robinson (p), John Woodall (p).
Date: 22 May 1746.

- bond of George Lewis administrator
  of Thomas Lewis. Sureties: William
  Gilbert, David Huxler. Also,
  renunciation of Phebe Lewis (widow).
  Date: 29 May 1746.
- bond of Jane Thomas & Benjamin
  Thomas executors of Trustram Thomas
  (Tully's Neck). Sureties: Baldwin
  Kemp, Henry Counsill. Date: 12 June
  1746.
- inventory of James Boon.

Peter Dent (g, PG) exhibited:
- inventory of John Williams.
- inventory of John Orchard.
- inventory of Thomas Middleton.
- inventory of Robert Newstubb.
- inventory of John Davison.
- accounts of John Haymond
  administrator of John Baldwin
  Adamson.
- accounts of Ann Adkinson
  administratrix of John Adkinson.
- accounts of Patrick Reding & his
  wife Sarah executrix of John
  Maudesley.
- accounts of Thomas Oweing
  administrator of Robert Newstubb.

20 July. Benton Harris (g, WO)
exhibited:
- will of Levin Disharoon,
  constituting Rebeckah Disharoon
  executrix. Said executrix was
  granted administration. Sureties:
  George Smith, Archabald Smith.
  Date: 5 June 1746.
- will of David Murray, constituting
  Hannah Murray executrix. Said
  executrix was granted
  administration. Sureties: James
  Martin, Patrick Glasgow. Date: 25
  June 1746.
- bond of Alexander Massey
  administrator of Tabitha Massey.
  Sureties: Peter Collier, William
  Kennett. Date: 30 June 1746.
- bond of Alexander Buncle
  administrator of John Evans Linton.
  Sureties: George Parker, Samuel

31:668

Parker.   Date: 10 June 1746.
- bond of Elisabeth Hill
  administratrix of Hutten Hill.
  Sureties: James Martin, Abraham
  Outten.   Date: 24 May 1746.
- bond of Rebeckah Bratten
  administratrix of Hugh Bratten.
  Sureties: James Martin, Abraham
  Outten.   Date: 27 June 1746.
- bond of Samuel Parker administrator
  of Leah Parker.   Sureties: Alexander
  Buncle, George Parker.   Date: 10
  June 1746.
- inventory of James Ewart.
- inventory of Benjamin Quillen.
- inventory of Robert Caldwell.
- inventory of Richard Hutson.
- inventory of Lucretia Claywell.
- inventory of John Burton.
- accounts of Anne Baddard executrix
  of Baddard Richard [!].
- accounts of John Teague
  administrator of John McCauley.
- accounts of John Taylor
  administrator of John Hopkins.

22 July.   Baptist Barber (SM) & his wife
Elisabeth vs.   Samuel Sothoron (SM) &
Richard Sothoron (SM) executors of John
Johnson Sothoron (SM).   Sheriff (SM) to
summon defendants to render answer.

29 July.   Col. Gabriel Parker (CV) to
examine accounts of:
- Kenelm Truman Greenfield
  administrator of Thomas Truman
  Greenfield (CV).

2 August.   Mr. Charles Hynson (KE) to
examine accounts of:
- Lambert Wilmer executor of Elisabeth
  Young (KE).

31:669   Executors of Richard Tootel creditor to
estate of Nicholas Hammond (AA) vs.
Mary Hammond (AA) administratrix of said
dec'd.   Sheriff (AA) to summon defendant
to render accounts.

5 August.   Exhibited from PG:
- accounts of Thomas Bowie (g)
  executor of James Bowie.

Col. Gabriel Parker (CV) exhibited:
- bond of Thomas Ireland, Jr. administrator of Thomas Cranford. Surety: William Ireland. Date: 24 May 1746.
- bond of Martha Brooke administratrix of John Brooke. Sureties: Joseph Skinner, James Brooke. Date: 24 June 1746.
- inventory of Hellen Susannah [!].
- inventory of Elisabeth Young.
- accounts of William Tayman & his wife Elisabeth executrix of Thomas Morsell.
- accounts of Thomas Brome administrator of Francis Spencer.
- accounts of William Hardisty executor of Thomas Hardisty.
- accounts of Isaack Monett & his wife Elisabeth administratrix of John Williams.
- accounts of Sarah & Michal Taney executors of Taney Michal [!].

6 August. Thomas Joyce father of Thomas Joyce (AA) vs. Anne Joyce widow of said dec'd. Sheriff (AA) to summon defendant to take LoA or show cause why LoA should not be granted to plaintiff.

7 August. Mr. John Needham who married Sarah Abington daughter of John Abington (PG, dec'd) vs. Dr. Andrew Scott & his wife Mary executrix of said dec'd. Sheriff (PG) to summon defendants to render final accounts.

8 August. Exhibited from BA:
- inventory & LoD of Samuel Gover.

31:670 Ennalls Hooper (g, DO) exhibited:
- will of Robert Clarkson, constituting Elisabeth Clarkson executrix. Said executrix was granted administration. Sureties: William Cannon, Jr., Joshua Cannon. Date: 25 April 1746.
- will of Henry Smith, constituting Mary Smith executrix. Also, widow's election. Said executrix was granted administration. Sureties: James Hall (p), David Williams (p).

Court Session: 1746

Date: 10 June 1746.
- will of Catherine Phillips. Also, bond of William Phillips administrator. Sureties: Joseph Shenton, John Phillips. Date: 29 April 1746.
- will of Charles Wheeler. Also, bond of Thomas Wheeler acting executor. Sureties: Phillip Tall, Stephen Ross. Date: 21 May 1746.
- will of John Hughs, constituting Catherine Hughs executrix. Said executrix was granted administration. Sureties: William Tregoe, Philemon Tregoe. Date: 3 July 1746.
- will of David Rogers, constituting Alice Rogers executrix. Said executrix was granted administration. Sureties: Francis Willey, William Willey. Date: 13 June 1746.
- will of John Willey, constituting William Willey executor. Said executor was granted administration. Sureties: Summer Adams, Andrew Insley. Date: 22 May 1746.
- will of William Wroughton, constituting Thomas Wroughton & Rachel Wroughton executors. Said executors were granted administration. Sureties: Edward Pritchett, Thomas Adams. Date: 21 May 1746.
- will of James Phillips, constituting John Salsbury executor. Said executor was granted administration. Sureties: Matthew Bright, Patrick Carawon. Date: 22 May 1746.
- bond of William Perry administrator of Adam Mears. Sureties: Levin Hicks, John Anderson. Date: 12 June 1746.
- bond of Rosanah Goldsborough administratrix of Howes Goldsborough. Sureties: Thomas Nevett, Levin Hicks. Date: 13 June 1746.
- bond of Elisabeth Turner administratrix of Henry Turner. Sureties: Andrew Gray, Richard Andrew. Date: 2 May 1746.

- bond of Evan Cornish administrator of Cornish Samuel [!]. Sureties: Joseph Thompson, Thomas Walker. Date: 31 July 1746.
- bond of John Pollard, Jr. administrator of George Williams. Sureties: John McKeel, John Brawhorn.

31:671 Also, renunciation of Susanna Williams (widow). Date: 11 June 1746. Witness: Levin Hicks.

- bond of Thomas Nevett administrator of Glode Lewis, Jr. Surety: Moses Poole. Date: 28 July 1746.
- bond of May Peirson administratrix of Benjamin Peirson. Sureties: Thomas Wheatley, John Brawhorn. Date: 11 June 1746.
- bond of Elisabeth Spencer administratrix of William Spencer. Sureties: Edward Dean, John Dean. Date: 25 May 1746.
- bond of William Murray administrator of Christian Mackormack. Surety: John Stephens (g). Date: 13 June 1746.
- bond of Elisabeth Bramble administratrix of Thomas Bramble. Sureties: George Selacum, Roger Hurley. Date: 21 May 1746.
- bond of Henry Wingate, Jr. administrator of Mary Wingate. Sureties: Phillup Wingate, John Willey. Date: 11 July 1746.
- bond of Levinah Tunis administratrix of Edward Tunis. Sureties: John Soward, Samuel Abbott. Date: 12 July 1746.
- inventory of Daniel Hill.
- inventory of James Vaulx, Sr.
- inventory of Burtonwood Allcock.
- inventory of Joseph Whiteacor.
- inventory & LoD of Thomas Phillups.
- inventory of William Scott.
- inventory of James Phillups.
- inventory of Charles Stapleford.
- inventory of Elisabeth Taylor.
- inventory & LoD of William Standford.
- inventory of John Cole.
- inventory of William Tregoe.
- inventory of John Jemison.

Court Session: 1746

- inventory & LoD of William Arnitt.
- inventory of Catherine Phillups.
- inventory of John Ogdon.
- inventory of William Jones.
- inventory of James Vaulx.
- inventory & LoD of John Pitt.
- inventory of Mary Wingate.
- inventory & LoD of William Hendrick.
- inventory & LoD of Grace Hooper.
- inventory & LoD of Richard Harvey.
- inventory & LoD of John Standford.
- inventory & LoD of Samuel Cole.
- inventory & LoD of Owen Connerly.
- inventory & LoD of Charles Standford.

31:672
- inventory & LoD of William Twyford.
- inventory of William Shegnasha.
- inventory & LoD of Robert Clarkson.
- inventory of Lewis Griffith.
- inventory of Sarah Langrill.
- inventory of Ephraim Trotter.
- inventory of Rosannah Reed.
- inventory & LoD of George Chillcutt.
- inventory of Margret Manning.
- accounts of Abigail Scott administratrix of William Scott.
- accounts of Margret Harper executrix of William Harper.
- accounts of Frances Brannock & John Brannock executors of Thomas Brannock.
- accounts of John Pattison & Mary Pattison executors of St. Leeger Pattison.
- accounts of Priscilla Rumbly executrix of John Rumbly.
- accounts of Rosannah Manning administratrix of Nathaniel Manning.
- accounts of Ann Coburn administratrix of Daniel Murphy.
- accounts of Ann Coburn administratrix of Hannah Hill.
- accounts of Edward Trippe & his wife Ann administratrix of John Trippe.
- accounts of Roger Adams administrator of William Adams.
- accounts of Richard Kendall Foxwell administrator of Robert Ross.
- accounts of Ann Rumbly executrix of John Rumbly, Jr.
- accounts of Roger Adams administrator of William Oston.

- accounts of Ann Coburn administratrix of Samuel Coburn.
- accounts of Margaret Brawhorn administratrix of Thomas Brawhorn.
- accounts of Richard Perray administrator of Hugh Perray.
- accounts of Elisabeth McDaniel administratrix of William McDaniel.

31:673
- accounts of John Robson & Joseph Shenton executors of Josias Mace.
- accounts of Diana Willey administratrix of Francis Willey.
- accounts of Mary Royall executrix of Thomas Royall.
- accounts of Thomas Williams administrator of William Stevens, during minority of Edward Stevens.
- accounts of Elinor Johnson administratrix of Henry Johnson.
- accounts of Elisabeth Prockter administratrix of Hugh Prockter.
- accounts of Cahterine White administratrix of Charles White.
- accounts of Mary Rimmer administratrix of Hugh Rimmer.

11 August. Thomas Aisquith (g, SM) exhibited:
- will of Thomas Notley Goldsmith, constituting John Goldsmith, William Goldsmith, & Michael Goldsmith executors. Said executors were granted administration. Sureties: James Mills, John Maddox. Date: 3 June 1746.
- will of Margaret Alvey, constituting Joseph Alvey executor. Said executor was granted administration. Sureties: George Graves, Arthur Alvey. Date: 3 June 1746.
- will of Joseph Edwards.
- bond of Elisabeth Hopkings administratrix of Luke Hopkings. Sureties: Thomas Allstone, Benjamin Reeder. Date: 3 June 1746.
- inventory of James Swann.
- inventory & LoD of William Phippard.
- inventory of Cuthbert Fenwick.
- inventory & LoD of William Billingsley.
- inventory & LoD of John Branan.
- inventory & LoD of Thomas Watts.

- inventory & LoD of Richard Hopewell.
- inventory of Timothy Joles.
- accounts of Thomas Beale & his wife Mary executrix of Richard Griffen.
- accounts of Winifred Burch administratrix of Benjamin Burch.
- accounts of Alexander Forguson & his wife Rebacca executrix of John Redman.
- accounts of Thomas Kirkley administrator dbn of Rebacca Colter.
- accounts of Thomas Pearce administrator of Elenor Pearce.
- accounts of Winifred Trepe executrix of Anthony Evens.
- accounts of Jane Chivirall executrix of Clement Chevirall.
- accounts of Edward Castor & his wife Sarah administratrix of John Redman, Jr.

31:674
- accounts of Thomas Cood one of administrators dbn of Joshua Guibert.

Exhibited from CV:
- additional accounts of Job Hunt executor of Sarah Hunt.

14 August. Mr. Peter Dent (PG) to examine additional accounts of:
- Josiah Beall & Lucy Beall executors of Virlinda Beall (PG).

15 August. Exhibited from AA:
- accounts of Benjamin Gardner executor of Thomas Mills.
- additional accounts of Richard Fowler & his wife Elisabeth administratrix of Stephen Stewart.

16 August. Exhibited from KE:
- additional accounts of John Rasin executor of Thomas Rasin.

19 August. Exhibited from BA:
- inventory of Rosannah Ogle.

21 August. Exhibited from AA:
- additional accounts of Ann & Jonathan Sellman executors of William Sellman.

23 August. Col. Gabriel Parker (CV)
exhibited:
- inventory of William Wood.
- inventory of John Griffin.
- accounts of Roseman Wilkinson administratrix of Thomas Wilkinson.
- accounts of Benjamin Elt administrator of Thomas Brittain.
- accounts of Elinor & John Dorrumple executors of John Dorrumple.
- accounts of Ann Wood administratrix of Edward Wood.

Brian Philpot & John Philpot (merchants, London) executors of
31:675 Godfrey Milner (merchant, London) executor of Isaac Milner (merchant, London) vs. Thomas White (g, BA). Sheriff (BA) to summon defendant to render answer.

Col. Gabriel Parker (CV) to examine accounts of:
- James Fraizier executor of Daniel Fraizer (CV).
- Elisabeth Fryer & John Fryer executors of Richard Fryer (CV).
- Lewis Welch administrator of Burdin Crosby (CV). Additional accounts.

25 August. Thomas Bullen (g, TA)
exhibited:
- will of Richard Grason, constituting Sarah Grason executrix. Said executrix was granted administration. Sureties: Aaron Higgs, Thomas Ray. Date: 13 July 1746.
- will of Robert Hopkins.
- will of Thomas Edward. Also, renunciation of executors.
- bond of Ann Davis administratrix of John Davis. Sureties: Thomas Bruff, Francis Armstrong. Date: 6 August 1746.
- bond of James Buckley & his wife Rachel administratrix of Isaac Edwards. Sureties: William Anderson, William Buckley. Date: 25 July 1746.
- bond of Rachel Thompson administratrix of Thomas Thompson.

Sureties: Abner Dudley, Abner Turner. Date: 27 June 1746.
- bond of Eve MacDaniel administratrix of Daniel MacDaniel. Sureties: William Richardson, John Hutchinson. Date: 20 June 1746.
- renunciation of Kathrine Skinner on estate of her husband. Date: 4 June 1746.
- inventory of John Powell.
- inventory of Susannah Powell.
- inventory & LoD of Michael Fletcher.
- inventory & LoD of Michael Fletcher [!].

31:676
- inventory of William Tipler.
- inventory of Michael Ryan.
- inventory of Ralph Robotham.
- inventory of Elisabeth Lawes.
- inventory of Lotan West.
- inventory & LoD of Robert Bettice.
- additional accounts of Jacob Gore administrator of John Sanckston.
- accounts of Rachel Williams acting executrix of Jacob Williams.
- accounts of Hannah West acting executrix of Loton West.

Exhibited from BA:
- will of William Mattingley.

26 August. Peter Dent (g, PG) exhibited:
- accounts of Jayne MackClash administratrix of William MackClash.
- additional accounts of John Child & his wife Elisabeth executors of Ann Demiliane.
- additional accounts of James Kingsbury executor of Elisabeth Kingsbury.

Exhibited from BA:
- bond of Constant Petty executrix of William Mattingley. Sureties: William Mills (p, AA), John Abercromy (cordwainer, AA), Barton Rodgett (perukemaker, Annapolis, AA). Date: 26 August 1746.

29 August. Exhibited from CV:
- accounts of Samuel Austin surviving executor of Henry Austin.

Court Session: 1746

Peter Dent (g, PG) exhibited:
- accounts of Mary Anne Atcheson executrix of John Atcheson.
- accounts of John Lawrance administrator of John Williams.

1 September. Exhibited from SM:
- additional inventory of James Mattingly. Also, additional accounts of Henry Sheircliffe administrator.

31:677 Lawrence Macnemara (CH) & his wife Elisabeth vs. Mary Ann Atcherson (CH) executrix of John Atcherson (PG). Sheriff (CH) to summon defendant to render answer.

2 September. Charles Hynson (g, KE) exhibited:
- will of Christopher Hall. Also, bond of George Wilson, Jr. acting executor. Sureties: James Ringgold, Jr. (g), John Wallace (g). Date: 11 April 1746.
- will of Edward Worrell, constituting Mary Worrell executrix. Said executrix was granted administration. Sureties: Isaac Crow, Edward Worrell. Date: 24 July 1746.
- will of Roger Hicks.
- will of Nicholas Neal, constituting Mary Neal & Charles Neal executors. Said executors were granted administration. Sureties: Daniel Dattehunty (p), Hanse Hanson (g). Date: 24 May 1746.
- will of Martha Miller, constituting Samuel Miller executrix. Said executrix was granted administration. Sureties: James Ringgold, Jr. (g), Hanse Hanson (g). Date: 24 May 1746.
- will of James Greenwood.
- bond of John Green administrator of Solomon Mason. Sureties: Joseph Mason (p), William Clark (p). Date: 17 June 1746. Also, renunciation of Sarah Mason. Date: 16 June 1746. Witness: William Clark.
- bond of James Younger administrator

of John Hamilton. Sureties: Aron
Alford (p), Nicholas Lynch (p).
Date: 26 August 1746.

- bond of Rebecca Rice executrix of
William Rice. Sureties: James
Smith, William Browning. Date: 24
July 1746.
- bond of Armerell Webb administratrix
of John Webb. Sureties: John
Falconar (p), John Miers (p). Date:
9 May 1746.
- bond of Martha Browne administratrix
of William Browne. Sureties: James
Ringgold, Jr. (p), Thomas Masun (p).
Date: 24 May 1746.

31:678 • bond of Daniel Cheston administrator
of Richard Walters Sureties: Charles
Hynson (g), Walter Dougherty (g).
Date: 5 May 1746.

- inventory of Edward Holman.
- inventory of William Crow.
- inventory of Jane Ball.
- inventory of John Bennett.
- inventory of Capt. Robert Dunn.
- additional inventory of Alexander
Adair.
- inventory of Christopher Hall.
- additional inventory of William
Woodland.
- inventory of Martha Miller.
- accounts of Isaac Freeman
administrator of John Bennett.
- accounts of Thomas Carwardin
administrator dbn of Robert Key.
- accounts of George Hall executor of
Benjamin Jones.
- accounts of Thomas Crow & his wife
Sarah administratrix of George
Skirven.
- accounts of Elisabeth Quinney
administratrix of Sutton Quinney.
- accounts of Mary Massey
administratrix of William Massey.
- accounts of Simon Wilmer
administrator of Patrick
Fitzgarrold.
- additional accounts of Elisabeth
Ringgold administratrix dbn of
William Burkham.
- accounts of Katherine Woodland &
James Woodland administrators of
William Woodland.

Court Session: 1746

- accounts of James Sterling & his wife Rebecca executrix of Arthur Holt.

5 September. Exhibited from QA:
- accounts of James Harvey & his wife Mary executrix of Benjamin Elliot.

8 September. William Rogers (g, AA) exhibited:
- will of James Mackelanan, constituting Charles Connant executor. Said executor was granted administration. Sureties: William Tillard (p), Richard Simmons (p). Date: 21 July 1746.
- will of Thomas Trott.
- bond of Dorothy Steel administratrix of Ralph Steel. Sureties: Jonas Green (printer, Annapolis, AA), William Butterfield (shoemaker, Annapolis, AA). Date: 27 May 1746.
- bond of Jeremiah Covell administrator of Mary Covell. Sureties: Benjamin Hall (p), John Forrest (p). Date: 16 June 1746.

31:679
- bond of Richard Harwood & Gassaway Watkins executors of Gassaway Watkins. Sureties: John Ijams (p), William Ijams (p). Date: 12 August 1746.
- bond of Mary Ruley administratrix of Thomas Ruley. Sureties: Robert Davis (p), William Davis (p). Date: 14 July 1746.
- bond of Ray Jones administrator of George Vennam. Sureties: Benjamin Fowler (p), Joshua Jons (p). Date 6 August 1746.
- inventory of John Young.
- inventory of Abraham Simmons.
- inventory of John Joyce.
- inventory of Ralph Steel.
- accounts of Thomas Wasson, Jr. administrator of Francis Sutor.
- accounts of Sarah Joyce administratrix of John Joyce.

Court Session: 9 September 1746.

32:1
Docket:
- Sheriff (PG) to render attachment to

Court Session: 9 September 1746.

Lingan Wilson (P)G administrator of
Joseph Wilson (PG) to render
inventory.

- Sheriff (PG) to summon James Wilson
  (brother) & Henry Wright Wilson
  (nephew) of Joseph Wilson (PG,
  dec'd) to show cause why they do not
  sign inventory as next of kin.
- Thomas Sligh & Henry Morgan sureties
  on estate of Buckler Partridge (BA)
  vs. Jane Partridge administratrix
  of said dec'd. Sheriff (BA) to
  render attachment to defendant to
  render accounts.
- Stephen Bordley procurator for
  Joseph Milburn Semmes & his wife
  Rachel (CH) vs. William Cumming,
  Esq. procurator for John Smith
  Prather, Thomas Prather, & Thomas
  Williams executors of Martha
  Yoakley.
  Text of libel. Plaintiff is late
  Rachel Pottenger widow of William
  Pottenger & daughter of Thomas
  Prather (dec'd). Mentions: Jane
  <torn> (widow, PG), grandmother of
  said Rachel, made her will in 1710,
  constituting

32:2   Thomas Williams & John Prather
executors. Said Rachel was then a
minor, remanded to care of her
mother Martha Prather (then a
widow). Said Martha married Capt.
Stephen Yoakley. Mentions: Negro
Esther (woman), Negro Punch (child).
Said Stephen Yoakley departed the
Province soon after 1723, & died
soon thereafter beyond the seas.

32:3   Mentions: Samuel Hanson (sheriff,
CH),

32:4   John Cook (sheriff, PG).
Text of answer of Thomas Williams &
John Smith Prather. Mentions: will
of Jane Smith, constituting William
Prather executor, & not Thomas
Williams & John Smith Prather.

32:5   Said Rachel married William
Pottenger 18/19 years ago. Said
Martha died in October 1742.

32:6   Mentions (2 justices of PG): George
Scott, James Edmondston.
Text of answer of Thomas Prather.

Page 214

Court Session: 9 September 1746.

32:7 ...
32:8   Ruling: dismissed, with costs to defendants.
32:9

- Thomas Clark on behalf of Margaret & Susannah Clark minors & orphans of Abraham Clark (CV, dec'd) vs. John Griffen (CV). Sheriff (CV) to summon defendant to show cause why some chattel is missing from appraisal.
- Henry Hooper administrator of Rosannah Reed (DO) vs. Sarah Dodd (DO). A. Muir (sheriff, DO) to summon defendant to show cause why she conceals estate of dec'd.
- Raymond Stapleford, Charles Stapleford, & Thomas Stapleford executors of Elisabeth Taylor (DO) vs. Dorothy Gollothon (DO) & Dorothy Loockerman (DO). A. Muir (sheriff, DO) to summon defendants to show cause why they conceal estate of dec'd.
- Sheriff (SO) to summon Thomas Morrison & his wife widow of Philip Ellis (DO) to take LoA.
- S.B. for Lawrence Macnemara & his wife Elisabeth (CH) vs. Edward Dorsey procurator for Mary Ann Atcherson executrix of John Atcherson. Libel.

32:10   Mentions: Samuel Hanson (sheriff, CH). Col. Robert Hanson and/or Dr. Gustavus Brown to take answer of defendant.

- S.B. for Baptist Barber & his wife Elisabeth (SM) vs. William Cumming, Esq. procurator for Samuel & Richard Southern executors of John Johnson Southern. Libel. Gilbert Ireland (sheriff, SM) to summon defendants to render answer.
- Executors of Richard Tootel creditors to estate of Nicholas Hammond (AA) vs. William Cumming, Esq. procurator for Mary Hammond (AA) administratrix of said dec'd. William Thornton (sheriff, AA) to summon defendant to render accounts.
- Mr. John Needham who married Sarah daughter of John Abington (PG, dec'd) vs. Dr. Andrew Scott & his

Page 215

Court Session: 9 September 1746.

32:11

wife Mary executrix of said dec'd.
John Cooke (sheriff, PG) to summon
defendants to render final accounts.
Said Mary Scott is NE.

- E.D. for executors of Godfrey Milner
  (BA) vs. Stephen Bordley, Esq. for
  Thomas White. Libel. John Risteau
  (sheriff, BA) to summon defendant.
- William Cumming, Esq. procurator for
  Elisabeth Gosling widow & executrix
  of Thomas Gosling (SM) vs. William
  Fowler (SM) administrator of said
  dec'd. Gilbert Ireland (sheriff,
  SM) to summon defendant to render
  accounts. Accounts exhibited &
  balance delivered.

Court Session: 1746

32:12

9 September. Thomas Bullen (g, TA)
exhibited:

- bond of James Acres administrator of
  Thomas Edwards. Sureties: Edward
  Harrison (p), Daniel Thompson (p).
  Date: 27 August 1746.
- accounts of Russel Armstrong & his
  wife Rebecca administratrix of Moses
  Clayland.

Exhibited from SM:

- accounts of Samuel & Richard
  Sothoron executors of John Johnson
  Sothoron.

10 September. Thomas White (g, BA)
exhibited:

- will of Rachel Paca, constituting
  Peregrine Browne executor. Said
  executor was granted administration.
  Sureties: Winston Smith, William
  Smith. Date: 23 June 1746.
- will of Susannah Stokes,
  constituting Peregrine Frisby
  executor. Said executor was granted
  administration. Sureties: James
  Phillips, Winston Smith. Date: 1
  May 1746.
- will of Henry Butler, constituting
  Susannah Butler executrix. Also,
  widow's election. Said executrix
  was granted administration.
  Sureties: Peter Bond, Benjamin Bond.

Date: 16 May 1746.
- will of Cassandra Coale.
- will of John Parish, constituting Elisabeth Parish executrix. Said executrix was granted administration. Sureties: Alexander Lawson, Richard Croxall. Date: 4 June 1746.
- will of John Rattenbury. Also, bond of Philip Jones acting executor. Sureties: Thomas Harrison, Cornelius Howard. Date: 4 June 1746. Also, renunciation of Margaret Rattenbury widow & executrix (with her father). Date: 22 May 1746.

32:13
- will of William Smith, constituting Johannah Smith (BA) & Thomas Smith (Lancaster Co. PA) executors. Said executors were granted administration. Sureties: Joseph Crockett, Samuel Crockett. Date: 10 June 1746.
- will of Isaac Wright.
- will of Samuel Underwood.
- will of Thomas Beton.
- bond of Ann Cadle administratrix of Benjamin Cadle. Sureties: George York, William York. Date: 16 June 1746.
- bond of John Kelly administrator of John Nugent. Surety: William Dougherty. Date: 26 July 1746.
- bond of Mary Griffith & Solomon Hillen executors of Samuel Griffith. Sureties: Abraham Raven, Isaac Raven. Date: 7 August 1746.
- bond of William Bond, Jr. administrator of Barnett Bond. Sureties: Walter Tolley, Amos Garrett. Date: 7 August 1746.
- bond of Charles Ridgeley administrator of John Huggins. Sureties: John Stinchcomb, Nicholas Gay. Date: 6 June 1746.
- bond of Thomas Sligh administrator of Rosanna Ogle. Sureties: Robert Wilkinson, John Searjant. Date: 4 June 1746. Also, renunciation of Heighe Sollers (next of kin), recommending Thomas Sligh. Date: 3 June 1746. Witness: Edward Bowen.
- bond of Amos Garrett administrator

of Annanias Mackfadden. Sureties:
Vincent Dorsey, William Copeland.
Also, renunciation of John
Mackfadden (eldest son),
recommending Amos Garrett. Date: 29
March 1746.

32:14
- additional inventory of John Taylor.
- inventory of William Maynard.
- inventory & LoD of Edmund Howard.
- inventory & LoD of Benjamin Cadle.
- inventory of Henry Butler.
- inventory of Annanias Macfadin.
- accounts of Tobias Stansbury administrator of William Mainer.
- accounts of Kezia Taylor executrix of John Taylor.
- accounts of Ruth Howard executrix of Edmund Howard.
- accounts of John Durbin acting executor of John Durbin.
- accounts of John Hall administrator of Thomas Johnson.
- additional accounts of William Standiford & his wife Christiana administratrix of Thomas Wright.
- accounts of Mary Stokes administratrix of Humphry Wells Stokes.
- accounts of Isaac Litton & his wife Mary executrix of Thomas Jones.
- Thomas White (Deputy Commissary, BA) certified on complaint of William Andrews who married a daughter of William Bond (dec'd) that part of said estate was concealed. Depositions taken at Joppa on 4 March 1746. William Bond administrator of William Bond.
  - Sarah Bond (widow of William Bond), age 50, deposed. Mentions: Capt. William Bond.

32:15
  - Thomas Horn, age 37, deposed that he was an overseer to William Bond (dec'd) at his plantation near White Marsh. Mentions: William Taman who became overseer.
  - James Billingslye, age 34, deposed that he was an overseer to William Bond (dec'd) at one of his plantations.
  - Walter Billingslye, age 31,

32:16

deposed that he was an overseer
to William Bond (dec'd) at one
of his plantations.
- Thomas Johnson, age 50, deposed
that he is entitled to a
dividend from the estate.
- accounts of Isaac Webster
administrator of Samuel Gover.

Mr. Thomas White (BA) to examine
accounts of:
- Susanna Butler executrix of Henry
Butler (BA).
- Winston Smith & his wife Susanna
executrix of George Stokes (BA).
Additional accounts.

Gabriel Parker (g, CV) exhibited:
- inventory of William Summers.
- accounts of Elisabeth & Absalom Kent
executors of Absalom Kent.
- accounts of Grace Parker acting
executrix of John Parker.
- accounts of James Richason executor
of Mary Manors.
- accounts of Kenelm Truman Greenfield
administrator of Thomas Truman
Greenfield (SM).

Exhibited from DO:
- inventory & LoD of Benjamin Pearson.

Exhibited from SM:
- 2nd additional accounts of Stourton
Edwards administrator of John
Edwards.
- William Fowler administrator of
Thomas Gosling.

12 September. Nehemiah King (g, SO)
exhibited:
- will of John Huitt Nutter,
constituting Ann Nutter executrix.
Said executrix was grantead
administration. Sureties: George
Hardy, John Nutter.

32:17

Date: 18 June 1746.
- will of William Harper, constituting
Edward Harper executor. Said
executor was granted administration.
Sureties: James Hayman, John Hayman.
Date: 20 August 1746.

- bond of Henry Lowes administrator of Obid Wolston. Sureties: John Williams, Moses Chelley. Date: 21 August 1746. Also, renunciation of Booz Walston & Joy Walston, Jr. next of kin to Obed Walston, recommending Henry Lowes (merchant, largest creditor). Date: 15 July 1746. Witness: Samuel Tull.
- bond of William Stevens administrator of John Hutchinson. Sureties: Samuel Handy, Stephen Handy. Date: 16 June 1746.
- inventory of William Dashiell.
- inventory of Thomas Newbold.
- inventory & LoD of Robert Boyer.
- inventory of John Hutchinson.
- inventory of John Huitt Nutter.
- inventory of Mary Sturling.
- accounts of Ann Pryor administratrix of Thomas Pryor.
- accounts of Alice Dunn (alias Alice Hopkins) administratrix of Richard Dunn.
- accounts of Roase Costin administratrix of Isaac Costin.
- accounts of Elisabeth Conner executrix of John Conner.
- accounts of Teague Dickeson administrator of David Wallace.

Exhibited from CH:
- accounts of William Carter administrator of William Carter.

16 September. William Tilghman (g, QA) exhibited:
- will of John Earle, constituting Hannah Earle executrix. Said executrix was granted administration. Sureties: Edward Browne, Sr. (p, KI), James Earle (mariner). Date: 17 July 1746.
32:18 - will of Henry Price, constituting Elisabeth Price executrix. Said executrix was granted administration. Sureties: Solomon Kentin, Henry Fiddeman. Date: 28 August 1746.
- will of John Fournier constituting Rebecca Williams executrix. Said executrix was granted

administration. Sureties: William
Newnam, John Hartshorn. Date: 9
September 1746.

- bond of Rebecca Mason administratrix
of Richard Mason. Sureties: John
Scott, Edward Godwin. Date: 23 July
1746.
- bond of Charles Connor & his wife
Mary administrators of Charles
Connor. Sureties: Andrew Price,
Jr., Samuel Osborne. Date: 24 July
1746.
- bond of Rebecca Curtis
administratrix of Thomas Curtis.
Sureties: Vincent Price, Giles
Hicks. Date: 14 August 1746.
- bond of Dinah Bryan administratrix
of John Bryan. Sureties: John
Sallaway, William Rabbits, Thomas
Harvey. Date: 27 August 1746.
- bond of Thomas Merridith
administrator of Sarah Owens.
Sureties: John Ruth, John Davis, Jr.
Date: 28 August 1746. Also,
renunciation of James Everrett,
recommending Thomas Meradith.
- bond of Ursula Saunders
administratrix of William Saunders.
Sureties: John Jarman, Amos Jarman.
Date: 4 September 1746.
- bond of Margaret Richardson
administratrix of John Thompson.
Sureties: John Johnston (Scotchman),
Thomas Meloyd. Date: 4 September
1746.
- bond of Daniel Ford & his wife Sarah
administrators of James Maud.
Sureties: William Seward, William
Birch. Date: 11 September 1746.

32:19
- inventory of John Jackerman.
- inventory of Thomas Sevil.
- inventory of James Hicks.
- inventory of John Hays, Jr.
- inventory of John Evans.
- inventory of John Carman.
- inventory of John Hawkins.
- inventory of James Hamilton.
- additional inventory of Timothy
Maynor.
- inventory of Thomas Lewis.
- inventory of Thomas Williams.
- inventory of William Primrose.

Court Session: 1746

- accounts of Robert Basnet & his wife Susannah executrix & James Maynor executor of Thomas Maynor.
- accounts of Ambrose Wright administrator of John Saunders.

18 September. Exhibited from SM:
- additional accounts of John Maddox executor of Samuel Maddox.

Exhibited from SO:
- inventory of Sarah Kellam.

Exhibited from DO:
- inventory of John Hays. Also, accounts of Bartholomew Ennalls administrator.

Exhibited from AA:
- 2nd additional accounts of Ann & Jonathan Sellman executors of William Sellman.

Exhibited from BA:
- inventory & LoD of John Rattenbury.

Mr. Thomas Bullen (TA) to examine accounts of:
- Jeremiah Nicols administrator of Michael Fletcher (TA).
- John Small & his wife Sarah executrix of Henry Oldfield (TA).
- Richard Gurling Robinson & his wife Judith administratrix of John Harrison (TA).
- Mary Davis & Perry Benson executors of John Davis (TA).
- William Trippe & his wife Elisabeth acting executrix of Wollman Gibson executor of Jacob Gibson (TA). Additional accounts.
- William Trippe & his wife Elisabeth acting executrix of Wollman Gibson executor of Jacob Gibson administrator dbn of Sarah Wollman (TA). Additional accounts.
- Robert Spencer & his wife Mary administratrix of Thomas Russell (TA).

32:20 19 September. Mr. John Thompson (CE) to examine accounts of:

- John Ricketts & Thomas Ricketts executors of Samuel Jones (CE).
- Joseph Thomas & John Rickets executors of Roger Mirick (CE).
- Richard Thomas surviving executor of Margaret Nicholas (CE).
- John Kankey administrator of Johannes Sluyter (CE).

Mr. Ennalls Hooper (DO) to examine accounts of:
- Jane Brown administratrix of John Brown (DO).
- Sarah Creek executrix of John Creek (DO).
- Josias Moore administrator of John Jamison (DO).
- Ann Hill administratrix of Daniel Hill (DO).
- Betty Cole administratrix of Samuel Cole (DO).
- Sarah Vaulx executrix of James Vaulx, Sr. (DO).
- Samuel Standford executor of William Standford (DO).
- James Langrill executor of Sarah Langrill (DO).
- Alace Warren administratrix of John Warren (DO).
- Rebecca Wall executrix of Charles Staplefort (DO).
- Martha Connerly executrix of Owen Connerly (DO).
- Mary Whitacre administratrix of Joseph Whitacre (DO).
- Phillis Clarkson executrix of Robert Clarkson (DO).
- Rosannah Standford & Thomas Standford executors of Charles Standford (DO).
- Margaret Arnall & Andrew Arnall administrators of William Arnall (DO).
- Ann Tregoe & William Tregoe administrators of William Tregoe (DO).
- Ramond Stapleford, Charles Stapleford, & Thomas Stapleford executors of Elisabeth Taylor (DO).
- Thomas Hutchins & his wife Hannah executrix of Ephraham Trotter (DO).
- Solomon Hubbert & his wife Margaret

executrix of Thomas Hayward (DO).
Additional accounts.

- Adling Cannon administratrix of
  William Cannon (DO). Additional
  accounts.
- Ebenezar Vaulx & his wife Jane
  administratrix of James Harriss
  (DO). Additional accounts.
- George Smith & his wife Alice
  administratrix of Jacob Covington
  (DO). Additional accounts.
- Grace Stogdell administratrix of
  Michael Stogdell (DO). Additional
  accounts.
- Hannah Reed administratrix of
  Ezekiel Reed (DO). Additional
  accounts.
- Sarah Cannon administratrix of James
  Cannon (DO). Additional accounts.
- Sarah Morriss administratrix of
  George Morris (DO). Additional
  accounts.
- Elisabeth Cock administratrix of
  Edward Cock (DO). Additional
  accounts.
- Sarah Stinson administratrix of
  Alexander Stinson (DO). Additional
  accounts.
- Elisabeth Jones executrix of Leonard
  Jones (DO). Additional accounts.

20 September. Mr. William Tilghman
(TA) to examine accounts of:
- Valentine Henry & his wife Sarah
  administratrix of George Sparks (son
  of John, QA).

32:21   23 September. John Thompson (g, CE)
exhibited:
- will of Charles Heath. Also, bond
  of Rebecca Heath administratrix.
  Sureties: John Baldwin, Dr. John
  Jackson. Date: 11 June 1746.
- will of Henry Nowland.
- will of James Wright. Also, bond of
  Elinor Wright & James Evans
  administrators. Sureties: David
  Creswell, Thomas Thompson. Date: 20
  August 1746.
- will of David Lawson. Also, bond of
  John Lawson administrator.
  Sureties: Peter Lawson, John

Court Session: 1746

Holland.   Date: 3 September 1746.
- bond of Elisabeth Bradford administratrix of Rev. John Bradford. Sureties: John Hamilton, Benjamin Bradford. Date: June 1746.
- bond of Rebecca Heath administratrix of James Paul Heath. Sureties: Walter Dulany, Benjamin Pearce. Date: 21 August 1746.
- bond of Rachel Knight administratrix of William Knight. Sureties: Walter Dulany, Benjamin Pearce. Date: 21 August 1746.
- inventory of Thomas Reynolds.
- inventory of Samuel Savin.
- inventory of John Bellarmine.
- inventory & LoD of Archibald Steel.
- accounts of John Savin, Jr. executor of Samuel Savin.
- additional accounts of John Stockton & his wife Elisabeth administratrix of Sigefridus Aldricks.
- accounts of Susanna Vandegrift administratrix of Nicholas Vandegrift.

Mr. Charles Hynson (KE) to examine accounts of:
- John Green administrator of Bowles Green (KE).
- Elisabeth Hickman & Henry Truelock administrators of John Hickman (KE).
- Elisabeth Miller administratrix of Nathaniel Miller (KE).
- Katherine Simpson administratrix of Thomas Simpson (KE).
- Collin Farguson executor of Robert Dew (KE).
- Oliver Caulk, Isaac Caulk, & Jacob Caulk executors of Mary Pearse (KE).

Mr. Thomas Aisquith (SM) to examine accounts of:
- Kenelm Boult, Edward Hilfard, & Ann Boult executors of Thomas Boult (SM).
- Athanasius Notingham administrator of Stephen Notingham (SM).
- Rachell Green executrix of John Green (SM).
- Peter Mugg & his wife Ann administratrix of Mathew Vowles

(SM).

32:22 Mr. John Thompson (CE) to examine accounts of:
- James Stevenson administrator of Robert Walker (CE).
- Margaret Alman executrix of Abraham Alman (CE).
- William Mackie & Samuel Walker executors of Hugh Walker (CE).
- James Foster & John Foster executors of William Foster (CE). Additional accounts.

Mr. Peter Dent (PG) to examine accounts of:
- Mary Wade & Zachariah Wade executors of Zacharia Wade (PG).
- Alexander Nolton & his wife Anne administratrix of Henry Jones (PG). Additional accounts.

Mr. Walter Hanson (CH) to examine additional accounts of:
- Walter Scott administrator of James Scott (CH).

25 September. Exhibited from KE:
- bond of John Galloway administrator of Richard Lux. Sureties (AA): Joseph Cowman (g), Samuel Galloway (g). Date: 25 September 1746.

Petition of Alex. Fraser. Edward Holmes (dec'd) was indebted to petitioner. Edward Holmes, Jr. took LoA. Bond on said estate assigned to petitioner.

GENERAL INDEX

(no surname)
    Abigail 195
    Christopher 190

Abbott
    John 67
    Samuel 28, 170, 205
Abell
    Edward 126
    John 158
    Samuel 158
Abercromy
    John 210
Abington
    John 84, 203, 215
    Sarah 203
Able
    Cuthbert 108
Ackworth
    Mary 9, 22
Acres
    James 216
Acwortt
    Thomas 22
Adair
    Alexander 16, 50,
       79, 212
    Christian 16, 50,
       79
Adams
    Elin 54
    John 155
    Luke 88
    Morgan 54, 124, 125
    Richard 54
    Roger 123, 124, 206
    Sarah 171
    Summer 54, 204
    Sumner 125
    Thomas 171, 176,
       204
    William 10, 46, 54,
       92, 124, 176,
       206
Adamson
    John Baldwin 85,
       98, 201
    Lucy 85
Addams

Roger 179
William 172, 173,
   179
Adkins
    Isaac 95
Adkinson
    Ann 150, 201
    John 150, 152, 201
Agway
    Richard 27
Airey
    Thomas 175
Airs
    Jacob 12
Aisquith
    Elisabeth 90
    George 158
    Thomas 10, 14, 16,
       28, 30, 32, 42,
       46, 48, 82, 86,
       89, 98, 108,
       116, 140, 142,
       150, 153, 154,
       158, 162, 168,
       169, 170, 188,
       194, 207, 225
    William 10, 47
Alcock
    Burton Wood 172
    Joanna 172
Aldrecks
    Sigefredus 193
Aldricks
    Sigefridus 225
Alexander
    Araminta 103, 105,
       179, 181
    John 161, 163
    Moses 9
    Paul 26, 94
    Thomas 161
    William 105, 115,
       161, 166, 179
Alford
    Aron 212
    Edward 7
    Joseph 122
    Mary 7
Allcock
    Burtonwood 205

Allen
Catherine 65
Francis 128, 147
Joseph 64
Mary 128
William 65
Alley
John 200
Allnutt
James 1, 40, 51
Sarah 1, 33, 40, 51
William 1, 112
Allstone
Thomas 207
Alman
Abraham 165, 226
Margaret 165, 226
Almesby
Sarah 197
Almsby
Sarah 180
Almsley
Sarah 184
Alney
John 48
Alricke
Elisabeth 77
Sickfredus 77
Alricks
Elisabeth 127
Sickfredius 168
Sigfredus 127
Alston
John 42, 105
Alstone
Drayden 194
John 38
Thomas 194
Alsworth
Isabella 112
Michael 112
Alvey
Anthony 142
Arthur 207
John 83
Joseph 207
Margaret 207
Amery
Samuel 148, 163, 199
Anderson
Alexander 10, 46
Henrietta 10, 46
John 86, 204

Michael 3, 14, 27
William 115, 161, 209
Anderton
John 90, 122
Andrew
Richard 204
Andrews
Alice 68, 69, 71, 84, 111
John 83
Stephen 65
William 45, 218
Ange
John 15
Anger
John 53
Annis
William 72
Ansil
William 21
APrice
Ann 82
Edward 82, 90
Eliza 83
Thomas 83
Archibald
John 77, 127
Ardery
Rachel 28
William 28, 61, 191
Argoe
Joseph 174
Armstrong
Ann 15, 93
Edward 3, 15, 93, 165
Francis 61, 132, 137, 209
John 106, 117, 185, 186
Rebecca 155, 194, 216
Russel 194, 216
Russell 155
Susannah 117
Thomas 157
Arnall
Andrew 223
Margaret 223
William 223
Arnatt
Andrew 173
Jonathan 175

Margaret 173
William 173
Arnitt
William 206
Ash
Thomas 64
Ashfield
Elisabeth 125
Eliza 99
John 99, 125
Askin
Vincent 148, 164,
166
Askings
William 109
Askins
William 140
Asten
Eleanor 188
Atcherson
John 199, 211, 215
Mary Ann 199, 211,
215
Atcheson
John 86, 185, 211
Mary Anne 211
Atchison
John 100, 150, 180
Mary Ann 100, 180
William 72
Atkinson
John 147
Michael 102
Thomas 102, 117
Auld
John 132
Aulthors
John 126
Austin
Henry 29, 138, 210
Samuel 84, 138, 210
William 29, 176
Austins
Henry 167
Aydelott
John 94
Ayres
Henry 129, 166
John 129

Badard
Ann 78, 181
Richard 78, 128,

181
Baddard
Anne 202
Richard 202
Badley
John 95
Richard 124
Samuel 95
Bagley
Drayden 89
Samuel 89, 126, 194
Bailey
John 45
Baker
Elisabeth 10
Eliza 47
Grace 117, 193
James 131, 177
Jane 131, 177
John 10, 46, 47,
117, 147, 193
Baldwin
John 3, 45, 180,
189, 224
Mary 45
Thomas 36
Baley
George 88
Ball
Benjamin 91, 92,
125
Elisabeth 91, 92,
125
Jane 78, 212
Ballard
Henry 8, 136
Baning
Charles 86, 164
Banks
Margaret 24
William 156
Banning
William 102
Barber
Baptist 116, 134,
202, 215
Elisabeth 116, 202,
215
Eliza 134
George 16, 54, 81
Barnard
Charles 144
Barnes
Abraham 48, 49, 158

Barbara 3
Ford 146
Godshall 164
Henry 3, 149, 164
Matthew 59, 164,
    188, 199
Thomas 149, 188
William 28, 42, 83
Barnett
James 65
Phebe 27
Thomas 27, 65
Barrock
John 190
Barrs
Aaron 1
Thomas 1
Barry
Andrew 93
Barton's Hope 105
Barwick
Edward 121
John 47
Rosannah 161
William 121, 161,
    190
Bashaw
Giles 110
Basnet
Robert 186, 222
Suanna 186
Susannah 222
Batchelder
Elisabeth 105
Batcheldor
John 86, 104, 190
Baton
Murdoc 188
Batson
Ann 90
John 90
Battee
Elisabeth 111
Ferdinando 111, 133
Samuel 111
Battson
John 152
Baxter
William 162
Bayard
James 189
Peter 92, 127
Baynard
Elisabeth 76, 80,

    117
Eliza 52
John 52, 76, 80,
    117, 161
Beach
Clement 69, 70
Beachamp
Elisabeth 11, 55
Robert 11, 55
Beale
Mary 150, 170, 208
Thomas 150, 170,
    208
Beall
Alexander 36, 64,
    141
John 19, 73
Joseph 2
Joshua 4
Josiah 97, 208
Lucy 97, 208
Mary 4
Ninian 36, 141
Robert 2
Samuel 97
Virlinda 19, 73,
    97, 208
William 36, 141
Bean
John 108, 140, 194
Mary 108, 194
Beanes
William 17
Beans
John 140
Beard
Lewis 135
Beaseley
Jeffery 35
Beastin
Thomas 165
Beauchamp
Turpin 176
Beavan
Blanford 49
Beazley
Elisabeth 77, 127
Jeffery 77
Jeffry 127
Beck
Ann 87
Matthew 87
Bedard
Mary 27

Beetle
  William 3
Bell
  Adam 69
  Christian 36
  Isaac 78, 132, 148
  John 36
  Katherine 89
  Middleton 198
  Moses 89
  Robert 13
Bellarmin
  John 178
  Mary 178
Bellarmine
  John 225
Bellos
  Francis 53
Belt
  Jeremiah 194
Bennett
  Edward 8, 96, 136
  Eliza 162
  George 8, 96, 136
  John 162, 212
  William 15, 18, 47,
    67
Bensford
  James 63
Benson
  Perry 222
Benston
  Alexander 5
  George 20, 25
  Thomas 92
Bernard
  Luke 131
Berry
  James 189
  Margaret 29
  Sarah 189
  William 51
Berwick
  James 187
Bessicke
  Absolom 69
Bessicks
  Absolom 128
Beton
  Thomas 217
Bettice
  Robert 190, 210
Bickam
  Francis 123

Bickham
  Francis 177
Biggs
  John 64
Billings
  James 11, 100, 124,
    131
  Katherine 9
Billingsley
  Bowles 28
  William 207
Billingsly
  Bowles 194
  Rachel 194
  William 169
  William Sumner 169
Billingslye
  James 218
  Walter 218
Birch
  Thomas 64
  William 221
Birckhead
  Christopher 47, 67
  Eleazar 57
  Eleazer 100
  Johanna 100
  John 57
  Nehemiah 57, 58,
    133
  Solomon 88, 116
Bird
  Arabella 160
  David 191
Birkhead
  Eleazar 57
  Joanna 57
  John 129
  Nehemiah 129
Bishop
  Elisabeth 66, 88,
    167
  Eliza 140
  Robert 66, 88, 167
  Roger 140
Bissco
  James 169
Black
  Alexander 31
Blackiston
  John 14
  Thomas 14
Blackston
  Thomas 141

Blackstone
  Richard 130
  Thomas 130
Blake
  John 93
  John Say. 43
  Philamon Charles 43
  William 73
Blanchet
  Henry 21
  John 21
Blanchett
  Henry 89
Bleuer
  James 75
Bleuett
  Thomas 160
Blewer
  James 160
  Margaret 160
Blewett
  John 95
Blewitt
  John 128
Blizard
  Richard 69
Blumfied
  James 90
Blunt
  Samuel 155, 160,
    183
Blyzard
  Richard 95
Boarman
  Francis Ignatius
    20, 37
  Ignatius 137
  James 20
Boddy
  Elisabeth 3
  Stephen 2, 3
Bold
  William 98, 127
Bolton
  Elisabeth 13, 52,
    76, 118, 150
  James 118, 150
  John 65
Bond
  Ann 45
  Barnett 217
  Benjamin 216
  John 126, 142, 169
  Joseph 54

Peter 216
Sarah 218
William 126, 217,
  218, 219
Zachariah 89, 169
Bonner
  Francis 36, 165
Booker
  John 47
Boon
  Abraham 29
  James 201
  Joshua 17
  Margaret 185, 187
  Moses 29
Boone
  Benjamin 121, 187
  Humphry 90, 101,
    114
  Jacob 121
  James 121
  Phebe 121
Booth
  William 42
Bordley
  Stephen 23, 24, 58,
    59, 68, 134,
    195, 214, 216
  Thomas 18, 119
Boswell
  John 26, 37
  Mary 21
  William 21
Bouchell
  Peter 93
Bouchelle
  Peter 165
Boulding
  Richard 36
  William 19, 36
Boult
  Ann 140, 225
  Kenelm 140, 225
  Thomas 140, 170,
    225
Bounds
  Joseph 75, 96
Bounton
  Joseph 28, 61, 62
  Thomas 28, 62
Bourdillon
  Benedict 77, 79,
    144
  Jannette Janssen 77

Bowden
    Jasper 13, 29, 43
Bowdle
    Loftus 179
Bowen
    Benjamin 63, 72
    Edward 217
    James 33, 156, 192
    John 11, 20, 63
    Mary 11
    Samuel 63
    Whittington 26, 147
Bowie
    Allen 49, 51, 64
    James 51, 86, 202
    John 51
    Priscilla 49, 64
    Thomas 51, 202
Bowley
    Daniel 106
    Elisabeth 106
Bowy
    John 17
Boyce
    Roger 48, 71, 138
Boyd
    Abraham 11
    George 142, 170,
        194
    Margaret 142
Boyer
    Robert 191, 220
    Sarah 191
Boyle
    James 93
Bozman
    Risdon 157
Bradburne
    William 158, 170
Bradford
    Benjamin 225
    Elisabeth 155, 183,
        225
    Eliza 141, 160
    John 141, 155, 160,
        183, 225
    Mr. 183
Bradley
    Charles 43
    Henry 11
    Richard 54
    William 11, 54
Brady
    Sarah 146

Terrance 146
Brahon
    Thomas 91
Bramble
    Elisabeth 205
    John 11
    Mary 11
    Thomas 205
Branan
    John 207
Brandon
    John 57
Brandt
    Ann 139, 164
    Randolph 125, 139,
        164
Brannock
    Frances 91, 178,
        206
    John 91, 178, 206
    Thomas 11, 55, 91,
        124, 178, 206
Bratten
    Hugh 202
    Rebeckah 202
Bratton
    Rebecca 5
Brawhan
    John 123
Brawhorn
    John 171, 205
    Margaret 171, 179,
        207
    Thomas 171, 176,
        179, 207
Brawner
    Elisabeth 20
    Henry 20, 37
    John 51, 87, 150
    Mary 87, 150
Brayfield
    John 37, 98, 125
Bredell
    James Stephen 78
Breeden
    James 188
    Thomas 188
Breeding
    Matthew 89, 187
Breeman
    Catherine 70, 95
    James 5, 70, 95
    Katherine 5
Brent

Ann 89
Jane 164
Randolph 89
William 26, 37,
    164, 188
Brereton
    Richard 20, 25, 31,
      142, 153, 159,
      183, 195, 196
    Thomas 20, 25, 31,
      142, 153, 159,
      183, 196
Brerewood
    Thomas 17, 31
    William 17, 18, 31
Brett
    George 99, 125
    Richard 21, 99,
      125, 138
Brewer
    John 85
    William 64
Brickhill
    Elisabeth 180, 184,
      196
Bright
    Mary 118, 150
    Matthew 204
    William 118, 150
Brightwell
    Eliza 35
    Richard 35
Brinkley
    James 33
Briscoe
    Elisabeth 116, 141
    John 12, 37, 83
    Mary 12, 37
    Philip 116, 141
Bristow
    William 127, 165
Brittain
    Thomas 80, 138, 209
Brittingham
    Isaac 94
Broadess
    Abraham 174
Broadway
    Sarah 18
Brohon
    Thomas 122
Brome
    Thomas 80, 203
Bronam

John 169
Brooke
    Ann 15, 51
    Baker 188
    Basil 88
    Isaac 97
    James 84, 203
    John 1, 203
    Leonard 15, 51
    Lucy 97
    Martha 203
    Mary Ashcom 56,
      130, 152
    Richard 20, 97,
      137, 188
    Roger 1
    Thomas 97, 185
    Walter 56, 130, 152
Brown
    Adam 116, 154
    David 41
    Francis 31, 44
    George 72
    Gustavus 194, 215
    Isaac 173
    Jane 173, 223
    John 164, 168, 173,
      176, 223
    Joseph 173
    Letitia 27
    Margaret 194
    Matthew 27
Browne
    Adam 88
    Anthony 82
    Charles 151
    David 8
    Edward 88, 89, 102,
      220
    Elisabeth 56, 118
    Gabriel 72
    James 82
    Jane 2
    John 85, 148
    John Elliott 56,
      118
    Letitia 14
    Martha 212
    Matthew 14
    Morgan 119
    Penelope 148
    Peregrine 216
    Rachel 89
    Susannah 30

Thomas 8
William 82, 212
Browner
  John 139
  Mary 139
Browning
  John 16, 53
  Rachel 16, 53
  William 212
Bruff
  Richard 189
  Thomas 132, 209
Brumley
  Nicholas 19, 64
Bryan
  Daniel 12, 37
  Dinah 221
  Frances 12, 37
  John 221
Bryant
  Daniel 119, 146,
    170
Bryon
  Henry 109
Buchanan
  George 129
  James 151
Buckham
  William 99, 120,
    193
Buckingham
  Henry 115
Buckinham
  Henry 104
Buckland
  William 52
Buckley
  James 209
  Rachel 209
  Richard 29, 102,
    117
  William 190, 209
Bullen
  John 99
  Thomas 9, 15, 17,
    18, 19, 27, 28,
    31, 43, 47, 61,
    62, 67, 74, 86,
    88, 94, 104,
    107, 115, 118,
    132, 137, 139,
    154, 155, 157,
    158, 161, 164,
    170, 178, 179,

189, 191, 194,
  209, 216, 222
Bullock
  John 11, 55
  Margaret 55
Buncle
  Alexander 25, 94,
    95, 128, 201,
    202
Bunt
  Amos 181, 184, 197
Burch
  Benjamin 89, 126,
    170, 208
  Justinian 148
  Thomas 148, 163
  Winefred 89
  Winifred 170, 208
Burdus
  Richard 18, 31, 68,
    69
Burgess
  Elisabeth 56, 107,
    154, 199
  Henry 61
  John 56, 111, 199
  Samuel 10, 56, 107,
    149, 154, 199
  Thomas 61
Burk
  David 53
  James 53
  Richard 77
  William 163
Burkham
  William 212
Burle
  John 90, 101, 114,
    117, 133, 141
Burman
  Ann 67
  Samuel 58, 67, 85
Burn
  James 140
  Michael 140, 158
  Patrick 149
  Priscilla 140
Burne
  James 22
  T. 140
Burnett
  Peter 136
Burt
  Henry 121

Burton
 John 78, 94, 147, 202
 Joshua 94, 95
 William 65, 70, 94, 95, 147
Busey
 Hezekiah 162
 John 150
 Samuel 150
 Sarah 150, 169
Bussell
 John 13, 30
 Margaret 13, 30
Bussey
 Hezekiah 142
 Rachel 142
Butcher
 Edmond 27
 Edmund 62
 William 27, 62, 145
Butler
 Ann 13
 Henry 2, 216, 218, 219
 John 64, 73, 138
 Susanna 219
 Susannah 216
 Thomas 13, 52, 76
 William 64, 138
Butt
 Richard 51, 64
Butterfield
 William 213
Byrd
 Thomas 21
Byrn
 Patrick 187
Byus
 Elisabeth 95
 Eliza 130, 177
 William 91, 95, 130, 177

Cadell
 John 37
Cadle
 Ann 217
 Benjamin 217, 218
Cahell
 Edmund 7
 Mary 7
Calder

James 165, 180
Caldwell
 John 193
 Joshua 135
 Mary 193
 Robert 22, 166, 202
Calk
 Elisabeth 74
 Lawrence 159, 171
 Mary 159, 171
 Peter 74
Callaway
 Joseph 75
Camper
 John 61, 159, 171
Campling
 Henry 175
Campton
 William 148
Camron
 Anthony 120
 Finley 29
Candle
 David 17
Canner
 Ann 121, 177
 Edward 121, 124, 177
 Thomas 121
Cannon
 Adling 54, 131, 177, 224
 Henry 122
 James 122, 124, 131, 177, 224
 John 172
 Joshua 203
 Sarah 122, 131, 177, 224
 William 54, 55, 122, 124, 131, 177, 203, 224
Cantwell
 Edward 45
Carawon
 John 92, 124, 131, 177
 Mary 91, 131, 177
 Matthew 92
 Patrick 204
Carbery
 John Baptist 158
Carey
 Dennis 7, 11

William 28
Carlett
    John 108
Carman
    John 185, 200, 221
    Rachael 200
    William 29, 187
Carmichael
    John 109
Carpenter
    John 45, 58
    William 163
Carr
    Francis 121
    John 60, 69, 81,
       189, 198
Carradine
    Ann 112, 121
    John 112, 121
Carrer
    Andrew 66, 76
Carroll
    Charles 20
    Dominick 45
    James 20, 149, 199
Carslake
    John 31, 61, 86,
       137
Carter
    James 7
    John 43
    Mary 6, 7
    Valentine 102
    William 64, 88,
       125, 149, 200,
       220
Cartwright
    Matthew 140
    William 23
Carvil
    John 58
Carvill
    John 4, 19, 24, 38,
       58
    Phebe 58
Carwarden
    Abraham 163
    Thomas 163, 170
Carwardin
    Thomas 212
Case
    James 29
Casel
    John 48

Sarah 48
Castor
    Edward 170, 208
    Sarah 170, 208
Caton
    Thomas 18, 31
Catrop
    Lemmon John 190
Catterton
    Michael 1
Caulk
    Eliza 47
    Isaac 66, 225
    Jacob 66, 225
    Oliver 66, 225
    Peter 47
Cawsey
    Thomas 91
Cawthren
    William 22, 60
Chamberlain
    Edward 174
    Samuel 168
Chambers
    James 35
    John 87
    Richard 23, 39, 41,
       59, 161, 191,
       192
Chandler
    William 26, 37
Chaplin
    James 154
Chapman
    John 187, 199
    Margaret 187
    Mary 187
    Richard 164, 188,
       199
Chapple
    James 118
Chase
    Richard 86, 152
Chauncey
    George 7, 22, 60
Cheiverell
    Clement 108
    Jane 108
Chelley
    Moses 220
Cheney
    Agnes 84
    Charles 84, 100,
       118

Thomas 30, 84
Chesley
    Robert 158
Cheston
    Daniel 38, 59, 212
Cheverell
    Clement 126
Chevirall
    Clement 208
Chew
    Joseph 67
    Mary 49
    Samuel 49
Chieverell
    John 29
Child
    Elisabeth 210
    John 210
Chillcutt
    Anthony 176
    George 176, 206
    Sarah 176
Chivirall
    Jane 208
Chocke
    George 32
    John 32
Christian
    James 163
Chunn
    Andrew 64, 148,
        199, 200
    John 28, 64, 73,
        148, 199, 200
    Richard 64, 148,
        149
    Samuel 141, 149
Cissell
    John 83
    Sarah 83
    William 83
Civil
    Thomas 187
Clark
    Abraham 71, 106,
        151, 153, 159,
        160, 171, 183,
        196, 200, 215
    Benjamin 79
    Elisabeth 48, 83,
        159, 171
    James 48, 83
    Jane 52
    John 88, 188

Leonard 83
Margaret 151, 153,
    159, 183, 196,
    215
Race 128
Robert 48, 83
Sarah 28
Susanna 151, 153,
    160, 183
Susannah 67, 196,
    215
Thomas 28, 151,
    153, 159, 183,
    196, 215
William 67, 78, 211
Clarke
    Benjamin 52
    George 141
    John 78
    Joshua 52, 76, 80,
        117
    Thomas 11, 91
    William 28, 74
Clarkson
    Elisabeth 203
    Phillis 223
    Robert 203, 206,
        223
Clavey
    John 152
Clay
    Thomas 120
Clayland
    Moses 18, 43, 155,
        194, 216
    Rebecca 18
Clayton
    Benjamin 156
    Edward 187
Claywell
    Lucretia 147, 202
    Peter 69, 95, 147,
        166
    Selby 69
    Thomas 5, 40
Clements
    Isaac 35, 50, 98,
        128
    Jacob 164
    Richard 73
Clift
    Henry 187
Clifton
    John 171, 191

Thomas 123
William 171
Climps
Thomas 9
Clocker
Daniel 83
Clough
Nathaniel 187
Cloyd
Robert 113, 150
Clubb
John 72, 89, 149,
200
Matthew 72, 149,
200
Coale
Cassandra 217
Thomas 13, 106, 109
Coburn
Ann 122, 178, 179,
206, 207
Samuel 122, 177,
178, 207
Cock
Edward 92, 125, 224
Elisabeth 92, 125,
224
Cockran
John 92, 168
Cockrin
James 18
Coffen
Thomas 4
Coffer
John 12, 37
Cole
Betty 173, 223
Elisabeth 176
Francina 99, 120
John 108, 166, 176,
205
Peter 99, 120
Richard 176
Samuel 173, 206,
223
Coleman
Joyce 17
Martha 88
Mordecai 65
Thomas 17, 88, 125,
149, 200
Collam
Sarah 109
Collier

Peter 201
Collings
Elisabeth 54
Patrick 54
Samuel 22, 39, 41,
59
Collins
Andrew 78
James 3
John 14, 43
Mary 14, 29
Richard 14, 43
Samuel 9, 161, 192
Thomas 14, 30
William 94, 95
Collison
Elisabeth 74
Colston
Henry 18
James 18
Colter
Rebacca 208
Rebecca 150, 170
William 152
Colvill
Thomas 127
Comegys
Cornelius 87
Edward 87
Commerford
Peter 189
Compton
Thomas 112
Condle
David 49, 64
Elisabeth 49, 64
Connant
Charles 213
Robert 133
Connell
James 89
Conner
Elisabeth 220
John 220
Connerly
Martha 173, 223
Owen 173, 206, 223
Thomas 173
Connor
Arthur 185, 197
Charles 221
Elisabeth 110, 193
John 67, 109, 136,
193

Margaret 185, 197
Mary 221
Phillip 2
Contee
  Alexander 5
  Jane 5
Cood
  Thomas 208
Coode
  Thomas 38, 39, 46,
    82, 140, 170
  William Gerrard 90
Cook
  Hercules 43
  John 68, 214
  Thomas 82, 169
  William 50, 93
Cooke
  John 39, 81, 134,
    182, 195, 198,
    216
  Thomas 3
Coombs
  William 14
Cooper
  Amelia 155
  Basil 83, 188
  Frances 139, 155,
    191
  Gabriel 12, 42
  John 34, 35, 36,
    100
  Richard 119, 134,
    143
  Thomas 12, 41, 42,
    155
  William 125, 139,
    155, 191
Copeland
  William 218
Copsey
  William 110, 193
Cornish
  Evan 205
  Samuel 205
Coster
  John 112, 138, 169,
    192
  William 112, 169,
    192
Costin
  Henry 29, 157, 186
  Isaac 147, 148,
    193, 220

Rebecca 157
Richard 157
Roase 220
Rose 148, 193
Cotman
  Joseph 96
Cotrell
  Andrew 17
Cotter
  William 17
Cottman
  Ebenezar 41
  Joseph 22, 136
  Nathaniel 41, 75,
    136, 147
  William 22
Counsill
  Henry 201
Countiss
  Peter 200
  Rebecca 200
Couran
  John 1, 150
Coursey
  James 66
  John 66
  William 187
Courson
  Thomas 11, 55
Courts
  John 89, 149, 164
Covell
  Jeremiah 213
  Mary 213
Coventon
  Henry 121, 140
  Jacob 124
  John 140
Covington
  Alice 91, 131, 177
  Henry 43, 65
  Jacob 91, 131, 177,
    224
  John 43
  Leonard 38, 64
  Priscilla 38, 64
Coward
  John 157
Cowman
  Joseph 49, 226
Cox
  Albert 36
  Edward 3
  William 7, 178

Coyle
   Elisabeth 20
Crackson
   James 28, 141
Cragg
   Thomas 6
Craig
   William 15, 93
Cramplin
   John 17
Crandall
   Francis 57, 67, 85,
      152
   Joseph 67
Cranford
   Thomas 203
Cranfurd
   David 100
Crawford
   David 17, 35
Craxon
   John 149, 164
Creagh
   Patrick 57, 84
Creek
   John 124, 176, 223
   Sarah 124, 223
Creswell
   David 224
Critchett
   William 27
Crittchett
   John 27
Crocket
   Gilbert 56
Crockett
   Gilbert 72
   Joseph 217
   Samuel 217
Crompton
   Mary 71
   Thomas 71
Crosby
   Burden 13
   Burdin 209
Crouch
   Isaac 8
   Joseph 182
   Mary 182
   William 2, 65
Crow
   Isaac 163, 211
   James 32, 39, 45,
      134, 155, 156

John 32, 39, 45,
   121, 134, 143,
   153, 155, 156
Juda 155
Judith 32, 39, 121,
   134, 143, 153
Sarah 15, 79, 162,
   212
Thomas 15, 79, 162,
   163, 212
William 163, 212
Croxall
   Richard 217
Crudgenton
   Roger 103, 156
Cruickshanks
   Christopher 21
Crupper
   Ann 52, 76
   Thomas 52, 76
Cullen
   William 167
Cullenbur
   Thomas 147
Cullens
   John 29, 30
   William 92, 114,
      125, 155, 160,
      180, 183, 184,
      196, 197
Cullinbur
   Thomas 138
Culver
   Henry 2
Cumming
   Magdalen 164
   Robert 164
   William 23, 30, 38,
      39, 57, 58, 59,
      68, 105, 134,
      214, 215, 216
Cunningham
   Daniel 119
   John 113, 149
Cunninghame
   John 163
Curlott
   John 162
Currant
   Ann 105
Current
   Ann 81
Currier
   John 93

Curtis
    Avarilla 45
    Benjamin 45
    Rebecca 221
    Thomas 221
Cutchin
    Robert 141
    Winifred 141
Cutler
    Ann 162
    William 162, 189

Daffin
    George 10
    Susannah 10
Daft
    Elisabeth 98, 127
    Matthew 108
    William 98, 127
Daggens
    Daniel 28
Dailey
    James 151
    John 2, 133, 157
Dale
    John 26
Daley
    John 151
Dallam
    Richard 146
    William 146
Dallas
    Walter 79
Dant
    John 14
Darnall
    H. 23
    Henry 12, 17, 97,
        133, 135
    John 97
Dashiel
    Matthias 135
Dashiell
    Esther 75, 110, 136
    George 75, 110,
        136, 160, 195
    Isabell 191
    Jessey 135, 191
    Joseph 96, 191
    Matthias 110, 146
    Mitchell 96, 196
    Priscilla 42
    Robert 75, 110, 136

Sarah 42
William 135, 191,
    220
Dattehunty
    Daniel 211
Davidge
    Azell 48
Davie
    Ann 24, 30, 32, 38,
        39, 59, 69, 81,
        98, 101, 102,
        114
    John 24, 38
Davis
    Allen 23
    Ann 209
    Benjamin 78
    Ishmael 69
    John 58, 61, 151,
        190, 209, 221,
        222
    Jonathan 23
    Margaret 25, 70
    Mary 222
    Richard 9, 51, 164,
        165
    Robert 213
    Ruth 51, 165
    Susannah 200
    Thomas 20, 113,
        128, 151, 185
    William 5, 25, 70,
        141, 144, 153,
        213
Davison
    Elisabeth 180
    John 180, 201
Dawkins
    James 40, 51
    Mary 40, 51
    William 1, 33, 80
Dawson
    Impey 15, 62, 74,
        104
    James 15, 62, 74
    John 180
    Mary 15, 62, 74
    Ralph 104
    Richard 123
Day
    Edward 72
    Francis 57
    John 72
    Matthias 16, 53,

Page 242

87, 99, 120
Nicholas 66, 88,
140, 167
Deak
John 34
Deakins
John 98, 113
Priscilla 98, 113
Deal
Agnes 118
John 118
Richard 33
Deale
James 44, 111, 133
Dean
Charles 95, 110,
191
Edward 205
Elisabeth 95
James 43
John 205
Mary 43
William 123
Deane
James 75
Dee
James 13
Mary 13
Deen
Elisabeth 7
John 7
Deford
Jacob 29, 52
Richard 106
Dehortee
William 26
Delihay
Thomas 15, 44
Demall
Mary 62, 63, 133
Demiliane
Ann 210
Dennin
John 128
Dennis
Daniel 26
Elisabeth 12, 26,
70, 78, 136, 147
John 26, 95, 134,
135, 136, 147,
191, 196
Lazarus 26
Wheatley 12, 70, 78
Dent

Peter 12, 15, 16,
19, 26, 34, 38,
49, 51, 56, 63,
73, 85, 86, 87,
97, 98, 100,
113, 118, 130,
131, 139, 150,
152, 165, 168,
180, 185, 186,
198, 199, 201,
208, 210, 211,
226
Denune
William 51
Denver
Richard 146
Derrickson
William 94
Devan
Thomas 33
Devene
Edmund 64
Devenish
Ishmael 106
Rachel 106
Rebecca 106
Deveron
Eleanor 63
Deverson
Humphry 97, 150
Dew
John 71
Robert 120, 145,
193, 225
Dick
James 18, 44, 57,
58, 65, 110, 111
Dickenson
Ann 129, 139
Daniel 171
Stephen 112, 129,
139
Dickerson
Ann 80
Stephen 80
Dickeson
Teague 96, 135,
193, 220
Dickinson
Daniel 171
Henry 171
James 51
John 171
William 161, 171

Dickson
    James 142
    John 194
Digges
    Charles 19
    Edward 36
    Ignatius 26
    Nicholas 26
    William 26
Dillon
    Lawrence 47
    Rebecca 47
    Richard 5, 25
Disharoon
    John 128, 147
    Levin 128, 201
    Rebeckah 201
Disharoone
    Lewis 128
Disney
    William 56
Dixon
    Benjamin 80, 117
    Christopher 10, 13
    Ellis 105, 138
    Gerrard 105
    John 44
    Mary 10, 13
    Obed 80, 138
Dobson
    Isaac 18, 132
Dockery
    Thomas 102
Dodd
    Sarah 181, 184,
        197, 215
Dodson
    John 154
    Robert 132, 155,
        171
    Walter 26, 37
Dolby
    William 5
Donaldson
    Jane 107
    Patrick 107
    Thomas 57
Doncastle
    John 25, 73, 118,
        138
Donoho
    John 5
Donohoe
    Daniel 5

Doran
    Patrick 47, 143
Dorman
    Nehemiah 41
Dorrumple
    Elinor 33, 193, 209
    John 1, 33, 80,
        193, 209
Dorsey
    Caleb 31, 57, 71,
        85
    Edward 31, 71, 134,
        182, 195, 215
    Henry 77
    John 57, 182
    John Hammond 72
    Joshua 31, 85
    Richard 71
    Vincent 72, 218
Dorumple
    John 106
Dossey
    James 1
    Philip 192
Dotson
    James 156
Dougherty
    Ann 37
    Walter 37, 212
    William 217
Doughterty
    Walter 37
Douglas
    Eliza 157
Douglass
    Archibald 50
    John 157
    Mary 50
    Thomas 21
Dove
    Rachel 191
    Richard 191
Downes
    Benjamin 149
Downs
    John 157
Doyne
    Ann 29
    Joshua 29
Drane
    Elisabeth 34
    James 34
Draper
    William 124

Dreaden
  William 109
Dreddon
  David 191
Driskell
  Moses 95
Driver
  Martin 80, 105, 117
  Matthew 124
Drummond
  Francis Thurrowgood
    41, 42
Drury
  Charles 57, 87,
    154, 182, 184
  George 167, 181,
    184, 197
Dudding
  William 43
Dudley
  Abner 161, 210
  Mary 104
  Richard 104
  Samuel 104
  Thomas 104
Duff
  Alexander 92, 93
  Simon 58, 99
Duffey
  Sarah 166
Duggens
  Daniel 158
Duggins
  Daniel 90
Dulany
  Walter 225
  William 102, 117,
    152
Dulen
  John 157, 190
  Mary 190
Dulin
  John 105, 115, 159
  Mary 115, 159
Dunahane
  Cornelius 59
Dunaly
  Daniel 112
Dunbar
  James 38, 39, 46,
    82, 170
Dunn
  Alice 95, 168, 220
  James 163

  Richard 95, 110,
    168, 220
  Robert 163, 212
Dunnahow
  Cornelius 38
Durbin
  John 120, 134, 143,
    153, 159, 167,
    183, 218
Dutton
  Robert 72
Duvall
  Elisabeth 49
  Mareen 49
  Marren 12
  Martha 6
Dyer
  William 86
Dyson
  Abigail 99, 125
  James 99, 125
  Joseph 148
  Mary 101
  Thomas 96, 101

Earle
  Hannah 220
  James 220
  John 220
  Joseph 52, 133,
    137, 151
  Michael 189
Ebernathy
  Ann 118
Ebernethy
  Ann 26, 73, 138
Ebtharp
  Thomas 3
Eccleston
  Charles 173
  Elinor 171
  Hugh 171
  John 171
  Thomas 171
Edelen
  Christopher 169
  Edward 164
Edelin
  Christopher 86
  Philip 149
Edgar
  Henry 54, 92, 125
  Ruth 54, 125

Samuel 111
Edge
  Margaret 7
  Thomas 7
Edgell
  Benjamin 173
Edger
  Henry 92
  Ruth 92
Edmondson
  Elisabeth 173
  John 165, 190
  Margaret 165, 190
  Solomon 6
  William 173
Edmondston
  James 41, 214
  Jane 41
Edmundston
  James 97
Edward
  Thomas 209
Edwards
  Ann 84
  Cadwallader 84, 85,
    184
  Edward 107
  Isaac 209
  John 43, 49, 219
  Joseph 169, 207
  Stourton 43, 90,
    219
  Thomas 216
Egan
  George 37
  Susannah 37
Eilbeck
  William 20
Elder
  John 114
Elgin
  George 16
  Susannah 16
Elliot
  Benjamin 213
Elliott
  Benjamin 102, 117
  George 187
  John 43, 65, 184
  Joseph 43
  Mary 102
  Susanna 184
  Susannah 43
Ellis

Alice 9
Owen 131
Philip 181, 184,
  197, 215
Robert 6
Ellt
  Benjamin 33, 66, 80
Ellwood
  Martha 19, 36
  Richard 19, 36
Elt
  Benjamin 209
Elzey
  John 9
Emerson
  John 97
  Philip 91
Emory
  William 157
England
  Sarah 27
English
  James 85
Ennalls
  Bartholomew 122,
    222
  Betty 172
  Henry 95, 131, 177
  J. 174
  John 172
  Joseph 95, 131,
    172, 174, 177
  Thomas 122, 172
Ensor
  John 44
  William 62
Esdell
  Thomas 58
Estep
  Joseph 97, 101,
    103, 162
Euart
  James 25
Eubanks
  George 132
Evan
  Ebineazer 78
  Sophia 78
Evans
  Anthony 46, 90, 170
  Ebeneazar 70
  Ebenezar 94
  Edward 84
  Elias 94

Gammage 78
Henry 37
James 224
John 22, 41, 51,
    141, 144, 150,
    151, 153, 157,
    159, 221
Jonathan 157
Philip 16, 47
Rowland 40, 99,
    143, 144, 153,
    159
Sophia 70
Evens
Anthony 208
Everrett
James 221
Ewart
James 202
Ewing
Alexander 98
Nathaniel 98
Exley
John 18

Fagin
Mercillas 9
Fairbrother
Nathaniel 67
Falconar
John 212
Falkner
Isaac 104
Fanning
John 162, 189
Mary 162
Fardery
Mary 82
Nicholas 83, 170
Fargason
Duncan 180
Farguson
Alexander 170
Colin 193
Collin 225
Rebecca 170
Farmer
Gregory 146
Mary 146
Peter 146
Farthing
James 10, 46
Fassitt

John 94
Mary 26, 40, 131,
    148
Rous 148, 192
Rouse 26, 94, 131
William 94, 166,
    192
Feddeman
Richard 157
Fell
Edward 48
William 79, 166
Fendall
Elisabeth 105
Fenwick
Benjamin 158
Cuthbert 158, 207
Enock 90
John 90
Robert 158
Ferguson
Collin 120
Fiddeman
Henry 220
Field
Bartholomew 35
Mary 48, 83
Sarah 35
William 48, 83
Fielder
Jane 82
William 90
Williams 82
Finch
William 49, 64
Fish
Thomas 142
William 61
Fisher
Henry 175
John Pritchet 123
Joseph 6, 82, 101,
    132
Mark 92, 114, 125,
    155, 160, 167,
    180, 181, 183,
    184, 196, 197
Matthew 146
Sarah 6
Fitzgarril
Patrick 119
Fitzgarrold
Patrick 212
Fitzgerald

Patrick 170
Fitzpatrick
    David 61
Fitzsimons
    Nicholas 18
Fleming
    Pearce 67
Fletcher
    Michael 210, 222
    Sarah 5, 75, 148
    Thomas 5, 147
Flintham
    William 63
Flower
    William 109
Forbes
    Dryden 23, 150,
        153, 189
    John 23
Forbush
    Mary 50, 53, 79,
        107, 120
Ford
    Daniel 221
    Peter 109
    Robert 30
    Sarah 221
    Thomas 187
    William 29, 65, 85
    Winefred 29
Foreman
    John 145
Foresith
    Thomas 5
Forguson
    Alexander 208
    Rebacca 208
Forrest
    John 213
    William 84
Fortune
    Henry 29, 66, 76
Foster
    James 19, 36, 168,
        226
    John 19, 35, 36,
        168, 226
    Rigby 190
    William 19, 36,
        168, 226
Fottrell
    Edward 10
Fountain
    Marsey 193

Mary 193
Nicholas 110, 193
Fouracres
    John 29
Fournier
    John 220
Fowke
    Gerrard 163
    Sarah 163
Fowkes
    Sarah 188
Fowler
    Benjamin 213
    Elisabeth 110, 127,
        208
    Eliza 20
    Henry 127
    Richard 20, 110,
        208
    William 89, 194,
        216, 219
Fox
    Nathaniel 18, 28
Foxwell
    Richard Kendall 91,
        131, 178, 206
    Thomas Adams 54
Fraizer
    Daniel 105, 147,
        209
    James 105
Fraizier
    James 209
Franklin
    Edward 147
    Jacob 67
    John 111
    Ruth 10
    Thomas 10, 96
Fraser
    Alex. 226
Frashier
    John 146
Frazer
    Ann 49, 64
    John 49, 63, 64
Freeland
    Robert 71, 129, 147
    Sarah 71, 129, 147
Freeman
    Archable 80, 139
    Isaac 162, 212
    James 21, 156, 179
    Jennet 21

Freestone
  Mary 145
French
  Otho 84
  Zerobabel 145
Frisby
  Elisabeth 77, 127
  Peregrine 45, 77,
    128, 133, 216
Froggel
  Jane 37
  Robert 37
Froggit
  Jane 16
  Robert 16
Fryer
  Elisabeth 156, 209
  John 156, 209
  Richard 156, 169,
    209
Furgoe
  Alexander 140, 158
  Mazolin 140

Gailshiott
  Lawrence 35
Gaither
  Alexander 111
  Benjamin 13, 62
  Edward 13, 62
  Henry 13, 62
  John 13, 62
  Samuel 13, 62
  Sarah 13, 62
Gale
  Benjamin 98, 127
  George 75
  John 75, 120
  Levin 30, 77
  Matthias 75
  Milcah 75
  William 185, 197
Galloway
  James 6, 55, 92,
    125
  John 49, 226
  Priscilla 34
  Richard 10, 103,
    107
  Samuel 226
  Sarah 107
  Sophia 11, 107
  William 6, 34, 55,

  92, 125
Gambell
  Abraham 122
Gamble
  Abraham 171
Gant
  Thomas 194
Gantt
  Edward 71
Ganyott
  Charles 90, 126
  Elisabeth 90
Gardiner
  Clement 188
  Elenor 188
  Ignatius 149
  John 20, 26
Gardner
  Benjamin 10, 13,
    111, 208
  Ephraim 60
  Henry 28
  Ignatius 166
  John 28, 60, 103,
    111
  Robert 117
  Wilfred 28
Garford
  Charles 156
Garner
  John 21
Garnett
  Joseph 78
Garrett
  Amos 217, 218
Gary
  William 61
Gass
  William 6
Gassaway
  Henry 152
  John 44, 152
  Nicholas 179
  Sarah 152
  Thomas 143, 152
Gay
  Nicholas 7, 72, 217
  Nicholas Ruxton
    146, 167
Geary
  Laurence 112
  Mark 111, 112
Gentle
  George 73

George
    Joshua 165, 189
    Robert 78
Ghiselin
    Reverdy 25
    William 24, 25, 47
Gibbens
    John 82
    Martha 82, 90
    Thomas 150
Gibbony
    John 77, 127
Gibson
    Alice 142, 194
    Jacob 222
    John 142, 194
    Richard 156
    Wollman 222
Giddens
    Morris 18, 28, 104, 115
Gilbert
    Michael 7
    William 201
Giles
    Jacob 146, 155, 167
    Richard 28, 105
    William 21, 135
Gillett
    John 70
    William 70
Gilligan
    Bryan 8
Gillis
    Thomas 135
Gilmore
    Edward 47
Gist
    Christopher 52
    Richard 3, 52
Gittings
    Thomas 72
Givan
    Robert 8, 22
Glanville
    Stephen 145
Glascock
    James 20
Glasgow
    Patrick 94, 201
Glover
    Samuel 50
Godfrey
    Ann Merida 26, 27, 78
    Ann Merrida 70
    Charles 27, 40, 70, 78
    George 88, 113, 188
    Joseph 27, 78
Godwin
    Edward 156, 221
    Mr. 157
Goff
    Peter 190
Goldsborough
    Howes 204
    John 189
    Nicholas 185, 197
    Rosanah 204
    William 161
Goldsbury
    Thomas 80
Goldsmith
    John 207
    Michael 207
    Thomas Notley 207
    William 207
Goley
    Thomas 188
Gollothon
    Dorothy 181, 184, 197, 215
Goodman
    Margaret 57
    Richard 36, 57, 110, 111
Goodrick
    Edward 164
    Francis 164, 199
    Mary 164
Goodwin
    Jacob 119
Gordon
    George 185, 198
    Robert 46, 105
    Thomas 17
Gore
    Jacob 67, 154, 210
Gorslyn
    John 122
Gorswick
    Nicholas 45
Gosle
    Mary 193
Goslee
    James 135, 147, 193
    Mary 136

Gosling
  Elisabeth 194, 216
  Thomas 89, 90, 194,
    216, 219
Gott
  Robert 7
  Walter 87
Gough
  John 33, 50, 106
  Joseph 74
  Mary 86, 126
  Peter 10, 46
Govane
  William 111
Gover
  Ephraim 84, 85
  Philip 84, 85
  Samuel 84, 143,
    203, 219
Gowtee
  Andrew 6
  John 54
Grace
  Alice 43
  Nathaniel 43, 61
Graham
  Comfort 173
  George 173
Granan
  James 188
Granger
  John 3
Grantham
  William 167, 181,
    184, 197
Grason
  Richard 209
  Sarah 209
Graves
  George 142, 207
  John 142
  Margaret 142
Gray
  Andrew 122, 204
  Ann 99, 113
  Dorcas 4
  Dorcus 34
  Jacob 123, 177
  James 199
  John 4, 34, 99,
    112, 113
  Joseph Cox 114,
    129, 177
  Rachel 177

Rosannah 114, 129,
  177
Sarah 22
Thomas 105, 156
William 22, 41
Graylis
  Owen 11, 55
  Timothy 6, 11, 55
Greaves
  George 108
  John 82, 170
  Thomas 108
Green
  Bowles 78, 120,
    144, 225
  Charles 14, 16
  John 78, 126, 142,
    144, 211, 225
  Jonas 84, 213
  Josias 47
  Leonard 149, 200
  Prudence 149, 200
  Rachel 126
  Rachell 225
  Valentine 30
  William 17, 35, 100
Greenfield
  Ann 140
  Gerard Truman 150
  James 200
  Kenelm Truman 89,
    202, 219
  Martha 56, 130,
    150, 200
  Nathaniel Truman
    169
  Thomas Truman 23,
    89, 126, 140,
    202, 219
Greenhough
  Thomas 190
Greenwell
  Mary 86, 127
  Thomas 86, 127
Greenwood
  Daniel 27
  James 211
  William 29
Gregory
  Edward 121
  John 121, 152
Gresham
  John 162
  Richard 119

Griffen
    Charles 46, 98
    James 158
    John 153, 160, 200,
        215
    Mary 46
    Richard 46, 83,
        150, 170, 208
Griffin
    Charles 127
    Elisabeth 192
    James 73
    John 71, 123, 151,
        176, 183, 192,
        196, 209
Griffith
    Charles 52, 53, 99,
        113, 145
    Frances 176
    George 11, 55
    John 88, 89
    Lewis 176, 206
    Martha 133, 135
    Mary 11, 55, 217
    Matthew 88
    Rachel 88
    Samuel 146, 217
    Sarah 52
Grimes
    Eliza 13
    William 13
Groome
    Amy 51, 63, 73, 185
Groves
    Issitt 2
    John 21
    Joseph 2
    Matthew 21
Grugun
    Ann 46
    Paul 46
Guibert
    Jane 38, 39
    Joshua 14, 39, 46,
        82, 141, 170,
        208
    Matthew 38, 39
Guichard
    Diana 103, 156
    Mark 103, 156
Gunbey
    John 161
Gunby
    James 136, 194

John 136, 194
    Sarah 136
Guy Williams
    John 18, 28
Guythers
    Thomas 188

Hacker
    Charles 41
Hackett
    Theophilus 122
    Thomas 55, 123
Haddaway
    William Hebb 104
Hadden
    John 20
Haddock
    John 108
Hadock
    Ann 5
Hagar
    William 72
Haile
    Thomas 21, 99, 139,
        149
Hall
    Abraham 89
    Andrew 93
    Ann 15, 117, 134,
        143, 153, 195
    Avarilla 75, 106
    Benjamin 213
    Christopher 15, 16,
        53, 99, 120,
        211, 212
    Cuthbert 145
    David 53
    Edward 17, 23, 38,
        56, 67, 75, 103,
        106
    George 15, 144,
        145, 162, 212
    Henry 67
    James 23, 38, 203
    John 4, 15, 45, 53,
        56, 67, 72, 111,
        117, 159, 218
    Mary 23, 38
    Parker 7
    Phenix 196
    Robert 26, 70, 132,
        155, 171
    Rosetta 145

Page 252

Sarah 64
Spence 26, 70
Thomas 64, 89
William 111, 142
Hallaran
Erasmus 190
Hambleton
Charles 4, 34
Elisabeth 4, 34
Philemon 62, 86,
157
William 62, 86
Hamblin
Francis 192
James 36, 73, 199
Hamersley
Francis 36, 88,
125, 200
Mary 88, 200
William 88
Hamill
John 100
Hamilton
James 185, 187, 221
John 57, 63, 187,
212, 225
William 26, 60, 187
Hamm
Abraham 35
Esther 35
Hammett
John 108
Hammond
John 56
Mary 36, 57, 202,
215
Mordecai 57
Nicholas 36, 57,
85, 202, 215
Philip 57
Thomas 57
Thomas John 56
William 167
Hampton
Mary 96
Hanbury
John 58
Hand
Peter 198
Handling
John 143
Handy
Isaac 75, 110
Jane 110

John 77, 110, 136
Samuel 220
Stephen 220
Hanson
Hanse 16, 47, 50,
79, 211
John 22, 60, 113,
199
Margaret 16, 47, 79
Robert 12, 37, 215
Samuel 134, 214,
215
Sarah 7, 22, 60
Walter 5, 12, 13,
16, 19, 20, 25,
36, 48, 59, 64,
71, 72, 73, 88,
98, 112, 118,
125, 126, 138,
139, 148, 149,
163, 166, 187,
188, 192, 199,
200, 226
William 149
Hardekin
Matthew 91, 161
Hardesty
Henry 138
Thomas 33, 66
William 66
Hardie
William 1, 33, 106
Hardikin
Edward 122
Harding
Elisabeth 170
Henry 170, 190
Robert 190
Hardisty
Thomas 1, 180, 203
William 180, 203
Hardy
George 22, 96, 148,
161, 219
James 41
Hargaton
Edward 173
Mary 11
Matthew 11, 55
Harper
Edward 94, 219
John 50, 54, 93,
192
Margaret 122, 178

Margret 206
Mary 94
William 3, 6, 15,
  44, 85, 122,
  177, 178, 206,
  219
Harrington
  Jane 19, 62
  John 27, 67
  Joseph 19, 62
  Richard 6, 19, 62,
    82, 101, 121,
    132
  Thomas 77, 81
  William 19, 62, 67
Harris
  Benjamin 67
  Benton 4, 5, 12,
    21, 26, 27, 40,
    69, 70, 78, 94,
    128, 129, 131,
    136, 147, 166,
    181, 201
  Frances 8, 12, 42
  George 4
  Henry 115
  James 79, 87, 91,
    124, 131, 177,
    193, 194
  Jane 131, 177
  Jean 91
  Matthias 87, 193
  Philip 96
  Richard 8
  Samuel 71
  Sarah 68
  W. 58
  Walter 182
  William 4, 8, 12,
    34, 41, 42, 71
Harrison
  Edward 154, 216
  James 56, 72
  John 104, 115, 154,
    171, 222
  Judith 115
  Mary 56, 72, 104
  Richard 67, 68
  Samuel 68
  Sarah 32, 67
  Thomas 87, 217
  William 115, 171
Harriss
  James 224

Hart
  Charity 53
  Elinor 55
  John 15, 53
  Katherine 15
Hartshorn
  Elisabeth 181
  John 181, 198, 221
Harvey
  James 213
  John 78, 128
  Martha 78
  Mary 213
  Newman 33, 71
  Richard 174, 206
  Thomas 221
  William 174
Harwood
  Peter 62, 86
  Rebecca 11, 55
  Richard 213
  Susannah 62, 86
Hassett
  Dinah 81
  Michael 80, 147
Hatch
  John 112, 199
Hatcheson
  Sarah 163
Hatton
  Elisabeth 48, 73
  George 37, 48, 73
Hawk
  John 3, 155
Hawkins
  Alexander 73
  Deborah 156
  John 156, 186, 221
  Sarah 99, 126
  Thomas 20, 99, 126
Hayman
  James 219
  John 219
Haymond
  John 85, 201
Hays
  Charles 168
  John 102, 187, 221,
    222
  Nathaniel 51, 168
  Sarah 187
  Thomas 51
Hayward
  John 6, 11, 55, 92,

125
  Margaret 121, 131,
    177
  Sarah 6, 92, 125
  Thomas 121, 124,
    131, 177, 224
Hayword
  John 55
Hazeldine
  Francis 15, 43
  Jane 15, 43
Heath
  Charles 224
  James Paul 3, 127,
    225
  Rebecca 224, 225
Heather
  Ephraim 94, 128,
    147
Hebb
  Edward Hilliard 90,
    140, 162
  Thomas 90
  William 90
Hedge
  William 81
Heighe
  James 80, 114, 130
Hellen
  John 24
  Peter 66, 169
  Susannah 169, 203
Henderson
  Ja. 197
  Jacob 6
  John 27, 40
  Mary 6, 133
  Robert 96
  Sarah 27
  Thomas 70, 133
Hendrick
  Catharine 176
  William 176, 206
Hennekin
  Elisabeth 125
  Eliza 98
  Matthew 98, 125
Hennes
  David 63, 64
Henry
  Sarah 224
  Valentine 224
Henton
  Allen 26, 37

Henward
  John 100
Herbert
  Elinor 77, 96
  James 49, 51
Hewes
  John 27
Heyden
  George 14
Hickman
  Elisabeth 144, 225
  John 145, 163, 225
Hicks
  Anne 187
  Giles 187, 221
  James 185, 187, 221
  Levin 96, 121, 204,
    205
  Roger 211
  Thomas 91, 175
  William 136
Higgens
  John 117
Higginbotham
  Charles 63
Higgins
  William 190
Higgs
  Aaron 138, 209
  Thomas 154
Highter
  John 99
Hilfard
  Edward 225
Hill
  Ann 172, 183, 223
  Clement 4
  Daniel 172, 205,
    223
  Elenor 183
  Elinor 120, 134,
    143, 153, 159
  Elisabeth 202
  Hannah 122, 176,
    206
  Hutten 147, 202
  Hutton 132, 147
  John 153
  Joseph 61, 68, 69,
    107
  Patience 97
  Rebecca 5, 27
  Sarah 107
  William 97

William Stephen 5,
    27, 70
Hillary
    John 63
Hillen
    Solomon 217
Hinderson
    Charles 137
Hindman
    Jacob 91, 161, 190
Hine
    Arabella 30, 98
    Joseph 30, 39, 98
Hines
    Arabella 32, 39,
        59, 69, 81, 101,
        102, 114
    Benjamin 52, 76
    Joseph 32, 39, 59,
        69, 81, 101,
        102, 114
    Thomas 4, 52
Hinesley
    Charles 29
    Nathaniel 76
Hitch
    Solomon 22
Hix
    Patience 109, 136
    William 109
Hobbs
    Absolom 8, 10, 42
    Joy 8, 10, 42
    Mary 9, 42
    Mercillas 10, 42
    Thomas 9, 42, 126
Hodgson
    Rowland 5
    Solomon 127
Hodson
    Charles 91
    John 122, 124, 125,
        172, 177
    Roger 122
Hoggard
    Andrew 2
Hogins
    Elisabeth 3, 93
Holland
    Benjamin 12, 70, 78
    Col. 39
    Elisabeth 59, 129
    Francis 88, 142
    Jacob 130

John 225
Margaret 168, 169
Richard 168
Susanna 88
Susannah 116, 142
Thomas 59, 71, 129,
    147
William 1, 28, 39,
    59, 150
Hollingsworth
    Mary 65, 144, 157
    Vincent 65, 144,
        157
Hollingworth
    Vincent 102
Hollis
    William 30
Holly
    John 97
    Thomas 97
Hollyday
    Catherine 80, 139
    Ja. 183, 198
    James 160, 196
    Leonard 44, 130
    Mary 68, 158
    Rebecca 70
    Thomas 44, 130
    William 68, 158
Holman
    Edward 52, 145, 212
Holmes
    Edward 226
    John 18
    Richard 65
    William 18
Holston
    William 128
Holt
    Arthur 79, 213
Holthun
    John 35
Holton
    George 50, 93
    Mary 50, 93
Hook
    William 69
Hooker
    Thomas 72
Hooper
    Ennalls 65, 90, 91,
        92, 95, 96, 100,
        114, 121, 130,
        171, 178, 203,

223
Grace 6, 125, 206
Henry 6, 7, 96,
    121, 174, 175,
    181, 184, 197,
    215
James 172
William 6, 55
Hope
    George 73
Hopewell
    Elisabeth 158
    Hugh 90, 158, 188
    Richard 30, 158,
        208
Hopkings
    Elisabeth 207
    Luke 207
Hopkins
    Alice 220
    Benjamin 18
    Gerrard 36, 57, 67
    John 57, 94, 128,
        202
    Joseph 189
    Margaret 56
    Philip 57
    Richard 57
    Robert 209
    Samuel 57, 69, 190
Horn
    Thomas 218
Horner
    George 8, 22, 96,
        136
    Martilda 8, 96, 136
    Nicholas 87
    Robert 148
Horney
    James 31
    Solomon 137
Horsey
    Hannah 10, 42
    John 109, 136
    Nathaniel 95
    Rachel 109
    Sarah 41
    Smith 8
    Stephen 8, 10, 42
Howard
    Ann 21, 89, 125,
        166, 184
    Anne 199, 200
    Cornelius 217

Edmond 146, 192
Edmund 167, 218
Eliza 22
Henrietta 48, 83
Ignatius 19
James 21, 48, 83
John 8, 16, 22, 37,
    42, 96, 136,
    179, 182
John Grinef 182
Michael 44
Penelope 19
Philip 143
Rebecca 16
Rebeccah 37
Ruth 167, 179, 182,
    192, 218
Samuel 143
Sarah 8, 96, 136
Thomas 22, 184
William 140
Howell
    Thomas 67, 175
Howerton
    John 192
Howison
    Anne 199
Hubbart
    Humphrey 7
    Titus 7
Hubbert
    Margaret 223
    Solomon 223
Hudson
    John 4, 92, 172
    Mary 166
    Richard 166
    Samuel 166
Hues
    John 167
Hufington
    John 41, 109
Huggins
    John 217
Hughes
    Mary 4
Hughs
    Catherine 204
    John 7, 181, 184,
        197, 204
Hugoe
    Ann 35, 98
    Israel 35, 98
Hukil

Page 257

Daniel 166

Hull
Daniel 145
David 19, 144
Elisabeth 158
Meverell 158

Hungerford
Benjamin 80
Elisabeth 66, 118,
147
James 66, 106, 118,
147
Thomas 89

Hunt
Job 30, 80, 208
John 44
Sarah 30, 33, 208
Thomas 5

Hunter
Mary 188
Walter 55, 92, 125
William 188

Hupper
Grace 173
Henry 173
John 173

Hurdle
Robert 88

Hurley
Roger 205

Huston
James 3

Hutchings
Hannah 176
James 4
Thomas 4, 43, 175,
176
Thomas Elliott 4

Hutchins
Burridge 1
Elisabeth 1, 4, 34
Francis 4, 34
Hannah 223
John 15, 44
Thomas 223

Hutchinson
John 189, 210, 220

Hutson
Richard 202

Huxler
David 201

Hyland
Nicholas 93

Hynson

Charles 3, 15, 19,
24, 38, 47, 50,
52, 58, 62, 66,
77, 78, 79, 87,
99, 107, 112,
119, 130, 139,
144, 146, 162,
170, 186, 193,
202, 211, 212,
225
Phebe 24, 38, 58
Thomas 145
William 58, 145,
163

Ijams
John 213
William 213

Inch
John 143

Ingalls
Thomas 98, 127

Ingram
Peasley 10

Insley
Andrew 204

Ireland
Gilbert 142, 215,
216
Thomas 179, 203
William 203

Jackerman
Ann 121
John 121, 198, 221

Jackson
Edward 139
Henry 139
John 14, 36, 102,
141, 224
Joshua 135, 136
Thomas 135
William 29

Jaco
Thomas 73

James
Howell 127
John 114, 130
Margaret 114, 130

Jameson
John 172

Jamison

John 223

Jane
   Thomas 113

Janes
   Thomas 10, 46

Jarboe
   Henry 14
   Ignatius 86, 127
   Monica 86, 127
   Peter 14, 86, 127

Jarman
   Amos 221
   Ann 128
   George 69
   John 40, 70, 221
   William 27, 40,
     128, 166

Jarrold
   Samuel 58

Jarvis
   Philip 2

Jemison
   John 205

Jenckins
   John 166

Jenings
   Ariana 18
   Bartholomew 103
   Edmond 18

Jenkins
   Ann 38, 39, 59, 71,
     89
   Edward 60
   George 188
   John 60
   Joseph 14
   Margaret 138, 149,
     200
   Mary 14
   Samuel 190
   Susannah 38, 39, 59
   Thomas 38, 39, 59,
     71, 73, 89, 161
   William 138, 149
   Willianm 200

Jennings
   Thomas 129

Johns
   Benjamin 1, 71
   Richard 45, 155,
     179
   William 11, 55

Johnson
   Affradozi 69
   Albert 65
   Alexander 15
   David 12, 42
   Edward 178
   Elinor 171, 179,
     207
   Eliza 53
   Ezekiel 7, 32, 54
   George 48, 99, 125
   Grace 86, 127
   Hannah 9
   Harman 172
   Henry 171, 176,
     179, 207
   James 190
   Jeremiah 4, 34
   John 20, 114, 140,
     158
   Peter 86, 127, 140
   Priscilla 7
   Robert 7, 32
   Thomas 72, 106,
     218, 219
   William 53, 128

Johnston
   Archibald 24
   John 221
   Rebecca 24

Joles
   Timothy 208

Jones
   Arthur 114, 130
   Benjamin 144, 162,
     212
   Caesar 81
   Charles 34
   Daniel 91
   David 161
   Edward 34, 63, 151,
     185, 199
   Eleanor 199
   Elianor 34
   Elisabeth 54, 76,
     92, 125, 224
   Evan 170
   Francis 104
   Henry 49, 64, 76,
     226
   James 75, 91, 96,
     193
   John 22, 85, 161,
     174, 190
   Jonathan 167
   Joseph 188

Leonard 54, 55, 92,
   125, 224
Lewis 18, 86, 104
Mary 53, 156, 188
Michael 17, 97
Mitchel 135
Morgan 182
Peter 53
Philip 87, 217
Rachel 55, 92, 125
Ray 213
Robert 77
Samuel 168, 223
Sarah 75, 193
Susanna 182
Thomas 160, 167,
   174, 218
William 58, 77, 97,
   126, 133, 135,
   160, 174, 206
Jons
  Joshua 213
Jordan
  Justinian 46
Jordon
  Alexander 15, 44,
    105
  Margaret 15, 44,
    105
Jowles
  Dryden 23
  Henry Peregrine 23
  Kenelem Greenfield
    189
  Kenelm 23
  Kenelm Greenfield
    150, 154
  Mary 23
  Rebecca 23
  Sibella 23
Joyce
  Anne 203
  John 84, 213
  Sarah 84, 213
  Thomas 203
Jump
  Van 151
Jumpe
  Benjamin 151
  Susannah 151
  William 151, 186

Kankey

John 127, 165, 178,
   223
Keach
  James 73
Kearney
  John 103
  Rachel 103
Keedle
  John 2
Kellam 41
  John 21, 110
  Sarah 21, 110, 222
Kelld
  Thomas 104
Kellet
  Edward 112, 199
Kelley
  Ann 2, 133
  Bryant 113, 194
  Edmond 133
  Edmund 2
  Joseph 113
  Katherine 4
  Margaret 78
  Mary 113
  Patrick 92
  Sylvester 4
Kelly
  John 217
  Mary 194
Kemp
  Baldwin 201
  John 167
  Mathew 195
  Matthew 22, 117,
    134, 135, 143,
    153, 159, 183,
    196
  Rachel 117, 195
Kenelm
  Greenfield Jowles
    28
Kennard
  John 66, 79, 107,
    120, 145, 163
  Richard 16, 54, 81
  Sarah 66, 79, 107,
    145
Kennerley
  Margery 7
  Thomas 7
Kennet
  Bridgett 94
  Martin 94

William 94
Kennett
   Martin 128, 166
   William 201
Kenney
   Alice 42
   John 42
Kenslaugh
   John 52
Kent
   Absalom 112, 219
   Absolam 186
   Absolom 156
   Elisabeth 112, 186,
     219
Kentin
   Solomon 151, 220
Kersey
   Jane 137
   John 31, 137
Key
   Elinor 1
   Mary 79
   Philip 39, 49, 82,
     100, 101, 134,
     158
   Richard Ward 142,
     162
   Robert 53, 79, 163,
     212
Keyberd
   Thomas 163
Keys
   Robert 170
Kidd
   William 40, 63
King
   Benjamin 106, 130,
     138
   Capel 186
   Capell 71
   Charles 10, 47, 158
   Ephraim 160
   John 172
   Nehemiah 8, 9, 12,
     21, 23, 30, 41,
     75, 76, 95, 96,
     97, 109, 110,
     135, 146, 148,
     160, 161, 168,
     191, 193, 194,
     219
   Richard 163, 188
   Robert 95

Thomas 85
Kingsbury
   Elisabeth 42, 62,
     210
   James 42, 62, 210
Kininmont
   Samuel 104, 138
Kinnimont
   Ambrose 47
   Catherine 47
Kirby
   David 18
   Elisabeth 9, 28
   Matthew 9, 28
Kirkland
   William 61
Kirkley
   Thomas 150, 170,
     208
Kirkwood
   John 49
Kirshaw
   James 1, 105
Knight
   John 50, 53, 93
   Rachel 225
   Richard 53
   Stephen 87
   William 3, 14, 19,
     35, 45, 50, 77,
     92, 98, 127,
     139, 167, 178,
     225
Knott
   George 48, 83
   Nathaniel 151
Knotts
   James 43
   Nathan 151
Knowles
   John 116
Knox
   James 45, 93
   Jane 45, 93

Lacey
   Margaret 60
   William 60
Lackey
   Alexander 22
   Ann 22
Lackie
   Alexander 12

Ann 12
Lacy
    Margaret 46
    William 45, 46
Lafee
    Lewis 75, 106, 186
    Sarah 75, 106, 186
Laking
    Abraham 31, 103
    Martha 31, 103
Lamaster
    John 89
    Joseph 89
Lambden
    John 152
    Thomas 42, 94
Lambdin
    Ann 121
    John 121
Lancaster
    Joseph 166, 199,
        200
Lane
    Joseph 142, 144,
        153, 154
    Timothy 102, 117,
        198
Lang
    John 74, 81, 101,
        114
Langnall
    George 91
    James 91
Langrill
    James 175, 223
    John 175
    Sarah 175, 206, 223
Langsdall
    William 75
Langston
    Judah 41
    William 41, 148,
        161
Larkin
    Jeremiah 166
Larwood
    John 76
    Mary 76
Lathbury
    Arthur 166
Lathinghouse
    Mary 181
    William 181
Lawes

Elisabeth 190, 210
    Panther 160
Lawrance
    John 35, 211
Lawrence
    John 19
Lawrensin
    Lawrence 165
Laws
    William 95
Lawson
    Alexander 88, 96,
        217
    David 224
    George 93, 193
    John 164, 224
    Peter 224
Layton
    Charles 11
    John 176
    Nichollson 11
    William 11
Lazenby
    Amy 157
    Henry 157
Leach
    Ambrose 1, 33
    James 1
    Mary 1, 33
    William 33, 112
Leak
    John 46
    Mary 47
    William 37, 47
Leake
    John 10
    Mary 10
    William 10
Lecompte
    Anthony 15, 47, 67
    Catherine 47, 67
    Charles 175
    Katherine 15
    Nehemiah 175
    Philemon 174
Lee
    Ann 25, 65
    Arthur 25, 65, 105
    Elisabeth 105
    Francis 11
    Hancock 105
    Henry 40, 51
    John 32
    Lettice 105

Philip 5, 17, 58,
     60, 69, 70, 71,
     105
Phillip 5, 11
Richard 89, 105
Robert 40, 51
Samuel 32, 142
Thomas 11, 58, 60,
     69, 70, 102,
     105, 157
Leech
  Rebecca 187
  Richard 187
Leftwich
  Thomas 113
Legoe
  Sarah 32
  Thomas 32
Lemaster
  Christian 24
  John 24
Lenard
  John 31, 62
  Sarah 31, 62
Letchworth
  Eliza 56
  Thomas 56
Letton
  John 85
Lewis
  Elisabeth 13
  George 149, 201
  Glode 205
  Phebe 201
  Stephen 73
  Thomas 13, 201, 221
Linch
  Alexander 128
  John 77
  Nicholas 77
Lindow
  Margaret 22
Lingan
  George 63, 152
  Joseph 60
  Martha 16, 34, 63,
     113
  Thomas 16, 34, 63
Linn
  Michael 127
Linton
  John Evans 201
Lisenby
  Amy 144

Henry 144
Lister
  Elinor 6, 92, 125
  William 6, 55, 92,
     125
Little
  Samuel 33, 63
  William 167, 181,
     184, 197
Litton
  (N) 167
  Isaac 167, 218
  Mary 167, 218
  Thomas 167
Llewellin
  John 162
Lloyd
  Alice 76
  Edward 49
  Elisabeth 14, 129
  John 13, 14, 52,
     76, 121, 129,
     189
  Robert 118
  Samuel 48
  Thomas 45
  William 111
Lock
  Mev. 90
  Richard 156
Lomas
  John 57, 84
Long
  Daniel 119
  John 25
  Rebecca 11, 55
  Samuel 191
  Solomon 20, 25, 41,
     109
  Thomas 11, 55
Longo
  James 191
Loockerman
  Dorothy 181, 184,
     197, 215
  Jacob 62, 79, 114,
     129, 177
  Rosannah 62, 79
  Thomas 6, 172, 174
Lord
  Andrew 175
Lorton
  John 90
  Susannah 90

Loton
  John 141
Louther
  Elisabeth 132
  Robert 132, 154
Love
  Thomas 179
Low
  Jacob 122
  William 88
Lowe
  Margaret 154
  Nicholas 132, 154
  William 75, 106,
    186
Lowes
  Henry 135, 220
Lucas
  James 160
Lucket
  Samuel 149
Lurty
  Mary 10, 46
  Patrick 10, 46
Lusby
  Milcah 24
  Robert 24, 112
  Thomas 112, 143
Lux
  Darby 106, 118, 129
  Richard 226
Lyle
  William 156
Lyles
  Robert 60
Lynch
  John 1, 33, 40, 53,
    63, 120
  Nicholas 120, 212
  Patrick 63, 72
  Sarah 63, 72
  Thomas 87
  William 1, 40, 63
Lyon
  Henry 28, 88

Maccubbin
  Nicholas 57, 111
  Samuel 111, 142,
    144, 153, 154
MacDaniel
  Daniel 210
  Elisabeth 123

Eve 210
  William 123
Mace
  Josias 6, 131, 179,
    207
Macfadin
  Annanias 218
Mackall
  Benjamin 112
  John 71
Mackallen
  Arthur 128
MackClash
  Jayne 210
  William 210
Mackelanan
  James 213
Mackemmy
  William 172
Mackemy
  Thomas 172
Mackey
  William 93
Mackfadden
  Annanias 218
  John 218
Mackie
  William 226
Mackimmy
  Roger 172
Mackland
  Margaret 17
  Matthew 17
Mackormack
  Christian 205
MacKready
  Alexander 23
  Margaret 23
Maclendon
  James 74
Macnemara
  Elisabeth 199, 211,
    215
  Lawrence 199, 211,
    215
  M. 9, 56, 67, 77
Maconchie
  Ann 12, 37
  John 12, 37
  William 13, 56
Macquire
  George 111
Maddox
  Benjamin 64

Edward 64
John 82, 207, 222
Samuel 222
Maddux
  Bell 21, 109, 110
Magee
  John 168, 194
Maglamery
  Ann 40
  Edward 40
Magruder
  Alexander 185, 186
  Nathaniel 118, 150
  Susanna 186
Mahone
  John 200
  Mary 200
  Robert 188
  Thomas 16, 53, 54,
    77, 87
Mahoney
  John 188
Mainer
  William 218
Majors 105
Malden
  Sarah 118, 186
  William 71
Malony
  John 163
Maners
  Mary 106, 117, 138,
    193
Mankin
  James 73
Manley
  Peter 120, 163
  Sarah 120
Manning
  John 59
  Margaret 172
  Margret 206
  Mary 59
  Nathaniel 123, 131,
    176, 177, 178,
    206
  Richard 131, 177
  Rosannah 123, 131,
    177, 178, 206
Manors
  Mary 219
Mapp
  Francis 68, 69, 84
Marbury

William 180
Mariartee
  Ninian 51
Markland
  Charles 28, 44
  Margaret 118, 150
  Mark 28
  Mary 44
  Matthew 63, 118,
    150
Marshall
  Daniel 115
  Thomas 74, 138, 180
Marten
  Matthew 199
Martin
  Grace 104
  James 21, 70, 201,
    202
  Jane 51, 98
  John 94
  Philip 104
  Samuel 104, 138
  Stephen 51, 98
  Thomas 8
  William 104, 179
Mason
  Joseph 78, 211
  Lawrence 90, 124
  Rebecca 221
  Richard 221
  Sarah 211
  Solomon 211
  William 90
Massey
  Alexander 40, 78,
    128, 201
  Aquila 13
  Henry 97, 198
  Katherine 53
  Mary 145, 186, 212
  Tabitha 201
  Thomas 53
  William 40, 53, 78,
    129, 145, 163,
    186, 212
Masters
  Nathan 17, 51, 68,
    87, 113, 139,
    150
  Robert 68
  William 9, 25, 38,
    59, 68
Mastin

Charles 16, 37
Francis 113, 138,
    188, 199
Winfred 188
Winifred 113, 199
Masun
    Thomas 212
Mathews
    Elisabeth 9
    Roger 9
Mathiason
    Mary 36
Mattenly
    James 154, 189
Matthews
    Elisabeth 29
    Eliza 45
    Hugh 165
    John 88
    Mary 134, 143, 144
    Patrick 110
    Roger 45
    William 110, 119,
        134, 143, 144
Mattingley
    John 28
    William 210
Mattingly
    Burton 20
    Clement 20
    James 109, 140, 211
    John 14, 86, 127
    Luke 48, 83
    Priscilla 48, 83
    William 62
Mattinly
    Grace 14
Maud
    James 221
Maudesley
    John 201
Mauduit
    William 35
Mawdesley
    John 17, 165
Maxwell
    James 66, 72
    Jane 7
    Samuel 7, 72, 140,
        167
Mayle
    Anthony 168
Maynadier
    Daniel 161

Maynard
    Law. 152
    William 218
Mayner
    James 157
    Susanna 157
    Timothy 157
Maynor
    James 186, 222
    Thomas 222
    Timothy 186, 221
Mayson
    William 102
McCabe
    Jesse 135
McCalley
    John 166
McCauley
    John 202
McClamey
    Woney 22, 25, 109
McClammey
    Woney 25
McClammy
    Wonny 20
McClash
    Jane 113
    William 113, 185
McClean
    Daniel 187
    Jane 187
McCleland
    James 108
McClester
    George 160
McCosh
    Samuel 187
McCounell
    John 35
McCoy
    Hugh 89
McCoye
    John 63, 64
McCready
    Alexander 42
    Margaret 42
McDaniel
    Ann 149
    Daniel 138, 149,
        188
    Elisabeth 178, 207
    William 176, 178,
        207
McDoggle

Hugh 30
McFall
  James 74
Mcferson
  John 126, 149
  Sarah 126, 149
McGill
  David 28
McGram
  Ellin 23
  John 23
Mchorne
  Elisabeth 163
  Robert 163
McKean
  George 107
  Patrick 107
McKeel
  Alice 123, 177
  Charles 123, 176,
    177
  John 171, 205
McKellvie
  Andrew 108, 126
  Ann 108
  John 86, 108, 126
McKelvey
  Andrew 189
  Ann 189
McLaran
  Alexander 48, 73,
    126, 149
  Janet 48, 73, 126
  Jannet 149
McLeod
  Alexander 163
  Elisabeth 58
McNeal
  Archibald 5
McWhorter
  Hugh 50, 93
  John 50, 93
Mears
  Adam 204
Mecotter
  Alexander 190
Medway
  George 112, 138,
    199
Meek
  James 56
Meekins
  Isaac 32
  John 6

Meeks
  Robert 120
Meloyd
  Thomas 221
Melton
  James 12
Melvil
  David 91
Melvill
  David 172
Meradith
  Thomas 221
Mercer
  Jacob 113
  Mary 113
Merchant
  James 104, 190, 191
  Mary 104, 191
Merrick
  James 190
Merridith
  Ann 2
  John 2, 36
  Thomas 221
  William 152
Merrill
  Luke 83
Metcalfe
  John 146, 167
  Thomas 85, 133, 182
Michal
  Taney 203
Middlemore
  Josias 22, 60
Middleton
  Holland 149
  Horatio Samuel 57
  James 59, 60, 149,
    166
  Thomas 73, 201
  William 73, 149
Miers
  John 212
Miles
  Mary 191
  Stacey 191
  Stacy 191
  William 22, 73, 191
Mill
  William 36
Millard
  Ezekiel 141, 144,
    153
Miller

Arthur 16, 79
Elisabeth 120, 225
Jacob 126, 149
John 156
Martha 211, 212
Michael 16, 79
Nathaniel 120, 145,
   163, 225
Samuel 120, 211
William 1, 33, 106,
   150
Milles
   William 85
Millhuse
   Bartholomew 19, 45
Millis
   John 105
Mills
   James 207
   John 182
   Peter 32
   Thomas 111, 208
   William 89, 210
Millward
   Charles 145
Milner
   Godfrey 209, 216
   Isaac 96, 209
Milstead
   William 21
Milton
   Abraham 78
Minskie
   Catherine 104
   John Samuel 104
Mirick
   Roger 168, 223
Mister
   Patience 41, 110,
     147
   William 41, 75,
     111, 147
Mitchell
   Isaac 22
   Jos. 109
   Joseph 90
   Peter 48, 73, 126,
     149
   Solomon 22, 147
   Stephen 22
   Thomas 40
Moasley
   James 6, 7
Mockbee

Mattheu 25
William 25
Mollihone
   John 126
   Mary 126
Mollohone
   John 141
Monark
   Monica 86, 127
Monarks
   Monica 28
Monday
   John 175
Monett
   Elisabeth 186, 203
   Isaac 186
   Isaack 203
Mong
   Robert 178
Monroe
   Thomas 100
   William 99
Monsieur
   William 29
Moody
   Abigail 2
   Roger 2
Moor
   William 190
Moore
   Anthony 44
   Francis 95, 110,
     168, 191
   Henry 99, 125, 149
   Isaac 191
   Jacob 95
   James 44
   John 41, 96
   Josias 172, 190,
     223
   Mary 95, 168, 191
   Rachel 164
   Samuel Preston 65
   Sarah 99, 125
   Tabitha 96
   Thomas 110, 135,
     174
   William 164
More
   John 21, 136
   Tabitha 21, 136
Morgan
   (N) 74
   Ann 106

Henry 77, 81, 101,
114, 134, 143,
152, 159, 183,
195, 214
James 146
John 109, 146, 151,
158
Thomas 112
Morris
Elisabeth 155, 179
George 91, 124,
131, 177, 224
Jacob 8
Margery 70, 95
Randolph 155, 179
Sarah 91, 131, 177
Thomas 28, 46
William 70, 95
Morrison
Thomas 215
Morriss
Sarah 224
Morrisson
Thomas 181, 184,
197
Morsell
Thomas 33, 63, 180,
203
Morss
Joshua 147
Mary 147
Morton
Alexander 64
Ann 64
Mosley
Robert 82
Mouett
William 106
Mugg
Ann 225
Peter 140, 169, 225
Muggleston
Barbara 21
Thomas 21
Mugleston
Barbara 89
Thomas 89
Muir
A. 215
Adam 90, 107
T. 160, 197
Thomas 90
Mulany
James 181, 184

Mullen
John 142, 153, 159,
183, 195, 196
Mullett
William 145
Mullhuse
Bartholomew 14
Bridget 14
Mullikin
Charles 4
James 4
Mulony
James 197
Mumford
John 29, 65, 106
Mumphord
James 27
Muncaster
James 163
William 188
Munroe
Thomas 113
William 20, 125
Murphey
Edward 72
Murphy
Daniel 122, 176,
179, 206
Eleanor 42, 79, 103
John 72
William 43, 65, 79,
103
Murray
Daniel 3
David 201
Dunken 94, 128
Elinor 130
Hannah 201
Henry 17, 30
William 7, 44, 130,
205

Nairne
Jennet 42
Nalley
Dennis 188
Elisabeth 188
Richard 188
Neal
Charles 211
Mary 211
Nicholas 211
Neale

Benjamin 164, 188
Henry 21, 26, 37
Mary 21, 36, 126,
    138, 164
Raphael 36, 126,
    138
William 20, 26, 37,
    88, 89, 164
Neall
    Ann 105, 115
    Edward 115
    Francis 105, 115,
        139
    Jonathan 115
    Samuel 115, 139
Nedels
    Edward 104
Needham
    John 203, 215
    Sarah 215
Negroes
    Bess 195, 196
    Dido 58
    Esther 214
    Grace 58
    Jack 196
    Jacob 195
    Jeffer 195, 196
    Moll 195, 196
    Nan 24
    Patience 58
    Penn 23
    Phillis 58
    Poll 59
    Punch 214
    Solomon 60
    Tom 155, 160, 167,
        180, 181, 183,
        184, 196, 197
    Toney 58
Neighbours
    John 17, 43, 118,
        138
    Margaret 18, 118
    Mary 138
    Thomas 190
Nelson
    Ann 76
    Elisabeth 108
    John 9, 76
    Joshua 108, 141
    Thomas 121
    William 20, 94
Nevett

Thomas 7, 91, 174,
    204, 205
Nevil
    Elisabeth 76
    John 156
    Walter 76
Nevill
    Elisabeth 14, 52
    Walter 14, 52
Newbold
    Purnall 191
    Thomas 191, 220
Newman
    Daniel 187
Newnam
    Catherine 74
    William 221
Newstub
    Robert 97
Newstubb
    Robert 201
Newton
    Edward 122, 174
    Elisabeth 80, 192
    Henry 80, 106, 192
    James 124
    William 122
Nicholas
    Margaret 168, 223
Nicholls
    John 122
Nicholson
    Elisabeth 96
    James 135
    John 145
    Joseph 29, 69
    Levin 96, 136
Nicolls
    Benjamin 11
    John 122
    Margaret 11
    Moses 6, 91
Nicols
    Jeremiah 222
    John 171
Nix
    George 15, 44
    Leah 15, 44
Noble
    Elisabeth 109
    John 54, 109
    Robert 132
Noblitt
    Francis 155, 160,

181, 183, 184,
196, 197
Noell
Ann 172
John 172
Nolton
Alexander 226
Anne 226
Norris
Clare 101
John 58, 67, 101,
111, 126
Mary 100
Thomas 58, 85
Norriss
John 86
North
Robert 84, 167
Norton
Alexander 49
Ann 49
Notham
Jemima 5, 40
John 5, 69
Notingham
Athanasius 108, 225
Stephen 108, 126,
225
Nottingham
Mary 98, 127
Matthias 98, 126
Nowland
Alice 132, 190
Augustin 132
Augustine 190
Henry 224
Nugent
John 217
Nuner
John 173, 174
Nuney
Michael 10, 47
Nuttawell
Mary 175
Richard 175
Nutter
Ann 219
Christopher 22, 75,
96, 148, 161
John 219
John Huitt 219, 220
Matthew 9, 23
Thomas 124

OBryan
Terrance 127
Thomas 151
Odell
Rignall 51
Ogden
John 174
Ogdon
John 206
Ogle
Rosanna 217
Rosannah 208
Ogleby
James 92, 168
John 33, 92, 127,
129, 130, 168
Sarah 33, 63, 129,
130
Oldfield
Barber 104
Henry 104, 154,
179, 222
Sarah 104, 179
Oldham
Edward 154
Oldson
Henry 157
John 157
ONeal
Charles 185
ONeale
Hugh 4, 37
ONeall
Lawrence 120
ONeil
Lawrence 79, 87
Oram
Cooper 99
Henry 99
Orchard
John 150, 201
Orem
Andrew 190
Orme
John 51, 73, 185
Robert 1
Orr
William 29, 108
Osborn
Benjamin 34, 100
Hannah 29
James 7
John 29

Osborne
    Mary 100
    Samuel 65, 221
    William 31
Osburn
    Benjamin 100, 131
    Mary 100, 131
Oston
    widow 123
    William 123, 206
Outerbridge
    John 12
Outten
    Abraham 21, 109,
       110, 128, 166,
       202
    Purnall 109
    Purnell 109
Oweing
    Thomas 201
Owen
    Joseph 90, 158
    Thomas 97
Owens
    Edmond 92, 177
    Edward 91
    Rachel 91
    Samuel 84
    Sarah 11, 55, 221
    William 11, 55

Paca
    Aquila 45
    Aunt 58
    John 146
    Rachel 45, 216
Paddison
    Vincent 132
Page
    Ra. 162
    Ralph 120, 162
Pain
    Catherine 47
    Ezekiel 47
    William 51
Palle
    Edward 123
Palluffus
    Joseph 89
Palmer
    Benjamin 119
Pardo
    Barrington 80, 169,

      192
    Liney 80, 169
    Lucey 192
    Lucy 118
Paries
    Moses 146
Parish
    Edward 58
    Elisabeth 217
    John 217
    Nicholas 6
Parker
    G. 39, 59
    Gabriel 1, 4, 16,
      31, 33, 34, 40,
      48, 50, 63, 66,
      67, 71, 74, 80,
      85, 100, 105,
      110, 112, 114,
      115, 117, 118,
      129, 130, 138,
      139, 147, 150,
      155, 156, 169,
      179, 180, 185,
      186, 192, 193,
      202, 203, 209,
      219
    George 96, 180,
      201, 202
    Grace 219
    John 219
    Leah 202
    Samuel 34, 35, 128,
      202
    Sarah 180
    Tabitha 147
    Thomas 96
Parks
    Bridget 19, 45
    John 19, 45
Parnham
    John 162
Parran
    Alexander 117
    Easter 100, 147
    Esther 24
    John 24, 50, 100,
      147
    Moses 80, 169
    Samuel 169
    Young 24, 100, 147
Parrott
    Francis 116
Parsons

John 102
William 93
Partridge
  Buckler 74, 81,
    101, 114, 134,
    143, 152, 159,
    183, 195, 214
  Isaac 6, 174
  Jane 74, 81, 101,
    114, 134, 143,
    152, 159, 183,
    195, 214
Pattison
  Jacob 37, 123
  Jane 37
  Jeremiah 36, 37
  John 123, 178, 206
  Mary 123, 178, 206
  St. Leegar 177
  St. Leeger 123,
    178, 206
  Thomas 32
Patton
  Dorothy 98, 128
  Robert 35, 98, 128
Paul
  William 35
Pavatt
  Isaac 158
  Joseph 158
Pavett
  Isaac 46
Peacock
  Ann 47
  Paul 47
Pearce
  Andrew 119
  Beartine 119
  Benjamin 225
  Elenor 208
  Elinor 83, 109, 168
  Gideon 119, 145
  Mary 66, 79
  Thomas 46, 83, 168,
    208
Pearse
  Mary 225
Pearson
  Benjamin 219
  John 54
  Noah 54, 123
Peck
  Bennett 61
Peele

Thomas 27
Peirce
  Margaret 48, 81
  Richard 147
Peirson
  Benjamin 205
  May 205
Pemberton
  Benjamin 9
  Grundy 9, 156
Pembrooke
  Agnes 126
  John 126, 142
Pennington
  John 36, 165, 178
  Mary 165
Peregoy
  Joseph 146, 151,
    158
Perkins
  Daniel 119
  John 4, 87, 99, 120
  Richard 45
  Thomas 18
  William 45
Perray
  Hugh 207
  Richard 207
Perrie
  Samuel 37
Perrin
  Thomas 90
Perry
  Charles 100, 129
  Hugh 171, 177, 179
  John 1
  Richard 171, 179
  William 173, 204
Peterkin
  James 179
  Mary 179
Petty
  Constant 210
Phillips
  Catherine 204
  Elinor 175
  James 88, 172, 204,
    216
  Jane 66, 150, 156
  John 36, 41, 66,
    81, 135, 146,
    150, 156, 204
  Richard 135
  Susanna 135

Thomas 135, 175
William 204
Phillups
    Catherine 206
    James 205
    Thomas 205
Philpot
    Brian 209
    John 209
Phippard
    Mary 169
    William 169, 207
Phippen
    Thomas 4
Phipps
    Thomas 40
Phips
    John 172
Pickeils
    Jeremiah 108
Pickerin
    Francis 132
Pickerls
    Jeremiah 141
Pickett
    Elisabeth 9, 98
    Eliza 45, 146
    Heathcoat 9, 45,
        146
    Heathcoate 98
Pickrin
    Stephen 35
Picton
    John 7, 8
Pierce
    Richard 80
    William 80
Piggot
    John 77, 127
    Rachel 77, 127
Piggott
    John 35
Pile
    Joseph 162
Piles
    Leonard 63
Pilkinton
    Hugh 10, 47
Pinar
    Elisabeth 16, 62,
        79
    Thomas 16, 62, 79
Pindall
    Elisabeth 2

Philip 2
Piper
    Christopher 9, 23,
        135, 147
    Rachel 135
Pitt
    John 175, 206
Pitts
    Ann 9, 76
    John 42
    Katherine 10
    Ketherine 42
Plant
    James 21, 99, 139,
        148, 149
Plumer
    Samuel 168
Plummer
    Elisabeth 41
    James 41
    Philemon 41, 63
Pointer
    Elias 166
    Ratclief 166
    Turville 166
Poleson
    Peter 35, 36
    Rachel 36
Pollard
    John 205
Ponder
    Ann 4, 52
    Morgan 52
    Morgin 4
Poole
    Edward 123
    Moses 205
Poore
    Nicholas 48
    Peter 81
Porter
    Eliza 137
    James 40, 98
    Joseph 40, 47, 74
    Joshua 8
    Philemon 137
    R. 43
    Richard 134
Posten
    Francis 20
    John 20, 21, 73
    William 20, 73
Poston
    John 48

Page 274

William 48
Poteet
    William 56, 72
Pottenger
    Rachel 129, 214
    Robert 129
    William 214
Potter
    Henry 21
Pottinger
    Samuel 34
Potts
    John 26
    Rachel 26
Powell
    Amy 65
    Charles 123, 173
    James 62, 66, 82,
        102, 103, 113,
        157, 160, 183,
        187, 196
    John 65, 133, 144,
        152, 157, 170,
        210
    Mary Ann 82, 103,
        157, 160, 183,
        196
    Rebecca 133
    Susannah 171, 210
    Thomas 66, 82, 103,
        104, 151
Power
    Nicholas 83
Powson
    William 97, 136
Prather
    John 214
    John Smith 117,
        134, 143, 214
    Martha 214
    Thomas 17, 117,
        134, 214
    William 214
Pratt
    Ann 146
    William 146
Presbury
    George 45
Prevatt
    Joseph 188
Price
    Andrew 43, 76, 221
    Ann 88
    Anthony 141

Dorcas 1
Elisabeth 48, 220
Henry 220
John 1, 135, 147
Richard 92
Sarah 141
Thomas 48, 116
Vincent 102, 187,
    198, 221
William 35, 190
Prichard
    John 6
Prickyard
    Benjamin 67, 111
Priestly
    James 3, 155
Primrose
    Bridget 156
    John 65, 66, 103
    Rachel 66
    William 156, 221
Prior
    William 200
Pritchet
    Elinor 49, 51
    William 49, 51
Pritchett
    Edward 91, 204
Prockter
    Elisabeth 207
    Hugh 207
Procter
    Elisabeth 178
    Hugh 176, 178
Proctor
    Elisabeth 123
    Hugh 123
Pryor
    Ann 109, 193, 220
    Thomas 109, 136,
        193, 220
Pullett
    Alice 7
    William 7
Purdey
    Edmund 104
Purnall
    Richard 100
Purnell
    John 5, 70
    Richard 101
Pye
    Edward 15, 64
    Walter 15, 64, 164

Quando
    Henry 17, 19
Quillen
    Benjamin 94, 202
    Joseph 94
Quiney
    Elisabeth 119
    Sutton 119
Quinley
    Margaret 73
Quinney
    Elisabeth 162, 212
    Sutton 162, 163,
        212

Rabbits
    William 221
Rackliff
    Nathaniel 26, 147
Railey
    John 156
Rake
    Richard 4
Raley
    Thomas 199
Ralph
    Thomas 22, 23, 76
Ramsey
    Hannah 56
    Johannah 72
    John 56, 72
Randall
    Bethia 145
    Richard 57
    Robert 145, 163
Randell
    Richard 152, 182
Ranhill
    Ann 179
    Thomas 179
Rasin
    John 208
    Thomas 208
    William 144
Rattenbury
    John 217, 222
    Margaret 217
Raven
    Abraham 217
    Isaac 217
Rawlings

Aaron 71
Daniel 66, 117
Edward 61
Elinor 57
John 67
Margaret 67
William 71
Ray
    John 15, 43
    Luke 34
    Thomas 15, 43, 132,
        209
Rayley
    Thomas 188
Read
    Elinor 98, 127
    John 16, 17, 54,
        77, 87, 98, 127,
        162
    Mary 16, 54, 77, 87
    Patrick 184, 197
    Zachariah 41
Reading
    Mary 187
    Richard 77, 120,
        187
    Sarah 165
    William 145
Realey
    John 127
Really
    Henry 108
Reckords
    John 135
    Thomas 135
Redach
    Joseph 93
Reding
    Patrick 201
    Sarah 201
Redman
    John 82, 83, 108,
        109, 170, 208
    Rebecca 108
    Sarah 82
Redus
    Catherine 50, 93
    James 35, 50, 93
Reed
    Ezekiah 161
    Ezekiel 90, 92,
        131, 148, 177,
        224
    Hannah 90, 92, 131,

177, 224
John 93
Juda 161
Judah 148
Patrick 175, 181
Rosannah 175, 181,
    184, 197, 206,
    215
Thomas 187
Reeder
  Benjamin 207
Reeves
  Samuel 20, 89
  Thomas 89
Rencher
  Thomas 8
Revell
  Katherine 10
  Randall 10, 42
Reyley
  John 64
Reynolds
  Deborah 119
  Edward 80, 110,
    115, 116, 147
  Jean 85
  John 61, 74, 85,
    111, 137, 154
  Margaret 165
  Sarah 31, 61, 62,
    137, 154
  Thomas 17, 34, 42,
    67, 80, 165, 225
  William 85, 119
Ricaud
  Benjamin 53
  Mary 53
Rice
  Rebecca 212
  William 212
Richard
  Baddard 202
Richards
  John 1, 85, 106
Richardson
  Ann 20, 144
  Benjamin 118, 129
  Daniel 61
  James 28, 148, 158
  John 75, 96
  Joseph 61, 107, 109
  Margaret 61, 221
  Mark 20, 58, 68,
    158

Mary 75, 161
Rachel 75
Richard 70, 79, 85,
    106, 107
Samuel 47, 109
Sarah 161
Thomas 70, 79, 85,
    106, 107, 144
William 8, 28, 40,
    61, 104, 210
Richason
  James 117, 219
Richison
  William 189
Rickards
  John 78, 132, 148
Rickason
  James 193
Rickets
  Elisabeth 84
  John 84, 168, 223
  Thomas 168
Ricketts
  Benjamin 30
  David 3, 165
  Elisabeth 47, 77,
    121, 139
  Eliza 30
  John 223
  Joseph 47, 77, 139,
    163
  Nathaniel 47, 77,
    139, 163
  Thomas 223
Rickords
  John 148, 161
  Thomas 148, 161
Ricords
  Joseph 173
Riddle
  Frances 17
  John 198
  Robert 17
Rider
  Charles 4, 6, 11,
    100, 131
  Willson 75, 136
  Wilson 23, 75
Ridgeley
  Charles 217
Ridgely
  Charles 17
  Henry 38
Ridgeway

William 54

Rigby
 John 76
 Lewis 76
 Nathan 45

Rigg
 James 131
 John 199

Riggen
 Ambrose 22, 76, 110
 James 76, 110
 Joseph 76, 110
 Mary 76, 110
 Teague 22, 76, 110

Riggs
 Elisabeth 97
 James 86, 97
 John 97

Rigsby
 Elisabeth 8
 John 8, 30
 Levin 8
 Lewis 8, 30

Riley
 Hannah 119
 Henry 83
 Isaac 119, 145, 170
 James 64
 John 28, 86, 146
 Mary 63, 98, 119
 Nicholas 119, 145
 Terrance 63, 73, 98

Rimmer
 Hugh 122, 177, 179, 207
 James 35
 Mary 122, 179, 207

Ringgold
 Charles 4, 52
 Elisabeth 3, 52, 99, 120, 193, 212
 James 3, 53, 120, 193, 211, 212

Risteau
 John 39, 77, 81, 134, 216
 Talbot 17

Riston
 Edward 85, 150

Ritchie
 Robert 84

Roach
 Michael 136

Roberson
 John 22

Roberts
 James 53
 John 136, 165
 Joseph 165
 Richard 80
 Robert 71
 William 24, 25, 53, 151
 Williams 24

Robertson
 Alexander 121
 John 41, 96
 Patrick 121, 152

Robey
 Benjamin 37, 99, 138
 Mary 99, 138

Robinson
 Charles 73
 David 115, 157, 190
 Diana 26, 51
 Dianah 199
 John 2, 128, 147
 Joseph 128
 Joshua 94
 Judith 222
 Mary 2, 48
 Peter 2
 Richard 146
 Richard Gurling 222
 Sarah 2
 William 26, 35, 48, 51, 102, 187, 199, 201

Robison
 Mary 73
 William 73

Robotham
 Mary Ann 132
 Ralph 132, 210

Robson
 Henry 190
 James 190
 John 131, 178, 207
 Lambert 190

Rock
 George 168, 178
 Mary 168

Rockhold
 Charles 1
 Elisabeth 1
 John 9, 182

Rodach
    Joseph 193
Rodgett
    Barton 85, 143, 210
Rodoch
    Joseph 127
Roe
    Edward 121
    James 179
    John 121, 187
    Thomas 76
Rogers
    Alice 204
    Ann 52, 76
    David 204
    John 52, 76
    William 45, 56, 57,
       61, 67, 68, 84,
       111, 133, 143,
       152, 182, 213
Rolle
    Fiddeman 132
    Francis 132, 157
Rolph
    Glanvill 16
    Glanville 47, 79
Ross
    Anne 199
    David 97
    Edward 91, 92, 177
    James 199
    John 182
    Mary 91, 177
    Robert 91, 124,
       131, 178, 206
    Stephen 123, 171,
       175, 204
    William 77
Rousby
    John 48, 49
Rouse
    Thomas 16, 107, 120
Rowles
    Sarah 116
    Thomas 84, 116
Royall
    Mary 124, 178, 207
    Samuel 124
    Thomas 124, 176,
       178, 207
Rozar
    Sarah 48, 99
Rozier
    Sarah 125

Rue
    William 163
Rule
    Elisabeth 90
Ruley
    Mary 213
    Thomas 213
Rumbly
    Ann 123, 178, 206
    John 122, 123, 176,
       178, 206
    Priscilla 122, 178,
       206
    William 122
Rumsey
    Sabina 36
    William 35, 36
Russell
    Luke 108
    Mary 94, 137
    Thomas 94, 108,
       137, 222
Ruth
    John 221
    Moses 3
    Thomas 151
Rutland
    Thomas 84
Ryan
    Dennis 68, 111
    Edward 35
    Elinor 68
    Hannah 74
    Michael 190, 210
    William 74
Ryland
    John 127
Ryon
    Joseph 150

Saile
    Gabriel 119
    George 119, 134,
       143, 144
    Mary 119, 134, 143
Saint Clare
    Dorothy 138
    George 138
Saintee
    Nathaniel 86
Sallaway
    John 221
Salloway

John 29
Salmon
  William 94, 128
Salsbury
  Elisabeth 3
  John 3, 204
Salter
  William 163
Samuel
  Cornish 205
Sanckston
  John 105, 154, 210
Sanders
  Elisabeth 174
  Francis 174
  James 74
  Jane 17
  John 102
  Robert 106
  Thomas 149
  William 154
Sankston
  John 67, 74
Santee
  Nathaniel 132
  Sarah 132
Sarson
  William 50
Satchell
  Tabitha 40
Saunders
  John 121, 186, 222
  Thomas 36
  Ursula 221
  William 221
Savin
  Cornelius Augustine 165
  John 165, 225
  Samuel 165, 225
  Thomas 165
Savory
  William 66
Scarff
  Nicholas 169
  Sarah 156
  William 156
Schoolfield
  Joseph 27, 69, 128
Scott
  Abigail 172, 206
  Andrew 38, 60, 69, 81, 83, 84, 189, 198, 203, 215

Ann 13, 52, 76, 149
Anne 200
Burridge 62, 77
Daniel 106
George 35, 64, 180, 214
James 19, 65, 192, 226
John 13, 52, 76, 109, 221
Mary 84, 203, 216
Nathaniel 13, 52, 76
Rebecca 77
Samuel 133
Solomon 13, 52, 76
Walter 19, 64, 192, 226
William 149, 173, 188, 200, 205, 206
Scrivener
  Richard 13, 52, 76
Scroggen
  John 16, 37
Searjant
  John 217
Sedwick
  Benjamin 33, 130, 169
  Betty 130
  John 33, 129, 130
Seeney
  Bryan 190
Selacum
  George 205
Selby
  Martha 5, 70
  Nathan 87, 133, 155, 184
  Samuel 19
  William 5
Sellman
  Ann 208, 222
  Charity 154
  John 36
  Jonathan 208, 222
  William 154, 208, 222
Semmes
  Clebburn 23
  Eleanor 24
  Henrietta 59
  Ignatius 19, 64

Joseph Milburn 19,
    64, 72, 134,
    143, 152, 159,
    195, 214
Marmaduke 60
Rachel 214
Serjeant
    Michael 187
Severson
    Thomas 50, 98, 128
Sevil
    Thomas 221
Seward
    William 221
Sewers
    James 174
Sexton
    Andrew 54, 55
    Rachel 54
Shakespear
    Joseph 30
Shanks
    James 66
Shannahan
    John 18
Sharp
    Ann 67
    Samuel 171
    Solomon 67, 171
    William 88, 116,
        154
Shaw
    Daniel 14, 16
    John 7
Shegnasha
    William 206
Shehawn
    Ann 50
    Miles Mason 99, 145
    Sarah 99, 145
    Thomas 50
Sheircliffe
    Henry 109, 154,
        189, 211
Sheldon
    John 69
Shenton
    Joseph 131, 178,
        204, 207
Shephard
    Thomas 105
Sheredine
    Thomas 130
Shermedine

John 24, 38
Sarah 24, 38
Sherwood
    Daniel 132
    John 157
    Lydia 157
Shery
    Job 5, 70, 128
Shiercliff
    William 19
Shipley
    Robert 114
Shockneshire
    William 175
Shores
    John 42
    William 8, 42
Shurmadine
    John 142
Sim
    Mary 5
    Patrick 5
Simmes
    Joseph Milburn 117,
        182
    Rachel 117, 182
Simmonds
    William 78
Simmons
    Abraham 68, 87,
        182, 213
    James 35
    Richard 213
    Samuel 111
    Sarah 182
    William 68
Simms
    Joseph Milburn 183
Simons
    John 66
Simpson
    Andrew 89
    John 57
    Katherine 145, 186,
        225
    Samuel 18
    Thomas 70, 78, 145,
        186, 225
Sirman
    John 22
Skillington
    Elijah 61, 185, 197
Skinner
    Elinor 32

Elisabeth 18, 80,
    169, 192
James 80
John 32, 71, 106,
    130
Joseph 203
Katharine 189
Kathrine 210
Leonard 80, 130
Nathaniel 56
Richard 189
William 18, 61, 80,
    106, 118, 132,
    169, 192
Skirven
    George 79, 162, 212
Skirvin
    George 15
Slacum
    George 174
    Job 171, 172
Slater
    Ellis 33, 80
Slaughter
    Elisabeth 77, 81
    James 77, 81
Slayton
    Esther 7
    James 7
Sledmore
    John 162, 189
    Mary 162
Sligh
    Thomas 3, 74, 81,
        101, 114, 134,
        142, 143, 144,
        146, 152, 153,
        159, 183, 195,
        214, 217
Slingoe
    Thomas 40
Slone
    James 55
Sluyter
    Johannes 127, 223
Slye
    Gerrard 48
    Mary 48, 126
Small
    John 104, 222
    Sarah 222
Smasha
    Naomi 69
    William 69

Smith
    Alice 224
    Archabald 201
    Basil 108, 115,
        116, 140
    Charles 52
    Charles Somerset 48
    Charles Somersett
        81
    David 78
    Dorothy 48, 83,
        108, 115, 116,
        140
    Elinor 40
    Elisabeth 1, 78,
        132
    George 128, 151,
        201, 224
    Henry 1, 150, 203
    James 1, 52, 77,
        97, 119, 120,
        166, 212
    Jane 214
    Johannah 217
    John 5, 27, 30, 31,
        43, 63, 65, 70,
        71, 76, 91, 92,
        121, 148, 163,
        185, 198
    Mary 78, 203
    Priscilla 29
    Richard 29, 111
    Samuel 42, 45, 68,
        69, 81, 84, 101,
        107, 111, 114
    Sarah 31
    Susanna 219
    Thomas 5, 30, 43,
        71, 86, 121,
        150, 169, 185,
        198, 217
    Walter 88
    William 22, 28, 41,
        45, 62, 75, 78,
        100, 128, 133,
        171, 172, 181,
        216, 217
    Winston 216, 219
    Zachariah 7, 45
Smithers
    John 15, 58, 112
    Katherine 15, 53,
        112
    Mary 19, 24, 38, 58

Thomas 53
William 145
Smock
   Henry 95
Smoot
   Ann 72, 166
   Barton 72, 113, 166
   Charles 73
   John 188
   Thomas 72, 166
Smullen
   Randolph 22
Snelling
   Mary 61, 88, 116
   Thomas 61, 86, 88,
     116
Snelson
   John 175
   William 30
Snowden
   Henry 6
   Richard 47, 61, 74,
     81, 84, 101,
     112, 114
Sollers
   Heighe 217
Somervell
   James 115, 135,
     183, 196
Sommervelle
   James 66
Soper
   John 12
Sothoron
   Benjamin 187
   John Johnson 23,
     83, 118, 202,
     216
   Richard 83, 202,
     216
   Samuel 83, 202, 216
Soumaien
   Samuel 143
Soumain
   Samuel 47
South
   Thomas 74, 81, 83,
     101, 114
Southern
   John Johnson 215
   Richard 215
   Samuel 215
Southorn
   Elisabeth 116

John Johnson 116
   Richard 116
   Samuel 116
Southoron
   Elisabeth 134
   John Johnson 134
   Richard 134
   Samuel 134
Soward
   John 205
Spalding
   Basil 88
   Benedict 2
   Charles 36
   Henry 2
   Thomas 2
   William 2
Spark
   George 29
Sparks
   George 224
   John 224
Sparrow
   Solomon 154
   Thomas 61, 111
Spaulding
   Charles 199
Spearman
   Francis 53, 99, 120
   Hester 53, 99, 120
Spencer
   Elisabeth 205
   Francis 80, 179,
     203
   Grace 6
   Henry 87
   James 55, 107, 132
   John 50
   Mary 222
   Robert 43, 107,
     132, 189, 222
   Sarah 50
   William 205
Spink
   Edward 14
   William 14
Sprigg
   Edward 11, 103
   Mary 103
   Osborn 11
Sprignal
   John 104
Spry
   Elisabeth 198

Francis 181, 198
John 181, 198
Thomas 189
William 181, 198
St. Clare
Dorothy 99
George 37, 99
Stacey
Rebecca 74, 105
William 74, 105
Stack
Patrick 176
Stafford
Abraham 123, 176
Henry 14
James 123
Mary 123
Robert 14
Stallings
Francis 71
Isaac 192
Kent 192
Richard 156
Thomas 33, 106
Stamper
Robert 19, 35
Standford
Charles 173, 174,
206, 223
John 173, 206
Rosannah 174, 223
Samuel 174, 223
Thomas 173, 174,
223
William 174, 175,
176, 205, 223
Standiford
Christiana 192, 218
Ephraim 106
William 192, 218
Stanford
Charles 122
Stansbury
Luke 2, 31, 44
Tobias 2, 31, 44,
218
Stapleford
Barnaby 115, 161
Charles 173, 175,
181, 184, 197,
205, 215, 223
Daniel 115, 161
John 161
Mary 115, 155, 171

Ramond 223
Raymond 173, 176,
181, 184, 197,
215
Robert 115, 155,
171
Thomas 173, 175,
181, 184, 197,
215, 223
Staplefort
Charles 223
Staples
Henry 145
James 9
Sarah 9
Starkey
Edward 15, 44
John 45
Jonathan 45
Joshua 45, 146
Susannah 15, 44
William 187
Steel
Ann 165
Archibald 165, 225
Daniel 5, 137
Dorothy 213
James 5, 137
Ralph 213
Stephens
Benjamin 29, 127
John 205
William 135
Sterling
James 213
Mary 191
Rebecca 213
Steuart
George 111
John 83, 86
Stevens
Abigail 195
Charles 56
Edward 122, 178,
207
Elisabeth 18, 44,
189
Isaac 117, 134,
143, 153, 159,
183, 195
Isaack 196
John 6, 7, 18, 43,
44, 172, 189,
195

Rachel 196
Richard 195, 196
Walter 171, 172
William 122, 124,
   178, 207, 220
Stevenson
  James 92, 226
Steward
  David 32
  Edward 32
  John 181, 184, 197
Stewart
  Alexander 9, 42
  Charles 19, 64
  James 113, 138, 199
  John 62, 87, 171,
   175
  Patrick 75
  Rebecca 9, 42
  Sarah 87
  Stephen 20, 110,
   208
  Thomas 6, 174
Still
  George 145
Stinchcomb
  John 217
Stinson
  Alexander 11, 92,
   125, 224
  Samuel 174
  Sarah 11, 92, 125,
   224
Stock
  Patrick 174
Stockton
  Elisabeth 168, 193,
   225
  John 168, 193, 225
Stoddert
  John 168
Stogdell
  Grace 122, 131,
   177, 224
  Michael 122, 124,
   131, 177, 224
Stokes
  George 219
  H. Wells 88
  Humphry Wells 167,
   218
  John 140
  Mary 167, 218
  Susanna 140

Susannah 216
Stone
  David 163
Stonestreet
  Butler 97
Storey
  Elisabeth 157
  Richard 157
Story
  Robert 3, 168
Stoughton
  William 196
Studham
  Jane 189
  John 189
Sturgis
  John 40
  Littleton 40
  Tabitha 40
Sturling
  Mary 220
Sulivane
  Daniel 173
  Florance 54
  Sarah 91, 177
  William 91, 177
Sulivant
  William 124
Suliven
  Daniel 46
Sullivant
  John 117
Summers
  William 179, 219
Sumners
  Thomas 7
Susannah
  Hellen 203
Sutcliff
  John 20
Sutcliffe
  John 99, 113
Suter
  Francis 143
Sutor
  Francis 133, 213
Sutton
  Ashbury 84
  James 65, 187
Swann
  Abigail 25, 37
  Ann 21
  Benjamin 73
  Edward 199

James 82, 169, 207
Mary 169
Samuel 21
Thomas 25, 37, 99,
    125
Sweat
  Elisabeth 61
  John 61, 74
  Varty 61, 105
Sweatnam
  Stephen 151
Swift
  Daniel 102
  John 13, 140
  Mary 13, 56
  Theophilus 13, 56
  William 13, 140
Sympson
  Andrew 72
  Ignatius 164
  Juliana 72
  William 164
Syng
  John 119

Taillor
  John 100, 114
Talbot
  John 84
Talbott
  Daniel 33
  Joseph 33
  Richard 33, 80
Tall
  Phillip 204
Taman
  William 142, 218
Taney
  Michael 1, 33, 107,
      108, 115, 118,
      186
  Michal 203
  Sarah 1, 107, 108,
      114, 118, 186,
      203
  Thomas 107, 114
Tanner
  Joseph 186
  Susannah 186
Tarlton
  James 82
  Mary 10, 46
  Thomas 10, 46

Tarr
  Samuel 132, 147
Tarvin
  Elisabeth 19, 139
  Eliza 37, 164
  G. 39
  George 24
  Richard 19, 37,
      139, 164
Tate
  Thomas 9, 22, 187
Taylard
  William 145
Taylor
  Abraham 109, 136,
      148, 161
  Ann 64, 73, 138
  Elisabeth 173, 181,
      184, 197, 205,
      215, 223
  James 14, 72, 86,
      89, 126
  John 34, 35, 40,
      57, 58, 94, 109,
      146, 148, 161,
      167, 202, 218
  Joseph 128
  Kezia 146, 167, 218
  Mary 128
  Patience 16, 47
  Rebecca 109
  Richard 3
  Solomon 50
  Thomas 8
  William 16, 43, 47,
      78, 91, 109,
      128, 147
  William Smallwood
      64, 138
Tayman
  Elisabeth 33, 180,
      203
  John 1, 34, 133
  Joseph 133
  Sarah 167
  William 33, 133,
      180, 203
Teague
  John 166, 202
Teal
  Emanuel 167
Temple
  John 86, 127
Tennant

John 52
Tennison
  Mary 127
  Samuel 28, 127
Terry
  Hugh 50, 93
  Rosamond 50, 93
Tharp
  Ann 47
  Elisabeth 162
  John 162, 163
  Samuel 47
Thomas
  Anne 200
  Benjamin 199, 201
  Christopher 200
  David 35
  Henry 79
  Jane 201
  John 126
  Joseph 7, 168, 223
  Mark 158, 170
  Philip 49, 57
  Richard 168, 223
  Samuel 145
  Sarah 7, 119
  Simon 7
  Tristram 88, 116,
    179
  Trust. 154
  Trustram 185, 200,
    201
  William 16, 28, 39,
    53, 54, 59, 79,
    86, 87, 94, 95,
    111, 119, 154,
    188
  Winefred 158
Thompson
  Daniel 216
  George 35, 158
  James 42, 83
  John 127, 165, 172,
    180, 189, 192,
    221, 222, 224,
    226
  Joseph 205
  Peter 46
  Rachel 209
  Richard 165
  Thomas 175, 209,
    224
  William 35
Thomson

William 6
Thornell
  Robert 176
Thornton
  John 120
  Katherine 163
  Posthumus 32
  William 84, 111,
    153, 159, 160,
    215
Thornwell
  Elisabeth 124
  Robert 124
Thrashier
  John 146
Tibbels
  Ann 137
  John 104, 137
Tibbett
  James 37
Tilghman
  Richard 137
  William 7, 13, 29,
    42, 51, 65, 66,
    76, 79, 82, 102,
    112, 116, 121,
    140, 144, 151,
    155, 156, 157,
    185, 186, 187,
    198, 200, 220,
    224
Till
  William 21
Tillard
  William 182, 213
Tilley
  Rebecca 6
Timbrell
  William 99
Tipett
  John 89
Tipler
  Ann 190
  William 190, 210
Tippens
  Edward 151
Tippett
  John 162
Titus
  Robert 124
Toadvine
  William 95
Todd
  Elisabeth 152

Lancelott 117
Tole
    Timothy 188
Toles
    Timothy 126
Tolle
    George 108
    Timothy 108
Tolley
    James 72, 83, 142
    Mary 72
    Thomas 167
    Walter 72, 142,
        167, 217
Tomlinson
    Saward 9
    Sayward 42
    Solomon 10, 42
Tootel
    Richard 202, 215
Tootell
    Helen 152
    John 152
    Richard 99, 152
Topham
    Christopher 27, 70,
        95
Topping
    James 3
    Sarah 4
Towgood
    Josias 100, 101,
        116
    Mary 100, 101, 116
Townley
    John 12, 15, 34, 35
    Mary 12, 15, 35
Townsend
    James 5, 95, 166
    Littleton 5, 70,
        128
    Solomon 5, 166
Towson
    Joseph 167
Train
    James 75, 136, 148,
        161
Traverse
    Henry 175
    John 55
    Matthew 6, 55
Trayman
    Thomas 105, 115,
        138, 155, 171

Tree
    John 165, 178
Tregoe
    Ann 175, 223
    Philemon 204
    William 175, 204,
        205, 223
Trepe
    Winifred 170, 208
Trippe
    Ann 122, 178, 206
    Edward 90, 173,
        178, 206
    Elisabeth 91, 148,
        185, 222
    Henry 6, 11, 12,
        32, 50, 54, 55,
        65, 91, 128,
        148, 185
    John 122, 124, 178,
        206
    William 222
    Winefred 46
Trott
    John 133
    Thomas 213
Trotten
    Luke 26, 60
Trotter
    Ephraham 223
    Ephraim 6, 176, 206
    Hannah 176
Truelock
    Henry 145, 225
    William 145
Trueman
    Henry 186
    James 51
Truitt
    George 40
Tubman
    Richard 173
Tucker
    Edward 103
    John 103
    Lewis 7
    Nathaniel 103
Tull
    Benjamin 26
    Isaac 166
    Richard 7
    Samuel 220
Tulley
    Benjamin 8, 41, 75,

96, 136, 148,
    161
  Elisabeth 41, 148,
    161
  James 41, 75, 97,
    136
  Joseph 41
  Richard 41, 96, 136
  Stephen 8, 41, 96,
    136
  Susannah 41, 97,
    136
Tunis
  Edward 205
  Levinah 205
Turbutt
  William 66
Turner
  Abner 210
  Elisabeth 204
  Henry 204
  Jonathan 50, 79,
    107, 120
  Samuel 36
Turpin
  Clarada 175
  John 175, 191
  Solomon 90, 122
  William 8
Turvile
  John 94
Turvill
  Presgrave 4
Twilley
  Robert 109
Twyford
  Jonathan 173
  William 123, 173,
    206
Tyler
  Robert 6

Underwood
  Samuel 217
Ungle
  Frances 178
  Friend 112
  Robert 112, 178
Uphill
  William 137
Urm
  John 165
Usher

Edward 45, 93
Usler
  William 120

Vadry
  Philemon 141
Vanbebber
  Adam 50, 93, 189
  Harmana 189
  Hermana 50, 93, 166
  Jacob 189
  Mary 50, 93
  Matthias 50, 93
Vandegrift
  Nicholas 225
  Susanna 225
Vanderford
  William 117
Vandergrift
  Nicholas 165, 166
  Susanna 165
Vane
  John 12
Vansandt
  Cornelius 145
  George 145
Vaughan
  Elisabeth 31, 34
  John 31, 33, 34
  William 22, 193
Vaulx
  Catherine 172
  Ebenezar 172, 224
  James 54, 172, 205,
    206, 223
  Jane 224
  John 172
  Sarah 172, 223
Vaux
  James 123
Veach
  Thomas 123
Veazey
  John 3, 127
Venatson
  Nathan 5
  William 5
Vennam
  George 213
Ventstone
  Jonas 85
Vickars
  Thomas 172

Vinson
 James 122
Vowles
 Mathew 225

Wabby
 John 57
Wade
 James 93
 Mary 97, 226
 Nehemiah 97
 Zacharia 226
 Zachariah 97, 113,
  226
Wakefield
 John 138
Wale
 Nathaniel 129
 William 26, 129
Walker
 Ann 160
 George 103, 180
 Hugh 93, 226
 James 87, 103, 116,
  133, 186, 190
 John 104, 116
 Mary 103, 180
 Robert 226
 Samuel 93, 226
 Thomas 35, 75, 93,
  96, 124, 148,
  161, 205
Wall
 Rebecca 175, 223
Wallace
 David 135, 136,
  193, 220
 Grace 160
 John 211
 Martha 135
 Matthew 160
 Richard 146, 160
 William 34
Waller
 Richard 41, 147
 William 75
Wallis
 George 90, 126
 Richard 91
Walston
 Booz 220
 Joy 220
 Obed 220

Walters
 Amelia 3, 14, 27,
  102
 Richard 212
 Robert 3, 14, 27,
  102, 117, 155
 Thomas 122
Walton
 Martha 69
Waple
 George 113, 164
Waples
 Paul 94
Ward
 Augustina 127, 180
 Benjamin 46
 Daniel 190
 Elisabeth 116
 James 29
 John 116, 127, 178,
  180
 Leah 46
 Mary 190
 Owen 92, 125
 Thomas 157
 William 14
Ware
 Francis 25, 73,
  118, 138
Warfield
 Absolute 113
 Alexander 113, 179
 Sarah 113
Waring
 Elisabeth 56, 74
 James Haddock 2
 Martha 56, 150
 Mary 130
 Richard Marsham 17,
  56, 74
 Samuel 150, 198
 William 137
Warner
 Charles 15, 132,
  154
 Garey 177
 Gary 131
 Richard 15, 132,
  154
 Solomon 104, 132
Warren
 Alace 223
 Alice 124
 John 124, 176, 223

Page 290

Thomas 126
Warsebury
  Ambrose 85
Wasson
  Thomas 133, 213
Waterfall
  Sarah 2
Waters
  Edward 191
  Elisabeth 142
  John 168
  Joseph 34, 35
  Littleton 4, 34
  Susannah 21, 199
  Thomas 142, 158
  William 21, 199
Wathen
  Hudson 164
  John 164, 199
Watkins
  Esau 15
  Gassaway 198, 213
  John 10, 83, 110
  Mary 110
  Rebecca 124
  Samuel 46, 60
  Sarah 15
  William 124, 176
Watson
  James 32
  John 95, 165, 166,
    189
  Joseph 32
  William 35
Watts
  James 188
  Jane 194
  John 38, 60, 69,
    81, 83, 189, 198
  Mary 188
  Richard 60, 69, 81,
    189, 198
  Thomas 188, 207
  William 126, 194
Wayman
  Deborah 11
  Leonard 11
Webb
  Armerell 212
  John 212
Webster
  Isaac 84, 219
  James 86, 88, 116
  Michael 84

Weden
  John 85
Week
  John 152
Weeks
  John 102, 198
  Matthew 102, 198
  Stephen 102, 198
Weems
  David 144, 182
  James 110, 115, 116
Welch
  Eliza 119
  Lewis 209
Wellman
  Joseph 170
  Thomas 82, 170
Wells
  Jane 192
  Martin 192
Welsh
  John 159, 160, 164
  Lewis 13
  Rachel 159, 160,
    164
  William 115, 116
Wentworth
  Thomas 163
Wenvier
  Thomas 162
West
  Benjamin 131, 194
  Hannah 115, 194,
    210
  Jean 82
  John 89, 125, 131,
    188
  Lotan 210
  Loton 115, 194, 210
  William 82, 90,
    168, 194
Westman
  Arthur 21
Wetheral
  Francis 120
Wetherall
  George 19
Wethered
  Issabella 87, 170
  Richard 52, 87,
    120, 163, 170
Wetherell
  Francis 78
  George 4, 53

Whaley
    William 157
Wharton
    Henry 162, 170
Wheatley
    Arthur 124
    John 20
    Joseph 10, 46
    Martha 10, 46
    Thomas 205
Wheeler
    Charles 204
    Henry 6, 124
    Isaac 94
    John 124
    Rachel 70, 95
    Thomas 204
    William 70, 95
Wheland
    Benjamin 91, 174
Wherritt
    John 169
    Thomas 169
Whichcoat
    Paul 38, 59
Whinfield
    Dorcas 33
    Dorcus 150, 169
    John 33
    Jonah 33, 150, 169
    Sarah 63
Whitacre
    Joseph 223
    Mary 223
Whitaker
    Charles 72
    John 72
White
    Archibald 109
    Cahterine 207
    Cassandra 154, 180
    Catherine 178
    Charles 122, 176,
       178, 207
    Elisabeth 34, 107,
       113, 120
    Eliza 16
    John 8, 16, 107,
       187
    Joseph 34, 73, 113,
       158
    Katherine 122
    Robert 52
    Samuel 41

    Thomas 7, 8, 9, 14,
       19, 22, 30, 44,
       46, 56, 60, 63,
       66, 71, 75, 87,
       96, 98, 106,
       140, 142, 146,
       166, 167, 186,
       192, 209, 216,
       218, 219
    William 154, 180
Whiteacor
    Joseph 205
Whiteacre
    Joseph 174
    Mary 174
Whiteaker
    Charles 46
    John 46
Whiteley
    Arthur 54
Whitely
    Arthur 91
    William 122
Whithers
    Robert 50
Whitley
    Thomas 92
Whitter
    George 46, 96, 101,
       103
    Mary 96
Whittington
    William 138
Wickes
    Joseph 141, 155,
       160, 163, 183
Wickham
    Nathaniel 131
Wilde
    Edith 157
Wilder
    John 148
Wildman
    Catherine 94, 128
    John 25, 94
Wiles
    Frances 27, 118
    John 27
    Thomas 27, 43, 118,
       139, 155, 191
Wiley
    John 92, 93
Wilkins
    Richard 85

Wilkinson
    Christopher 52,
        133, 137, 151
    Elisabeth 137, 151
    Eliza 52, 133
    John 108
    Robert 217
    Roseman 105, 209
    Thomas 105, 137,
        147, 209
    William 23
Willett
    Edward 85, 113, 185
    William 85, 185
Willey
    Diana 178, 207
    Dianah 171
    Francis 171, 176,
        178, 204, 207
    John 204, 205
    William 204
Williams
    Abraham 198
    Ann 35
    Billy 123
    Charles 3
    Christopher 112
    David 203
    Elias 35
    Elisabeth 80, 82,
        86
    Esther 112
    George 123, 175,
        205
    Jacob 74, 105, 155,
        190, 191, 210
    James 57, 86, 115,
        159, 171
    Jervis 119
    John 26, 51, 80,
        95, 106, 123,
        186, 191, 199,
        201, 203, 211,
        220
    John Guy 18, 28
    Joseph 18, 64
    Lewis 16, 53
    Mary 55, 57, 92,
        125
    Merida 173
    Monica 54, 55, 92,
        125
    Nathaniel 35
    Nehemiah 123, 176,

        177
    Rachel 74, 155,
        191, 210
    Rebecca 162, 187,
        198, 220
    Susanna 205
    Thomas 16, 53, 87,
        117, 122, 134,
        143, 178, 187,
        207, 214, 221
    William 48, 54, 55,
        56, 82, 92, 99,
        125, 126, 162,
        191, 192
Williamse
    Thomas 126
Williamson
    John 45, 130
    Thomas 58, 85
Willis
    Barnaby 191
    Richard 11, 55
Willmott
    William 80
Willson
    James 34
    John 12
    Joseph 81
    Priscilla 12
Wilmer
    Lambert 16, 53,
        130, 202
    Simon 119, 170, 212
    William 163
Wilson
    (N) 60, 68
    Ann 198
    David 196
    George 211
    Henry Wright 182,
        183, 195, 214
    James 17, 57, 60,
        85, 111, 115,
        182, 183, 195,
        214
    John 42
    Joseph 49, 69, 101,
        110, 114, 115,
        116, 134, 143,
        152, 159, 182,
        195, 214
    Joshua 169
    Lawrence 85
    Lingan 49, 60, 69,

81, 101, 114,
133, 143, 152,
159, 167, 182,
195, 214
Phineas 198
Priscilla 9, 16,
17, 25, 38, 42,
59, 68, 87, 113,
139, 150
Richard 162
Samuel 160, 191
Thomas 16, 24, 30,
32, 38, 39, 51,
59, 69, 81, 87,
98, 101, 102,
113, 114, 115,
138
William 115
Wimsett
Thomas 48, 83
Winall
Clarana 33, 139
Claranna 129
William 33, 40,
129, 139
Winard
Thomas 14
Winchester
Jacob 76, 136
Mary 76, 136
Winder
Alice 135
Thomas 135, 161
Windows
Henry 55
Wing
Ann 50, 131, 177
Robert 50, 131, 177
Wingate
Henry 205
Mary 205, 206
Phillup 205
Winstandly
Modling 121
Thomas 121, 124
Wintersell
Elisabeth 49, 61
William 49, 61
Wise
Christopher 104
Matthew 70, 95
Thomas 5, 70, 95
Wiseman
John 82

Withers
Robert 93, 192
Wolliston
Cornelius 93
Wollman
Sarah 222
Wolston
Obid 220
Wood
Adam 27
Ann 1, 138, 194,
209
Edward 33, 114,
130, 138, 169,
194, 209
James 3
James Greenfield
149
John 156
Joseph 15, 28, 93,
139, 166
Martha 15, 93, 139,
149, 166
Thomas 8
William 8, 156, 209
Woodall
John 201
Woodard
Jane 37
John 37
R. 111
Wooden
John 133
Thomas 111
Woodhead
George 168, 180
Woodland
James 119, 186, 212
Katherine 119, 186,
212
William 119, 145,
175, 186, 212
Woodward
Abraham 85, 111,
133, 186
John 82
Mary 44
Priscilla 111
Thomas 44, 60, 72
William 111
Woolford
John 8
Thomas 175
Wooliston

Cornelius 50
Woolley
    Robert 3
Woollford
    John 180, 184, 197
    Margaret 180, 184,
        197
    Thomas 50
Wootton
    Elisabeth 44
    Turner 60
    William 44, 113
Worrell
    Edward 4, 52, 211
    Mary 211
Worthylake
    Margaret 42
Worton
    Mary 198
    Rebecca 181, 198
    Robert 181, 198
Wrench
    William 200
Wright
    Ambrose 29, 102,
        186, 222
    Ann 99, 144, 153,
        159
    Benjamin 2, 70
    Elinor 224
    Fairclough 76, 102,
        157
    Frances 76
    Henry 2, 70
    Isaac 217
    James 224
    John 68, 99
    Nathan 187
    Nathaniel 102
    Peter 99, 144, 153,
        159
    Richard 113
    Robert Norris 137
    Samuel 13
    Sarah 13
    T. H. 82
    Thomas 113, 192,
        218
    William 9, 45, 98,
        146
Wrightson
    Eleanor 86
    Francis 86, 132
Wroughton

Rachel 204
Thomas 204
William 204
Wyate
    Thomas 53, 99, 120
Wye
    Rebecca 93
    William 93, 127

Yates
    Ann 12
    Robert 12, 25, 65,
        149
    William 158
Yealdhall
    Gilbert 34
Yewell
    Christopher 117
Yoakley
    Martha 117, 134,
        143, 153, 159,
        182, 183, 195,
        214
    Stephen 214
York
    George 217
    William 217
Yorkson
    Frances 168
    Thomas 168
Young
    Elisabeth 16, 33,
        53, 74, 192,
        202, 203
    Eliza 106
    John 33, 53, 102,
        156, 182, 213
    Joseph 181
    Margaret 182
    Mary 52, 141
    Rebecca 48, 71
    Richard 4, 34, 103,
        105
    Samuel 1, 48, 71,
        103
    William 52, 102,
        141
Younger
    James 211

INDEX OF EQUITY CASES

Alexander vs. Young 103

Barber vs. Sothoron & Sothoron 116, 134, 202, 215
Black vs. est. of Brerewood 31
Blunt vs. Bradford 155, 160, 183
Boone vs. Burle 90, 101, 114
Brereton vs. McClammy, Long, & Benston 20, 25
Brereton vs. Mullen 142, 153, 159, 183, 196

Clark vs. Griffen 151, 153, 160, 183, 196, 215
Cooper vs. Matthews 134, 143
Crow vs. Crow 32, 39
Cullens vs. Brickhill, Woollford, & Almsby 180, 184, 197

Darnall vs. Griffith 133, 135
Dorsey & Dorsey vs. est. of Dorsey 31
Dyson vs. Estep 97, 101

est. of Milner vs. White 216
est. of Tootel vs. Hammond 202, 215

Gale vs. Skillington 197
Goldsborough vs. Skillington 185
Gordon vs. Smith 185, 198
Gosling vs. Fowler 194, 216
Guibert vs. Coode & Dunbar 38, 39

Hall vs. Hall 23, 38
Hall vs. Kemp 117, 134, 143, 153, 159, 195
Harrington vs. Slaughter 77, 82
Hartshorn vs. Spry, Spry, & Worton 181, 198
Hellen vs. Parran & Parran 24
Hill vs. Durbin 120, 134, 143, 153, 159, 183
Hill vs. Kemp 183
Hooper vs. Dodd 181, 184, 197, 215
Hynson vs. Carvill 24, 38, 58

Jenkins vs. Jenkins 38, 39, 59
Joyce vs. Joyce 203

Lang vs. Snowden 74, 81, 101, 114

Macnemara vs. Atcherson 199, 211, 215
Masters vs. Wilson 9, 25, 38, 59, 68
Millard vs. Davis 141, 144, 153

Needham vs. Scott 203, 216
Noblitt vs. Cullens 155, 160, 183, 196

Noblitt vs. Grantham, Hughs, Little, & Drury
    181, 184, 197
Noblitt vs. Mulany, Bunt, Steward, & Reed 181,
    184, 197

Philpot & Philpot vs. White 209
Purnall vs. Towgood 100, 101

Ridgely vs. est. of Alstone 38
Roberts vs. Ghiselin 25
Roberts vs. Johnston 24
Roberts vs. Lusby & Lusby 24

Semmes vs. Lemaster 24
Semmes vs. Prather, Prather, & Williams 117,
    134, 143, 153, 159, 183, 195, 214
Shermedine vs. Wilson 24, 38
Sligh & Morgan vs. Buckler 195
Sligh & Morgan vs. Partridge 74, 81, 101, 114,
    134, 143, 152, 159, 214
Sligh vs. Lane 142, 144, 153
Smith & Mapp vs. Hill 68, 69
Sothoron vs. Forbes 23
Stapleford, Stapleford, & Stapleford vs.
    Gollothon & Loockerman 181, 184, 197, 215

Taney, Taney, & Taney vs. Smith 108, 115
Thomas vs. Holland 28
Thomas vs. Holland & Holland 39
Thomas vs. Holland, Holland, & Holland 59

Watts & Carr vs. Scott 60, 69, 81, 189, 198
Wilson vs. Hines 30, 32, 39, 59, 69, 81, 98,
    101, 102, 114
Wilson vs. Weems & Parker 110, 115
Wright vs. Evans 144, 153, 159